LONG

LIVE

LATIN

LONG LIVE LATIN

The Pleasures of
a Useless Language

NICOLA GARDINI

Translated from the Italian by Todd Portnowitz

Farrar, Straus and Giroux
New York

Farrar, Straus and Giroux
120 Broadway, New York 10271

Library of Congress Cataloging-in-Publication Data
Names: Gardini, Nicola, author. | Portnowitz, Todd, 1986– translator.
Title: Long live Latin : the pleasures of a useless language / Nicola Gardini ; translated
from the Italian by Todd Portnowitz.
Other titles: Viva il latino. English
Description: New York : Farrar, Straus and Giroux, 2019. | Includes bibliographical
references and index.
Identifiers: LCCN 2019020200 | ISBN 9780374284527 (hardcover)
Subjects: LCSH: Latin language. | Latin philology.
Classification: LCC PA2057 .G37313 2019 | DDC 470.9—dc23
LC record available at https://lccn.loc.gov/2019020200

Designed by Jonathan D. Lippincott

Our books may be purchased in bulk for promotional, educational, or business use.
Please contact your local bookseller or the Macmillan Corporate and Premium Sales
Department at 1-800-221-7945, extension 5442, or by e-mail at
MacmillanSpecialMarkets@macmillan.com.

www.fsgbooks.com
www.twitter.com/fsgbooks • www.facebook.com/fsgbooks

1   3   5   7   9   10   8   6   4   2

Published by arrangement with the Italian Literary Agency.

To Rosanna Crocitto

Contents

LONG
LIVE
LATIN

Ode to a Useless Language

For many people, Latin is *useless*. I won't enter into a discussion on the meaning of "utility," a concept with variations and stratifications that are centuries in the making, and which itself merits an entire book. What I will say here, however, is that those "many people"—civilians, politicians, professionals in every field—have a sadly (and dangerously) limited idea of education and human development. What their focus on "utility" betrays is the belief that, in the end, knowledge amounts to know-how, that thought should be immediately adapted toward a practical aim. But if that were the case, knowledge would hardly be useful: we'd have surgeons, plumbers, and not much else, given that machines are growing more and more responsible for satisfying our primary needs. Eventually the surgeon or plumber will disappear too. And if such is the fate of knowledge, that it be surrendered to machines—or, as we put it more often these days, to technology—what exactly will there be for humans to *know*? Of course, we'll have to learn how to build the machines and keep them functioning, and to dispose of the remains when they become obsolete, and to procure the materials necessary to build new machines. In short, all in service of machines, with the idea, no doubt, that machines are fundamental, the only truly useful thing, the all-encompassing solution . . . But what about the rest? Those needs that aren't immediate, that aren't practical or distinctly material, and yet are no less urgent? The so-called spirit? Memory, imagination, creativity, depth, complexity? And what about the larger questions, which are common to other essential domains of knowledge, including biology, physics, philosophy, psychology, and art: where and when did it all begin, where do I go, who am I, who are others, what is society, what is history, what is time, what is language, what are words, what is human life, what are feelings, who is a stranger, what am I doing here, what am I saying when I speak, what am I thinking when I think, what is meaning? Interpretation, in other words. Because without interpretation there is no freedom, and without freedom there is no happiness. This leads to passivity, a tacit acceptance of even our brighter moods. One becomes a slave to politics and the market, driven on by false needs.

Then there are those, perhaps a smaller group, who maintain that Latin does in fact have a purpose. Latin, according to this camp, teaches us how to reason and instills a certain discipline, which can then be applied to any other task. So Latin is just like math. I can't tell you how many times I heard this growing up, and how often I hear it still! They defend Latin by granting it the merits of other branches of knowledge, while ignoring its own unique merits—without recognizing that Latin offers something that math can't offer, just as math offers things that Latin can't.

Neither argument—that of the "usefuls" nor that of the "uselesses"—is quite what engenders and nourishes a love for Latin. The objection given by the uselesses is just as weak as that of the usefuls: that Latin's purpose is to train the mind. Its rich morphology for jogging the memory, its syntax for stimulating our logical-deductive capacity, and so on . . . All true. But if Latin is this alone, an exercise gym, it would be all the same to study other complex languages, such as German, Russian, Arabic, and Chinese, which have the added benefit of being still in use. And wouldn't algebra serve just as well to reinforce our memory and logical skills? Or chemistry? Even a mystery novel might do the trick!

The frail argument offered by the usefuls has, for decades, helped to prop up shaky pedagogical and rhetorical methods, only adding fuel to the fire of the uselesses. The structure won't hold anymore. No, the study of Latin—demanding, challenging, exhausting, and, like a good hike through the mountains, restorative in and of itself—must not be treated like a cognitive boot camp. Next we'll be going to the Louvre and the Metropolitan Museum to sharpen our vision and to La Scala to improve our hearing. Divers and ballerinas have beautiful physiques, no doubt, but they've built those muscles so they can dive and dance, not to look at themselves in the mirror. When we study Latin, we must study it for one fundamental reason: because it is the language of a civilization; because the Western world was created on its back. Because inscribed in Latin are the secrets of our deepest cultural memory, secrets that demand to be read.

One other minor contention against the usefuls and the uselesses: Latin is *beautiful*. This fact undergirds all that I will be saying in these pages. Beauty is the face of freedom. What all totalitarian regimes have most strikingly in common is their ugliness, which spreads to every aspect and form of life, even to nature. And by the adjective "beautiful" I mean to say that Latin is various, malleable, versatile, easy and difficult, simple and complicated, regular and irregular, clear and obscure, with multiple registers and jargons, with thousands of rhetorical styles, with a voluble history. Why give ourselves practical reasons for encountering beauty? Why impede ourselves with false arguments about *comprehension*? Why submit ourselves to the cult of instant access, of destination over journey, of answers at the click of a button, of the shrinking attention span? Why surrender to the will-less, the superficial, the defeatists, the utilitarians? Why not see that behind the question "What's the point of Latin?"—perhaps posed unassumingly—rests a violence and an arrogance, an assault on the world's richness and the greatness of the human intellect?

I would like to put the reader on guard against one more noxious cliché. Even among specialists one hears the term "dead language" thrown around. This characterization arises from a misconception of how languages live and die, and a hazy distinction between the written and the oral. Oral language is linked immediately with the idea of being alive. But this is a bias. Latin, even if it's no longer spoken, is present in an astounding number of manuscripts—and writing, particularly literary writing, is a far more durable means of communication than any oral practice. If, therefore, Latin lives on in the most complex form of writing we've yet imagined, namely literature, is it not absurd to proclaim it *dead*? Latin is alive, and it's more alive than what we tell our friend at the café or our sweetheart on the phone, in exchanges that leave no trace. Think of it on an even larger scale. In this very moment the entire planet is jabbering, amassing an immeasurable heap of words. And yet those words are already gone. Another heap has already formed, also destined to vanish in an instant.

It's not enough that the speaker is living to say that the language he or she speaks is alive. A living language is one that endures and produces other languages, which is precisely the case with Latin. I'm not referring to the Romance languages, which were born from spoken Latin, or to the massive contribution of Latin vocabulary to the English lexicon. What I mean to say is that Latin qua literature has inspired the creation of other literature, of other written works, and, as such, distinguishes itself from other ancient languages: those that, even with a written record, are truly dead on the page, since they served in no way as a model for other languages. Dante would never have composed

his *Divine Comedy* without the model of the *Aeneid*, nor Milton his
Paradise Lost; Machiavelli could not have written his *Discourses
on the First Ten Books of Livy* without Livy's history; nor Castigli-
one his *Book of the Courtier* without the paradigm of Cicero's *De
oratore*; Shakespeare's rise would have been inconceivable without
the influence of Ovid's *Metamorphoses*. We could fill hundreds of
pages with such examples, coming from every age, even our current one, and from every cultural tradition on earth. Written Latin
gradually became the voice of the past, and this voice struck up
a dialogue with posterity. And there's no truer or more moving
representation of this conversational power, I believe, than Machiavelli's letter to his friend Vettori. Machiavelli, having been
expelled from the world of politics, describes the consolation he
finds in reading the ancients. But reading, in this letter, becomes
an exchange, a dialogue, and it takes on the appearance of a real,
physical encounter. Here, the books stand in for the authors, alive
and well despite their temporal remove, and his study becomes
the magical space of an initiation ritual. In his words:

> [. . .] once properly attired, I step into the ancient courts
> of ancient men, where, a beloved guest, I nourish myself
> on that food that is mine alone and for which I was born;
> where I speak to them without inhibition and ask them
> the reasons behind their actions; and in their humanity
> they reply; and for four hours I feel not a drop of boredom,
> think nothing of my cares, am fearless of poverty, unrat-
> tled by death; I transfer all of myself into them. (Letter to
> Francesco Vettori, December 10, 1513)

One's encounter with the ancients, we note, even has its own
dress code. It's not a private matter but a public ritual. Note also
that Machiavelli calls this encounter a "conversation." A metaphor, of course—not a fly could be heard buzzing in his study,

I imagine. And yet that silence has all the power of a real verbal exchange, resounding and alive, though bound within the perimeter of his mind.

However unique Machiavelli's "conversation" appears to be, we all do something similar when we approach a classical text: we participate in the growth of tradition. Our very act of reading is not simply a private practice, but posits itself within the overarching temporality of cultural transmission, which takes centuries. By reading, we are not just living today: we are living in history, transcending our biographies and entering a much broader chronology.

Despite this similarity, we must also remember that the culture to which Machiavelli belonged, the Renaissance, was *profoundly* Latin.[1] Indeed, the Renaissance came about as a direct result of the revival of Latin antiquity, developing in strict dialogue with its texts, even when the authors chose to express themselves in the vernacular. Of course, Latin was also crucial to the development of vernacular literature before the Renaissance, and to some extent we could even claim that there was a revival of the Latin classics in the Middle Ages, before the times of Petrarch. Dante is a case in point. His *Divine Comedy* could never have been written if Dante the author had not elected the pagan Virgil as a teacher of his textual double, Dante the Pilgrim. Though Dante remains an exception in his century, and his relationship with the Latin classics is conditioned by a strict Christian censure, the fact remains that the father of European vernacular literature conceived of his poem as a companion piece to Latin's greatest epic. Today, more than ever, the *Divine Comedy* strikes us as a magnificent and exemplary fusion of ancient and modern.

Over the course of the fifteenth and sixteenth centuries, science grows in influence. Religion's grip on society weakens and, even in a persistently Christian climate, a passionate interest in rediscovery takes hold, giving new clarity to the once clouded perception of antiquity. The recovery of Latin texts becomes a field of study in and of itself, bringing about shifts in pedagogical thinking and literary taste, and elevating grammar to the science of sciences. One thinks of Lorenzo the Magnificent, or of Aldo Manuzio's editorial work, founded entirely on the spread of Graeco-Latin antiquity. A new religion sweeps the world, one might say, a perfectly human religion: one of textual precision and purity; a cult of the word as a living, evolving trace of man's existence. The university, the library, the private study all rise to the level of sanctuaries. Texts are carefully analyzed and annotated, combed through for even the subtlest glimmers of meaning. The interpreter bows humbly before the author's complexity, allowing it to resonate—as exemplified in the Florentine lectures held by Agnolo Poliziano, one of the most brilliant minds that Europe has ever produced (his teachings receive international acclaim, prompting the admiration of such prestigious personalities as Erasmus of Rotterdam). Whether annotating Persius's *Satires* or Virgil's *Georgics*, Poliziano scrutinizes each and every word or expression that he deems worthy of consideration, determining its exact meaning and textual form. His preferred method is to illuminate a single linguistic element by turning to passages from other ancient authors, even those distant in time from the author being analyzed. He situates and considers each individual word within a network, a civilization, or a tradition, and only there can its true meaning emerge. It's not a case of establishing, as did Dante, how Christian Virgil already was. With Poliziano, the task is to establish who the author in question *truly* and *specifically* was, what the words of the Latin language mean *in relationship to ancient culture as a whole*. No longer is it a search for oneself in the other, but for the other as other, as a historical product, perfect and beautiful in his historical completeness. Beauty and truth become one, to put it in John Keats's words. In his letter to Vettori, Machiavelli reveals a respect for the ancients on par with that of Poliziano, if less technical. Knowledge is described

as "food," or nourishment, a source of life. But what's most striking in the letter quoted above is the verb *trasferire* (to transfer): that
need to enter the world of the ancients, the very opposite of the
desire to haul them into the present age. To enter into contact with
the ancients requires a transference of oneself, as clearly indicated by the Latin preposition *trans*: this is an effort to understand
historically, to step out of one's individual identity and approach
the other. Only then can the past take on meaning and give pleasure. Mere *pastism*? An inability to live in the present? Not at all.
In the next paragraph of this same letter, Machiavelli goes on to
describe his work on *The Prince*, one of the most innovative texts
of all time. In fact, he even intends to intervene in the present with
this treatise, providing drastic solutions to the current crisis.

The Renaissance is philology, the scientific study of ancient
words, their forms and meanings. But it is also the defiant response of those who, centuries later, felt themselves caught in the
same ceaseless, destructive current, the same perishability that
Latin sought to oppose and from which, in part, it has managed
to escape. Through the passionate study of antiquity, the present
discovers its own historicity and attempts to moor itself against
time's ruinous momentum.

It's not even true to say that Latin has disappeared completely
from the oral landscape. Latin is still spoken in the church:
Pope Benedict XVI gave news of his resignation from the pa-
pacy in Latin, evidently assuming—given the great intrigue of
the announcement—that his audience was filled with advanced
Latin speakers. It is also practiced in certain international confer-
ences, and among enthusiasts from everywhere around the globe.
I've met doctors and engineers, in Italy and elsewhere, who speak
it as their mother tongue. I too, every now and then, find myself
exchanging a few emails in Latin, with a friend who makes his

living as an accountant. Not to mention a Finnish radio station that broadcasts news only in Latin.

But, most of all, Latin is alive in what we the living read and translate, and in the work done at schools and universities. Literary Latin has never been a spoken language. No literary language has, in truth. Who among Cicero's contemporaries spoke the way he wrote? Nobody. Not even Cicero himself, who carefully went back over the transcripts of any speeches he gave in court. And what about an even more modern writer, such as Henry James or Virginia Woolf? Can you imagine a contemporary speaking in such sentences? All literature—if we're using the criterion that a language must be spoken—is dead, because it is art, and so a construction, a calculation, stylized, like music or painting. Notes and colors are everywhere around us, but Beethoven's Ninth and the Sistine Chapel won't be found except in the unique combinations given to them by an individual, through brilliance and intention, selecting and arranging each element according to a precise plan. Virgil's *Aeneid* is no different from Beethoven's Ninth. And the same is true of all great literature, ancient and modern. Who would ever mount an argument against reading Proust in the original on the basis that spoken French is a different language?

Some might object that literature is filled with regular speech. But let's dispose of yet another misconception: that literary dialogue is the speech we hear in real life. Literary dialogue is a *simulation* of speech. The very moment that speech or a spoken expression enters the realm of artistic writing, it changes in value; it becomes *style*, and not the spontaneous expression of everyday language. Dialogue can certainly add color, it can be ironic, it can create the illusion of reality. But it isn't speech, not in the empirical or sociohistorical sense.

Literature is life, and it lives because it generates more writing, and because readers exist, and because interpretation exists, which is a dialogue between thought and the written word, a dialogue between centuries, which halts time on its ruthless march and continually renews our potential for permanence. To label as dead a language that's written but no longer spoken is to deny the power of reading, to misunderstand how knowledge operates—even more, it is to commit an act of violence, a harebrained and arrogant act of violence; it would be like burning down the National Gallery or the Metropolitan Museum. You're dead because I don't believe you're alive, because it doesn't matter to me that you're living, and so I'll bury you without a thought for your echoing voice. But the dead and dying are those who don't listen, not those who speak. And violence done to another turns automatically into self-amputation and self-destruction—because to not listen is to empty oneself, to flatten out, to grow dull, to disappear. It's true that this self-destructive instinct is part of the human condition, as any number of TV shows will attest to. Literature helps to contain this instinct; literature preserves our capacity for peaceful and respectful relationships, without which nothing else can survive. The name that Latin gives to this capacity is *humanitas*, and those who possess it *humani*. Both of these terms, which are derived from *homo* (human being), appear with great frequency in Cicero. *Humanitas* can even be specifically understood to mean literature *tout court*, literature being the space in which we express spiritual nobility through linguistic excellence. Looking back at Machiavelli's letter to Vettori, we can now see just how much semantic weight lies behind that word "humanity."

This book, in short, is a defense of Latin and a tribute to it and to the literature that has been written in that language since antiquity, as well as an invitation to study Latin. The present indifference toward Latin—though not universal—and often the rejection and boycott of the language (even from on high, even from within) are symptoms of a systematic attack on literature and on the functions that literature has traditionally served, and is still quite capable of serving, better than any other form of knowledge or communication: giving order and meaning to the human experience through story and metaphor; broadening the scope of the visible by imagining potential worlds; forming and disseminating paradigms of thought and action; representing ideas and modes of living that are still resistant to, or already exist beyond, institutionalization; giving form to feelings and emotions and moral values; reflecting on justice and beauty, and constructing cultural centers out of otherwise distant and fragmentary communities; and, not least, uplifting a national language to the level of art. And, in doing all this, allowing for a particular kind of pleasure: the pleasure of understanding through interpretation.

Literature, in any language, is rarely ascribed such responsibilities and such dignity today. High school and university programs have withered. Students are reading less and less. As for the good of society, our mental health, the beauty of sentences—as for the *education* of the spirit, in other words—we no longer seem to give them any thought, betting all our happiness on material wealth. And so our taste decays, along with our expectations. Our words turn anemic, signifying less and less, sounding more and more like white noise, like traffic, or like certain politicians. Words! Our greatest gift, our most fertile ground.

Let's start over again with Latin.

1

A Home

Not without a certain vaingloriousness, I had begun at
that time my methodical study of Latin.

—Jorge Luis Borges[1]

How does one come to love a language? And a language like
Latin?

I fell for Latin at an early age. I'm not exactly sure why. When
I try to make sense of it, all I can ever dig up is a memory or
two, not necessarily linked to any reason. It's hard to explain an
instinct, a calling. The best you can do, perhaps, is tell the story.

Latin helped me excel in my studies, find my way toward poetry and literature, fall in love with translation; it gave my divergent interests a common goal; in the end, it's even earned me a
living. I taught Latin at the New School in New York, at one high
school in Lodi and another in Milan. And even now, at Oxford,
where I teach Renaissance literature, I use this language every
day, because there's no such thing as the Renaissance without
Latin. Growing up, I wielded it like an amulet or a magic shield, a
bit like Stendhal's Julien Sorel in *The Red and the Black*. When I

went to my rich friends' houses in Milan, where I grew up, I always made a good impression, precisely because of my reputation as a good Latin student. And later, with my brand-new classics degree in hand, when I began a doctorate in comparative literature at New York University, it was my knowledge of Latin that American professors valued most. Only then, in that American world, where who you are matters more than your parents' surname, did I understand how fortunate I was. Thanks to Latin, I was never alone. My life stretched for centuries and across continents. If I've done any good for others, I've done it through Latin. And whatever good I've done myself—that, without question, I owe to Latin.

Studying Latin set me in the habit early on of thinking about language in terms of discrete sounds and syllables. It taught me the importance of musical language: the soul of poetry. At a certain point, words I'd used every day began disassembling in my mind and swirling around, like petals in the air. Thanks to Latin, every word I knew doubled in sense. Beneath the garden of everyday language lay a bed of ancient roots. This is true of Italian and the other Romance languages, but it also applies to English, whose vocabulary is mostly derived from Latin, either directly or through French. The double origin of the English vocabulary is obvious in the different roots of semantically related nouns and adjectives: consider, for example, the pairs "sun/solar," "moon/lunar," and "tooth/dental." The noun is Germanic, the adjective is Latin. Even the most Germanic-sounding word may have sprung from Latin. Take "laundry": it derives from the Old French *lavanderie*, which derives from the Latin gerundive *lavandum*, "that which must be washed." It makes perfect sense, no? The same root *lav-* (wash) is to be found in "lavatory," or even in "lavish," taken from the Old French *lavasse*, "deluge of rain": hence the notion of abundance, which originally applied to speech. We now forget that there is a connection between, say, a lavish banquet, an overflowing amount of water, and an excessive discourse. But the connection—a metaphorical one—is definitely there.

If on the one hand this multiplicity of meanings requires an understanding of history and a faith in even the most remote connotation, on the other it makes one alert to insidious nuance, to the splendor of figurative language, and therefore to ambivalence, elusiveness, mystique, and the gift of saying two or even three things at once.

I was drawn to Latin as a child because it was ancient, and I've always loved antiquity. Or to put it more accurately, certain images of the ancient world have always given me a special pleasure, along with something like tachycardia—the pyramids, or the columns of Greek temples, or the Egyptian mummies. I also recall a passage in my elementary school textbook about the *domus*, the house of patricians, and the *insulae*, where everyone else lived. My family and I, I discovered, lived in an *insula*.

It wasn't until my second year of middle school that I came to own an actual book in Latin. And there it was, the *domus*, described in detail. Alongside it was a wealth of architectural terms, my first Latin words: *impluvium, atrium, triclinium, tablinum, vestibulum, fauces*. I then overlooked the fact that this terminology came from a book by Vitruvius, one of the most influential figures in history. Who would have dreamed: a house that let the rain in through a hole in the roof and collected it in a basin below, that had columns and rooms atop rooms; a house so big you could hide in it and never be found! So, yes, Latin became entangled with my desire to, in a certain sense, climb the social ladder: the dream of a magnificent home. More precisely, it became a space in my imagination where I could live happily: *the* happy place. And it wasn't solely internal, this space: uncontainable, it slipped out of me into my drawings. Everywhere I could I sketched plans for this *domus*, filling in every box with its proper Latin term, certain that

I too would one day have my own *domus*. My apprehensive parents tried to justify the habit by saying I'd grow up to be an architect.

Nor, in truth, could Latin have been anything other than an imaginary space to me at the time. In 1977, the year I entered middle school, it was deleted from the required curriculum. My dutiful teacher, Ms. Zanframundo, went on dedicating an hour of her class to Latin, more out of habit than any particular belief, though she never expected too much of us students. I learned the first and second declensions on my own, as a labor of love, without bothering to understand the logical functions of their different inflections. But what a pleasure just to know the names of the cases: nominative, genitive, dative, accusative, vocative, ablative.

There was, now that I think about it, one other factor that affected my imagination: the example of my mother. On some level, I can say that even before encountering it I considered Latin a maternal language (as it was for Montaigne, who, by his own account, learned to speak it even before French)—or if not maternal then certainly natural, something born from emotion. As a girl, before emigrating to Germany, my mother had lived for a time in a convent, in Aquila degli Abruzzi, where she'd learned several prayers in Latin: the *Requiem aeternam*, the *Pater noster*, the *Ave Maria* . . . This was enough to convince me that she knew Latin. She, to be sure, had never claimed such knowledge; in fact, by her account she didn't know the language at all. Like the other girls, she had learned to parrot what she heard in Mass every morning, noon, and night, spitting back who knows how much nonsense. Yet I needed no further evidence than her parroted prayers; stilted and incomprehensible as it was, I thought her Latin was perfectly fluent. Thanks to those strange utterances, she became in my eyes the magnificent matriarch of the equally magnificent home I would one day build—with Vitruvius's simple words.

I learned Latin during my first two years of *liceo classico*—the humanities track at an elite high school, where I was initiated into classical languages—and perfected it in the final three. At university, I simply read a lot of poetry and prose in Latin. I always had very capable and demanding teachers. But Latin, I can say without presumption, I learned on my own: with passion, dedication, and curiosity. If my teacher assigned us a passage to translate, I turned in three or four versions. I translated every day, whether there was homework or not. In addition to the one we used for class, I picked up two or three translation exercise books from the teacher's library, from which I could pluck at will. The best time to translate, I found, was in the evenings, just before bed. I'd scan the text for those passages marked by three asterisks—the most difficult. Nights, I muttered Latin in my sleep. Or so claimed my father, drawn by the sound of my voice.

I never put my translations to paper: I did them in my head and committed them to memory. If called on in class, I'd reproduce them, or else retranslate the passage then and there, with the Latin text in front of me. I never liked fixing *one* version to the page. Writing, I felt, served only to legitimize the imperfection of a particular phrasing, to set errors in stone. Better left to the mind. There you could improve the translation, dispensing with any vagueness, filling in any gaps—for memory has little interest in the disagreeable, and even less in the incomplete.

And here I am today, writing a book that communicates, or tries to communicate, my love for, and faith in, Latin, to put into words that joyous atrial flutter, that sense of expansion I still feel, despite my accruing experience, whenever I read the language. Not a grammar book, not a history of language or literature, but an essay on the beauty of Latin, which may ultimately encourage readers to refresh their Latin or even start learning it from scratch.[2]

If in part I draw on my long study of the literature, what you'll find in these pages comes fundamentally from a renewing of my vows, so to speak: a revived effort of intuition and penetration founded upon rereadings and reconsiderations, which nurtured the writing of this work at every step, calling upon my entire sensibility—the very same sensibility, I believe, that I bring to the drafting of a poem or the structuring of a novel.

In each chapter, I'll focus my attention on specific authors and passages, keeping technical discussions to a minimum, and avoiding any detailed accounts of the close ties between Latin and Greek, else we veer too far off course. Authors and excerpts, to be clear, do not figure here as they would in a history of Latin literature. In this book, they stand as "episodes" in the life of Latin, and not necessarily in chronological order; they are examples of what Latin has accomplished, what it has gained at a certain moment, in certain circumstances and conditions, and handed down to its long—and still living—tradition. The authors, therefore, do not function as individuals but as linguistic instances. When we encounter Cicero or Virgil, we won't speak of the particular Latin of Cicero or the particular Latin of Virgil. Rather, we'll consider what Latin gained and accomplished when expressed in Cicero's style or Virgil's style. And even here we must distinguish, given that Cicero and Virgil are not *people* but sums of linguistic phenomena, as the differing forms, styles, and rhetoric of their works demonstrate. Besides, I've always believed, even beyond the field of Latin, that individual authors are only embodiments of the empirical conditions that allow a language to break new ground or transform itself. We speak often, of course, of personal style, how style separates one thing from another; but style, ultimately, is only an event in the life of a language.

This is a book, above all, for young students, the most eager among us to make sense of what they do and see. Though I hope, in truth, to say something in these pages to the not-so-young as well, whether or not they are Latinophiles; perhaps even to help a few former high school students rediscover the pleasure of their longed-for or abandoned studies; to communicate something vital and necessary to politicians and teachers, businesspeople and doctors, lawyers and writers; and even to those who've never once asked themselves the question of Latin, and who, today, without bias, without fear or vague excuses, decide they'd like to know a little more about it—just because, out of *curiosity*.

It will have been enough even if I succeed in helping only a few readers to see the importance of the Latin language, why knowing it, or at least understanding its properties, can truly add life to your years.

2

What Is Latin?

Latin is the language of ancient Rome and the civilization that took root there; expanding through the centuries to cover a remarkably vast territory, the so-called empire, it became a means of expression and communication for a large part of mankind, on the page and in the public sphere, serving even in the modern age—long after spoken Latin forked into distinct tongues (the so-called Romance languages) and loaned thousands of terms to Germanic languages such as English—as a means of expression for poets, intellectuals, and scholars across various disciplines.

Latin is the language of our legal institutions, of architecture, engineering, the military, science, philosophy, worship, and—of greatest relevance here—a flourishing literature, which served as a model for all of Western literature in the centuries to follow. No field of knowledge or linguistic creativity exists that has not been expressed in Latin with superb and exemplary skill: poetry (epic, elegy, epigram, etc.), oratory, comedy, tragedy, satire, personal and official letter writing, the novel, history, dialogue; along with moral philosophy, physics, jurisprudence, the culinary arts, the theory of art, astronomy, agriculture, meteorology, grammar, ancient studies, medicine, technology, systems of measurement, and religion.

Through literature, in hundreds of masterpieces, Latin speaks of love and war, explores body and soul, proposes theories on the meaning of life and the duty of the individual, the destiny of the soul, the structure of matter; it sings the beauty of nature, the greatness of friendship, pain at losing what we love; it challenges corruption, and meditates on death, on the arbitrary nature of power, on violence and cruelty; it constructs images of our inner states, gives shape to our emotions, formulates ideas about the world and about civil life. Latin is the language of the relationship between the one and the many; of the complex confrontation between freedom and constraint, between private and public, between the contemplative life and the active life, between province and capital, between country and city. And it is the language of responsibility and personal duty; the language of inner strength; the language of property and of will; the language of servitude that questions the abuse of power; the language of mourning. Intention speaks Latin; protest speaks Latin; confession speaks Latin; belonging speaks Latin; exile speaks Latin; memory speaks Latin.

Latin is our most striking monument to the civilization of the human word and to faith in the possibility of language, as, for example, extolled by Pliny the Younger (c. 61–112 C.E.). I'm thinking of one of his letters that praises the versatility and linguistic skill of a certain Pompeius Saturninus. Pliny speaks of his "ingenium [. . .] varium, flexibile, quam multiplex," where for *ingenium* we are to understand a natural propensity, or, to use another word of Latin origin, "talent." Pompeius Saturninus, in other words, is *talented* at any form of verbal expression: a legal document, a historical account, poetry, letters. He lacks nothing: his words are fluid and sublime, light and weighty, bitter and sweet, as the case demands. Pliny never ceases reading and admiring him, as one of the greats of antiquity. It is a sincere shame that—as with many other luminaries—not a single work of his remains.

To speak of "Latin" is first and foremost to speak of a complete dedication to organizing one's thoughts in a profound and measured discourse, to select meanings in the most pertinent manner possible, to arrange one's words in a harmonious order, to give verbal evidence of even the most fleeting states of our inner self, to believe in verbal expression and in demonstration, to record the contingent and the transient in a language that survives beyond all circumstance.

3

Which Latin?

There are, in truth, several different Latins, all of which are represented by a staggering number and variety of texts: the Latin we find in literature, in the church, in scholastic philosophy, science, law, and marble inscriptions. And studies of Latin also come in every color. There are scholars who explore the relationship between Latin and the Romance languages; who reconstruct spoken or vernacular Latin through written texts, literary and otherwise; those who focus on medieval Latin and those who focus on sectional Latin. Even defenses of the language have been approached from different perspectives, at times contradictory, determined by personal tastes, concrete aims, or the cultural specificity of the countries for which they were written.[1] Looking only at Italy, it's possible to see the ideological distortions that Latin and the idea of imperial Rome underwent during fascism.[2] Consider even just the varying pedagogical importance that the study of Latin has held depending on time and place: it's one thing to teach and learn it in Italy, another in America, in the U.K., or in France; one thing today, another yesterday, or in the fifteenth century. After all, even the study of a modern language such as English begs a question similar to the one with which I opened this chapter: Which English? Shakespearean English or Woolfian English? The English spoken in Manhattan or in Manchester? The verbal fireworks of Joyce or early Beckett (and what a lot of Latin there!) or the lyrics to a pop song? New Zealand slang or Mississippi blues? Or the rudimentary English from the back of a travel guide?

Every cultural phenomenon casts its own aura, what we believe we know about it, its charm, its prestige, its historical importance—something that stretches beyond its surface value. Latin's aura is the most susceptible to transformation and diminution. Today it seems to have disappeared. What matters now, or seems to matter, is something quite different: technology, spontaneity, the easy, the ephemeral, the new at any cost and in every instance. Few are those who believe—and none, unfortunately, among the political or economic elite—that newness and renewal depend on engaging with those very things that seem obsolete or old.

In this book, unlike other defenses of the subject, my focus is on literary Latin, the Latin that helped form my character as a man and as a writer, the Latin I continue to read and that I still believe must play a central role in any serious and historically conscious pedagogy: the Latin of authors such as Cicero, Sallust, Lucretius, Catullus, Virgil, Livy, Ovid, Horace, Propertius, Seneca, Tacitus, Augustine, Jerome, and many others who lived centuries later, long after the vernacular tongues had taken hold. Because even after Italian, or French or English, arrived on the scene, Latin continued to represent, through the model of its ancient proponents, the language of literature: Petrarch (immortal even just for his *Epistolae familiares* and other epistolary works), Leon Battista Alberti, Enea Silvio Piccolomini, Marsilio Ficino, Agnolo Poliziano, Giovanni Pico della Mirandola, Giovanni Pontano,

Jacopo Sannazaro, Pietro Bembo; and on through the nineteenth and twentieth centuries, with Giovanni Pascoli, right up to the recent past, with Fernando Bandini. Even Ariosto, another great master of vernacular Italian, like Petrarch, wrote poetry in Latin. And that's covering only Italy. In France, du Bellay composed in Latin—the very poet who defended the power of his native tongue in *La Défense et illustration de la langue française*—as did Milton, another hero of his country's vernacular, in England, and innumerable others throughout Europe, both in prose and in poetry. In fact, some of the very works we identify with the rise of modernity were themselves composed in Latin, such as Erasmus of Rotterdam's *In Praise of Folly* and Thomas More's *Utopia*. We're not speaking merely about erudite, formulaic, or passively imitative texts. We're discussing, rather, a remarkable body of verbal art, into which these authors poured their technical knowledge and passion.

The influence of Latin has been spreading now for several centuries. Its thoughts on what it means to be alive and participate in society continue to reach us. Latin is alive. Indeed, without Latin I would not be who I am, and I'm sure there are others who could say the same. It formed the society and the sentiments in which we live. Without Latin, the world would be otherwise.

To engage with the complexities of Latin, to perceive its etymological resonances, to disentangle its structures and relish its stylistic beauty—these are all means of knowing oneself better, of finding solutions before the problems even arise. At the same time, it's a way of sharing in an utterly unique form of happiness, the happiness born, to echo Aristotle, from the desire to interpret, to go a step beyond what's evident. Really, why limit knowledge to only the immediate, to the practicality of mechanical response? Why forgo reflection and intellectual adventure? Why believe that the present is just the moment you live in and antiquity so much junk to stuff in the attic? Why not recognize that the story of our lives is just a fraction of all history, that life began long before we were born, and that an individual's existence is far more authentic when set in a context that transcends census records?

4

A Divine Alphabet

It has been a known fact for centuries now that spoken, or "vernacular," Latin generated a host of modern languages, the so-called neo-Latin or Romance languages: Italian, French, Spanish, Portuguese, and Romanian the most common among them.

But how did Latin itself come to be?

Virgil tells us in the *Aeneid* that the Roman people of Latium were born from a fusion of Trojan refugees and the local population. The goddess Juno, toward the end of Virgil's narrative, convinces Jupiter to let the language of Rome, this new city, remain that of its first inhabitants: the "indigenas Latinos," or "native Latins" (*Aeneid*, XII.823). Latin, therefore, according to the myth, would be a product of the original population, as it indeed proves itself to be through linguistic analysis. At the very beginning, it was the tongue of a small community, the people of Rome. With the years and the centuries, and in proportion to the growth in power and prestige of its city, Latin became the language of an enormous empire, which at the height of its expansion, under the emperor Trajan (the beginning of the second century C.E.), stretched from the Atlantic to Mesopotamia, from what is today Great Britain to the coasts of North Africa.

Though its origins are traceable to a circumscribed territory and population, Latin is no desert flower. It belongs to an extended linguistic family, which boasts some eighty members, among them ancient Greek, Sanskrit, and the Slavic and Germanic languages. Nor was Latin's rule uncontested at the outset. As numerous inscriptions testify, Latin had to clear its path in a crush of concurrent languages: Etruscan, Oscan, Umbrian (known also as the Sabellic languages, and found to have minor regional variants), Faliscan (Latin's closest of kin), Messapian, Venetic, Greek, of course (spoken by emigrants), and many others, a number of which we can assume have disappeared without a trace.

In that distant, primordial past, no trails are yet blazed—as Varro put it in his *De lingua Latina* (V.3)—and you wander through the shadows, stumbling over the earth, while waves of contrasting forces clash, and instincts and erratic desires struggle to emerge, as in a witch's boiling cauldron. Confusion gropes for order. Forms appear and are lost below the roiling surface, their remains morphing into new forms: an organism is coming to life, wrestling into a recognizable shape, gathering strength for its survival.[1]

Among these new forms, somewhere between the ninth and eighth centuries B.C.E., arose the alphabet, developed on the model of the Greek alphabet (which was itself derived from Phoenician), perhaps by the Etruscans. In the final tale of the *Fabulae* by Hyginus—an author of the early imperial age and a freedman of Augustus—we read that Evander, an exile from Arcadia, brings the Greek alphabet with him to Italy. There, his mother, Carmenta, transforms the letters into Latin, fifteen in all. Apollo will supply the rest. As Ovid tells us in the *Fasti* (I.461–586), Carmenta has prophetic powers and is considered a goddess. Virgil speaks of her too, in the *Aeneid* (VIII.336), in his account of Evander's reign. Giovanni Boccaccio, the author of the *Decameron*, also addresses the alphabet myth, expanding upon and embellishing it in his *De mulieribus claris (On Famous Women)*. A Latin work composed late in his life, and to much acclaim, *On Famous Women* gives us a catalogue of the most notable women of all time, both mythical and historical, beginning with Eve, though drawn principally from the ancient world (and notable, most often, for their vices rather than for their virtues). Carmenta, as Boccaccio recounts, prophesying the grand future of the Roman people, refuses to let their story be told in foreign letters. And so, rallying all her mental strength, she creates an entirely new alphabet, like no other in the world. God assists her in the effort, and its success guarantees her a devoted following and eternal fame.

Besides being a far richer and more eloquent account than the one provided by his ancient sources, Boccaccio's text presents a fiercely proud, impassioned, and all-encompassing ode to the Latin alphabet, one of the highest tributes to the power and glory of these letters that would make their way to modern literature:

> God so favored Carmenta's achievements that the Hebrew and Greek languages have lost the greatest part of their glory while a vast area covering almost all of Europe uses our alphabet.
>
> An infinite number of books on all subjects has rendered the Latin alphabet illustrious: in its letters is preserved a perpetual remembrance of divine and human accomplishments so that with the help of Latin characters we know things which we cannot see. In Latin characters we send our requests and receive with trust those made by other people. Through these characters we enter into friendship with people far away and preserve it by reciprocal correspondence. Latin characters describe God for us insofar as that can be done. They show forth the sky,

the earth, the seas, and all living things; there is nothing open to investigation that one cannot understand by careful study of its letters. In short, Latin characters enable us to entrust to faithful guardianship whatever the mind cannot embrace and retain. [. . .] Neither the rapacity of the Germans, nor the fury of the Gauls, nor the wiles of the English, nor the ferocity of the Spaniards, nor the rough barbarity and insolence of any other nation has been able to take away from the Latin name this great, marvelous and serviceable glory.[2]

Evident lexical and grammatical similarities, not attributable to chance or to borrowings, demonstrate that all of the languages I have mentioned above—the Italic languages, with the classic exception of Etruscan, and those from beyond the peninsula—are descended from a common source. Though we have no direct account of it, this source can be reconstructed through comparative means. Linguists have called that source "Indo-European."[3] Exactly how this process of descent took place is still a point of contention and speculation. What's certain is that whatever picture we paint of its development, it will be based on hypothesis.

This is not the place to delve into the minutiae of Latin's Indo-European roots. It's enough to say that from Indo-European Latin derives one of its most characteristic traits: its system of grammatical cases. A word, in Latin, changes its inflection not only to demonstrate number—that is, whether it is singular or plural—but also according to the logical function it serves within the sentence. There are six logical functions in all, and therefore six inflections (the grammatical cases): nominative (which marks the subject), genitive (used to express possession), dative (which marks the recipient of an action), accusative (which marks the direct object of a verb), vocative (used to address someone or something), and ablative (used to express separation, or the means by which an action is performed, often preceded by a preposition). Each word, in this way, has twelve different inflections, six in the singular and six in the plural. Taken all together, this is known as a word's declension. Indo-European included two additional cases: the locative and the instrumental. In Latin, they've been absorbed by the ablative, though now and then we find a fossil or two of these ancient grammatical cases.

Old Latin is attested to in hundreds of epigraphs, which give records of wars, administrative matters, religious rituals, and deaths. It is a coarse language, far from anything we might call literature: its orthography varies and its grammar is incoherent. To find examples of a more evolved form of writing, we have to wait until the second half of the third century. By then, it could be said, a certain linguistic order had been established: one even senses a budding aesthetic awareness. Though the evidence is still only fragmentary, scholars have nevertheless been able to trace the physiognomy of certain individuals through an abundance of relics. Among them are Cato the Elder (234–149 B.C.E.) and the comedic playwright Plautus (c. 250–184 B.C.E.), a truly ingenious linguist. Their lives coincide with the period in which Rome established its dominance over the Mediterranean. The year 146 B.C.E., just three years after the death of Cato the Elder, saw the fall of both Carthage and Corinth. The dreaded North African enemy was no longer, and Greece had become a Roman protectorate (it would be made a province in 27 B.C.E.).

Cato the Elder, the renowned Censor—antiaristocrat par excellence and the archenemy of Carthage—left us with a farming manual, *De agri cultura*. The sole surviving text of his vast body of work, *De agri cultura* would give rise to a new genre in Rome, championed by several authors (Varro, Columella, not to mention the giant, Virgil). Here, it could be said, is the beginning of Latin literature, the *Latinitas* that would endure for centuries and with which we would come to identify an ethics of language and thought. Cicero himself, whom we'll look at shortly, considered Cato the Elder to be the first prose writer in the tradition: nothing that came before him was worth reading (*Brutus*, XVII.69). The text Cicero refers to most often is Cato's discourses—sadly lost to us now but for a few indirect quotations.

In the work by Cato the Elder that we do possess, there's still something primitive, a list-like quality, which is not derived solely from the prescriptive nature of the genre: do this, do that; don't do this, don't do that; it's done this way, it's not done that way. Indeed, the syntax is limited to a few recurring structures and tends to be formulaic. Nonetheless, Cato's prose has its undeniable artistic force. It is clear, assertive, effective, concise. Read, for example, this passage on curing ham, with which he concludes the text:

> In fundo dolii aut seriae sale sternito, deinde pernam ponito, cutis deosum spectet, sale obruito totam. Deinde alteram insuper ponito, eodem modo obruito. Caveto ne caro carnem tangat. Ita omnes obruito. Ubi iam omnes conposueris, sale insuper obrue, ne caro appareat; aequale facito. Ubi iam dies quinque in sale fuerint, eximito omnis cum suo sale. Quae tum summae fuerint, imas facito eodemque modo obruito et componito. Post dies omnino XII pernas eximito et salem omnem detergeto et suspendito in vento biduum. Die tertio extergeto spongea bene, perunguito oleo, suspendito in fumo biduum. Tertio die demito, perunguito oleo et aceto conmixto, suspendito in carnario. Nec tinia nec vermes tangent. (*De agri cultura*, 162.1–3)

I'll translate this shortly. Let's focus for one moment on some linguistic features that should be obvious even without deeper understanding. The passage consists in large part of a string of future imperatives ending in *ito*; certain verbs repeat (*obruo, com-*

pono) as do certain structures (*ubi* . . .). One can also sense Cato's skillful use of homoeoteleuton—or the repetition of words with like endings (e.g., *sternito/ponito*)—and of alliteration, the repetition of words with the same opening consonant in close succession (*caveto/caro/carnem*; *fuerint/facito*). Even without knowing what the text says, we can see the author's careful attention to aesthetics: a sense of rational order, the willingness to make one operation descend from the preceding one, a clear vision deriving from a prefashioned set of gestures, which correspond to recurring grammatical features. No less remarkable is his simple ability to tackle the subject whole hog, so to speak, leaving nothing unsaid—no matter the banality of the topic. Here's my translation:

> Spread salt along the bottom of a jar or barrel, then place in the ham, skin side up, and cover in salt. Place another ham on top of the first and salt it in the same way, taking care that meat does not touch meat. Salt them all over. Once they're neatly arranged, fill the barrel with more salt until they're completely buried; level the mixture. Let them sit for five days in the salt, then remove them, still salted, from the barrel. Swap the hams so that the one on top before is now on bottom, and again arrange and cover. After twelve full days, remove the hams, brush off the salt, and hang to air-dry for two days. On the third day, scrub them thoroughly with a sponge, rub them in oil, and hang them to smoke for two days. On the third day, remove them from the smoke, rub them in a mixture of oil and vinegar, and hang in the pantry. Neither moth nor worm will touch them.

5

Understanding Latin with Catullus

Among the more satisfying experiences of my first year of high school was the discovery of Catullus. It was just after Christmas, I remember, and I stumbled upon him on my own. I was glancing through the introduction in my Latin textbook, a section our teacher had decided to skip. The topic, after all, was meter, or the structure of the line, still quite foreign waters to us beginners. We had plenty else to learn before learning the rules of Latin poetry: endings upon endings, both for nouns and for verbs; and then the lists of exceptions. Meter we would get to later, if at all.

Our teacher had good reason for adopting the lesson plan she did, and even for limiting our curiosity—mine, case in point—lest it lead us into a bog or over a cliff. My compassionate Chinese teacher, years later, would take a similar attitude: everything in good order, cover one issue at a time, don't ask too many questions, or be paralyzed by the sight of too much complexity. I can't help but think of poor Semele, who dared look directly at Jupiter in all his splendor and was turned to ashes. In truth, as I'd grasped even then, when learning a language—be it Latin, Chinese, or English (another of my oldest loves)—it's a *good thing* to follow your curiosity where it leads, to be open to all paths, to trust yourself at every bend. No risk of incineration, in this case. If anything, the light will not destroy you but illuminate the way.

But as I was saying, among the examples included in that overlooked section of my Latin textbook was a poem by Catullus, quoted in its entirety: eighteen lines on the death of a sparrow. What lay before me—though I had no sense of it at the time—was one of the most celebrated texts in Western literature. I read and reread it, until it lodged in my mind, right where it lives today. How much of it could I grasp? My Latin was still only remedial, but I understood a good bit. I understood more than our step-by-step lesson plan would yet have me understand. (No offense, of course, to our good teacher, who from the very first day of class, and rightly so, warned us against the phonic similarities of Latin and modern languages, which were "almost always misleading.")

> tam bellum mihi passerem abstulistis
> o factum male! o miselle passer!
> tua nunc opera meae puellae
> flendo turgiduli rubent ocelli.

> You took my beautiful sparrow
> O cruel deed! O pitiable sparrow!
> Because of you, my girlfriend's eyes
> are swollen red from crying.

There, in the first line, was *bellum*, which referred to the *passerem*: no chance here that it could mean "war," from the neuter *bellum*, one of the most common words in our translation exercises. It had to mean plain-old *bello*, "beautiful" (and recognizable in "embellishment"!), just like in Italian, even though we'd learned that "beautiful" in Latin was *pulcher*. Of course, some of what I recognized were things we'd studied. Like *deliciae meae puellae*, "my girl's delight," one of the first declension's "peculiarities" (as we referred to "exceptions" in grammar class): the word *deliciae*, along with a group of other feminine words (*indutiae*, "truce"; *nuptiae*, "nuptials"; *Athenae*, "Athens"; *divitiae*, "wealth"; etc.), exists only in the plural (indeed, this word group is known as the *pluralia tantum*, or "plurals only") but with a singular meaning (though Italian would eventually wrangle *deliciae*'s form too into the singular, unlike with words that remained in the plural, such as the word for *nuptiae*—*le nozze*—which in English is also in the plural, "nuptials").

If I'd been asked at the time to explain what Catullus's poem was really about, I wouldn't have been able to give a good answer. What mattered to me was the Latin, for some deep-rooted reason—similar to the way some people are driven to play soccer and others to play the cello. Already I'd intuited that with literature, whether poetry or prose, a purely rational understanding is neither possible nor necessary. In truth, even when the meaning of every word comes to light, some sense of mystery remains; an aura, a shadow, whatever you want to call that nebulous ring that surrounds the chain of signs and sounds, and which belongs to a primitive stage of language, when graphic symbols weren't yet readily associated with codified meanings. To know Latin, even just a little, is to take part in that mystery, to experience a sort of wonder, which is the utterly unique wonder reserved for sublime and foundational events in the history of language, for the power of speech qua speech.

I know far more Latin today than I did in high school, and I can say in full honesty that I still feel this sense of wonder; and even though I've been reading Latin now with relative confidence for many years, I'd never want that fascination to fade. Nor did my wonder for the poem on the death of the sparrow fade when an old friend of mine, Dino, who sat next to me in class and knew of my love for Catullus, gave me the complete poems in translation for my birthday. Indeed, my wonder only grew with understanding, and this book planted in me the seed of a desire that I would come to realize several decades later: to produce my own translations of Catullus.[1]

In my second year of high school, our teacher went on maternity leave, and the substitute taught us a few of Catullus's epigrams: one on the contrast between love and hate; one in which Catullus tells Julius Caesar that he could not care less "if he's black or white" (a metaphor for top or bottom—an allusion to Caesar's homoerotic inclinations); one on a man named Arrius, who aspirated any word that began with a vowel in order to pass himself off as refined. His poem on the death of the sparrow was never assigned. It remained my little secret, which was fine by me.

School syllabi, for all of their glory, are strange affairs. They seem dead set on concealing, or even canceling outright, a fundamental element of education: the very reason for which we go to school. We study Latin so we can read the authors of antiquity. And yet we've long been studying Latin for abstract reasons. I'm not arguing, and I never would, that Latin should be studied like a modern language (if there are people out there who speak it, good for them). It should be studied, again, for the literature in which it is manifested. But what happens in reality is that the literature—the great original works—winds up being largely ignored through the first years of study. Students, instead, are drilled with phony sentences, made up on the spot (female servants sacrificing mules on altars for goddesses, poets loving Muses' roses, schoolgirls praising their teachers, etc.), which neither help them speak the language—which was never the school board's intention in the first place—nor call attention to the literature. In theory, these practice sentences should be there to help students interpret real sentences, those taken from authentic texts, which they'll soon be drowning in. So then why not begin directly with the real sentences—that is to say, with the authors themselves? Even the least inquisitive students will find themselves asking, "When am I ever going to need this stuff? What's the point of me knowing that you can only use *deliciae* in the plural?" Confronting a poem by Catullus head-on would put an end to such disconcerting and legitimate questions. It just takes a bit of care in selecting the more accessible texts at first.

Yes, Catullus is a great place to start. His texts are brief, so less of a burden on a beginning reader; he addresses matters that, as specific as they are to their historical period, still offer something familiar: disappointment, love, suffering, friendship, rivalry. Catullus knows how to move, to engage, to please, even to draw a smile. And his language, for all its formal refinement, is fresh and to the point. We've already seen his use of *bellum* (which we find even as far back as Plautus or in Cicero, the classic of classics). But what about a phrase like *da mi basia mille* (Catullus 5.7, "give me a thousand kisses")? Or of course, the unforgettable *odi et amo*, from epigram 85: "I hate you and I love you":

Odi et amo. Quare id faciam fortasse requiris.
Nescio, sed fieri sentio et excrucior.

I hate you and I love you. Why do I do this, you might ask.
I do not know, but I feel it happening and I'm tortured.

Odi et amo is Catullus's trademark—the key to his entire sensibility and the expression of a conflict that stretches well beyond the personal: the mental and emotional impasse we face when we can no longer find conciliation in our lives, public or private. Such is the economy of the Latin language. And besides, what better way than this epigram to introduce the so-called defective verbs? *Odi, coepi . . .* , verbs that possess forms only in the past perfect system, though they are present in meaning. In that same epigram, we encounter another curious verb: *fieri*. It is the passive infinitive of *facio*, or "to be done/made," though it can also mean "to happen" (as it does in this epigram) or "to become." A famous example: *Fiat lux*, "Let there be light" (from Genesis I). An exhortative subjunctive in the third-person singular.

To learn the exhortative subjunctive, one need only flip to Catullus 5: "vivamus [. . .] atque amemus" (let us live [. . .] and love!). The opening line of Catullus 14 is ideal for teaching the conditional—the third conditional, in this case, dealing with the counterfactual: "Ni te plus oculis meis amarem / [. . .] / odissem te . . ." (If I didn't love you more than my own eyes / [. . .] / then I would hate you . . .). Poem 51 introduces us to one of the most Latin of Latin words in existence: *otium*. Catullus, addressing himself by his own name (as he does elsewhere), says: "otium, Catulle, tibi molestum est" (51.13, "Idleness, Catullus, is destructive to you"). We're here in the midst of a rather special composition, a translation of a lyric by the Greek poet Sappho—one of the few substantial fragments of her work to survive. The line cited above, which includes the name of the poet-translator and begins the piece's final stanza, functions as a signature, or as a declaration of ownership. But what is this *otium* (root of the obscure English adjective *otiose*) that does the poet so much harm and, as the final lines proclaim, has brought kings and entire cities to ruin? For the Romans *otium* was a way of life—the opposite of *negotium*, political activity or public activity in general—synonymous with study and contemplation. Running between the two ideals is an often conflicting tension. In theory, they should complement one another; in practice, they're mutually exclusive. *Otium*, for the Romans, was not something you chose but something forced upon you, an exile from *negotium*, which in the Republican age stood firmly as the highest form of life. For Catullus, however, *otium* was a polemical choice, a disengagement for the purpose of writing poetry—though by no means an apolitical disengagement, rather one filled with civil passion and disdain. Indeed, his poetry, as fresh and individualistic as it may seem, aimed to reform the social ethics of the day by defending values such as loyalty and justice. Catullus detested corruption, betrayal, and frivolity, as much in the people he cared for as in those who ran the government, Julius Caesar first among them.

Another memory from my school days: In my third year of high school, we started taking art history. Our teacher was one Ms. Gilli, a remarkably qualified expert in architecture and painting, well-known for her restoration work with stained glass, versed in semiotics and structuralism, and even something of a classicist. One morning, she set about covering the chalkboard with Latin swear words. This was her method of explaining the concept of style. Every word on the board, she informed us, could be found in Catullus. Of course this display of linguistic boldness made her far more popular than our Latin and Greek teacher.

High school students' enthusiasm for profanity is the expression of an inviolable need for truth: curse words have nothing at all to do with grammar books; curse words are true by their very nature—they're authoritative, they're authentic. No one can curse on another's behalf. And that's exactly the point: to study Latin seriously and productively is to train oneself in the authenticity of language, profanity included. But more on profanity later.

6

Cicero's Star-Studded Sky

The Latin we learn at school is literary Latin. This is an artificial language, a codified language; but no more so, in any case, than that of Petrarch or Shakespeare. As we all should know, written language is more enduring than spoken language, and allows for certain traits not available to oral communication, though not themselves true vestiges of speech.

Its uniformity derives less from an extensive, grammatical coherence than from a widespread "artistic will," and from the commitment to sustaining a tradition, or, taking into account the various genres, a series of traditions. For which reason, even when the irregularities, idiosyncrasies, and departures are evident—irregularities, idiosyncrasies, and departures of which the authors themselves are aware—we still recognize a continuity and a shared sense of purpose. Ovid, to give just one example, is wildly different from Virgil, and yet he's among his inheritors. This lineage is essential, even between authors from distant centuries.

Latin became "classical" in the last years of the Republican era, when an entire culture developed around the regularization and codification of language—a true "grammatical ideology." In a time of political upheaval, and in a final attempt at cultural self-legitimation, the Romans sought to establish statutes and credit in relation to, and even in concurrence with, the great tradition of Greek oratory, as represented by Isocrates and Demosthenes in particular. The resulting characteristics of this "new Latin," which found its most paradigmatic form of expression in oratory, were regularity, orthographic uniformity, semantic clarity, and a syntactical complexity, so-called hypotaxis, or subordination, in which the subjunctive plays a starring role and is used according to predetermined criteria. These very traits will be maintained by *literary* Latin (I again emphasize) for all the centuries to come, despite the divergent approaches of its many authors and its great variety of genres. As such, it distinguished itself sharply from the so-called scholastic Latin of the Middle Ages (blunt, graceless, tone-deaf), as well as from the "Esperanto Latin" (which was meanwhile developing a long life of its own) used in international communication, bureaucracy, antiquarian research, the church, law, and science. When Petrarch railed against Dante's Latin (the Latin of the Middle Ages) and only a few decades later Lorenzo Valla, with increasing competence, labored to restore the elegance of classical standards, it was this literary Latin that they had in mind—a Latin that, though it hadn't exactly gone extinct in the medieval period, had been buried or reduced to a few trickling and aimless streams.

The theoretician and living symbol of this "high" Latin was Cicero, with whose name we've long since come to associate, both in school and out, the very concept of the Latin language and a universal classicism. Petrarch's Latin letter of gratitude, written fourteen centuries after Cicero's death, is worth all the tributes ever penned for him. Addressing Cicero directly, he calls him "supreme father of the Roman language" and the source of whatever greatness his successors achieved (*Familiares*, XXIV.4). His numerous surviving works—which demonstrate excellence in the rhetorical treatise, the philosophical essay, the linguistic essay, juridical oration, and the private letter—have been a trove of examples of proper usage, stylistic devices, and oratorical forms since ancient times.

Cicero's Latin is in fact a self-describing and self-analyzing Latin; it reveals itself as the fruit of a rigorous and rational thought process. What results is a language capable of describing, commenting, expressing passions and emotions, debating, and speculating. Latin, which had already produced wondrous evidence of its expressivity, begins with Cicero to reflect on itself, to codify a way of being. The most extensive treatise on the instruction of oratory written in the imperial age, Quintilian's *Institutio oratoria*, upholds Cicero as the supreme master. And nothing could be more representative than the Cicero-worship professed by Saint Jerome, though he accompanied it with a healthy dose of Christian guilt (more on this later).

Cicero, in the end, came also to represent a model human being: a model of political and moral dedication, an unrivaled example of the power of words, a hero and a martyr of democratic freedom, Catiline's enemy and Mark Antony's bloody casualty, a sensational victim—his hands and head severed—who still today has the power to stir our emotions, even in certain TV depictions of the Roman Empire (I'm thinking of the HBO series *Rome*, 2005–2007). Though not even a man of such high distinction is free from criticism and antipathy. Petrarch, again, is a good example here—for all his admiration of Cicero's style, in another letter of his *Familiares* Petrarch has no problem accusing his idol of opportunism and excessive ambition.

Even just dipping into an anthology of Cicero's letters, one gets a clear sense of his substantially public and competitive character. Different times, yes, different mores, a different culture, in which the individual emerged from a flurry of social functions, and privacy, not surprisingly, was held as the ideal antidote. Cicero outshone his peers through his intense and unceasing social activity: pulling strings, building friendships, recommending one man, cozying up to another, attacking his enemies, making peace, courting favor and alliances, recriminating, justifying himself, defending himself from envious rivals.

The syntax for which Cicero became known as a champion of the Latin language reflected his frenetic social activity. His is a syntax that seeks to examine every corner, to throw light in all directions, to flush out every source of possible opposition and silence it in advance. The result is clear and ordered sentences, complex but not complicated, where everything holds, where one phrase justifies the next and there's no room for doubt or vagueness. Cicero's elegance is in his fullness and thoroughness: in his habit of exhausting the entire potential of the subject, stretching thought to the limits of reason. There's something of a warrior's pathos in his cold, composed reflection: even in his improvisations there's something definitive, something calculated.

With an author of such depth and range, there's no one right place to turn for an example. Almost at random, I can pull down one of his most enjoyable texts from the shelf—his treatise on friendship, composed toward the end of 44 C.E. (Cicero died the following year.) Here's an intriguing bit:

> Sed quoniam amicitiae mentionem fecisti et sumus otiosi,
> pergratum mihi feceris, spero item Scaevolae, si quem
> ad modum soles de ceteris rebus, cum ex te quaeruntur,
> sic de amicitia disputaris quid sentias, qualem existimes,
> quae praecepta des. (*Laelius de amicitia*, IV.16)

This sentence presents remarkable complexity. The concatenation of its various elements is total. Each leans on the one before it and the one that follows. Not a single crack or gap. Here is a word-for-word translation of the Latin:

But since you've mentioned friendship and we aren't busy, I'd be very pleased—and I hope Scaevola would too—if, as you often discuss other matters when they're put to you, you'd tell us your thoughts on friendship, its nature, what lessons you draw from it.

Good Latin, as Cicero saw it, requires not simply a respect for usage (*consuetudo*), which can lead one astray, but obedience to a method (*ratio*) and to clear principles (*Brutus*, 258). That said, Cicero never allows a purist application of the rules to derail his own grammatical plan. At heart is always his own stylistic ideal, which marries, in his own long practice of the art, the history of language, usage, and regularity; in other words, an ability to adapt to the circumstances while nonetheless always pursuing grammatical excellence and formal elegance.

Take note of his clarity, above all: "oratio [. . .] lumen adhibere rebus debet," "language must shed light on things" (*De oratore*, III.50). Language must be coherent and morphologically correct, must avoid ambiguity and excessive metaphor, must not prolong or break up sentences at whim, and must outlaw archaisms and uncouth expressions—that backwoods coarseness (*rusticitas*) which in the past was welcomed as a sign of distinction and a token of tradition. Linguistic orthodoxy, in this way, is elevated to a prerogative of citizenship, *urbanitas*, since the capital of the empire (*Urbs*) is also the stage on which this enduring language is taking shape.

At the core of Cicero's linguistic theory is command of the lexicon, which one must work to achieve from childhood on through the study of literature and daily practice: to choose the words most fitting to the topic and the times—and not culled from a specialized vocabulary but from the language of all, rhetoricians and civilians alike—and to combine them with a proper syntax and sense of rhythm. Musicality is considered essential. One must string words together in phrasings that please the ear, as in poetry. And the sentence must end with a gratifying succession of sounds, because it's there, at the end of a passage, that the reader is most attentive. The words, in short, must flow melodically, though without pleasing too thoroughly or giving the impression of an artificial arrangement: they must be free and controlled at once. The example I'd like to look at here, however, is one that demonstrates how rhythm (*numerus* in Latin) is far more than euphonic harmony. In Book VI of *De re publica*—Cicero's treatise on political philosophy composed between 54 and 51 B.C.E.—Scipio Aemilianus, the destroyer of Carthage, dreams of an encounter in heaven with his ancestor Scipio Africanus, the victor of the Second Punic War. In the course of their conversation, he discovers the structure of the universe, the tininess of earth, the immortality of the soul, and the vanity of glory. The passage—one of the high points of Latin literature—proved a favorite in late antiquity and the Middle Ages. In *De oratore*, Cicero describes the properties of rhythm using the very same vocabulary that Scipio uses to describe the sonic harmony of the celestial bodies in his dream: *intervalla, distinctio, conversio* (a sentence's syntax in one case, a celestial orbit in another[1]), *extrema* (for Cicero the conclusion of a discourse, for Scipio the most distant celestial bodies) (*De oratore*, III.186, and *De re publica*, VI.18). By carefully alternating the musical "note lengths" in a sentence, it is as if one can mirror the order of the cosmos itself.[2] It should not surprise us, then, that in a passage of his *Tusculan Disputations* (I.63) Cicero sets the discovery of rhythm and the observation of the stars in direct relationship.

As I've already indicated, word choice is Cicero's highest priority. The pursuit of clarity demands a continual labor of semantic adjustment, which develops into a true art of terminology. Let's look at an example from *In Verrem*. The work dates to 70 B.C.E., when for the first time Cicero dons the robe of prosecutor, delivering a series of speeches against the former governor of Sicily,

Verres, who partook in every brand of corruption during his years in power, from art heists to the murder of innocent men. The trial presented Cicero with a ripe opportunity: to rise up and defend legality, restoring the credit and prestige of the senatorial class, and to give his own work the importance of a national mission. Here are his words:

> Non enim furem sed ereptorem, non adulterum sed expugnatorem pudicitiae, non sacrilegum sed hostem sacrorum religionumque, non sicarium sed crudelissimum carnificem civium sociorumque in vestrum iudicium adduximus. (*In Verrem*, II.1.9)

> Indeed the man we've brought before this court is not a thief but a despoiler, not an adulterer but a conqueror of chastity, not a plunderer of temples but an armed enemy of the sacred and of religious practice, not a killer but a cruel executioner of citizens and allies.

The scrupulous prosecutor, in order to maximize the effect of his attack, puts his precision on display, demonstrating a thorough mastery of the language. And not only that—he demonstrates with enviable confidence his knowledge of which words most accurately describe reality. Behind such exactitude is a profoundly positive view of speech: a faith that all is expressible, as long as one has the tools. If we take a closer look at the terms he chooses in this passage, we get a clear sense of Cicero's lexical brilliance: *furem* (from *fur*) is a thief (the root survives in the English word "furtive"); *adulterum* is not specifically an unfaithful husband but anyone who practices illicit love (from *adulter*, "one who nears another"); *expugnatorem* (from *expugnator*) is a military term, most commonly used in relation to *urbium* (city), though clearly used as a hyperbolic metaphor here, when placed next to *pudicitiae* (chastity; feminine modesty); *sacrilegum* (from *sacrilegus*) means "one who defiles sacred places," with the idea of sacrilege further expressed by *hostem sacrorum religionumque*, where *hostis* is yet another military metaphor; *sicarium* (from *sicarius*) is your generic killer (from *sica*, "dagger"), while *carnificem* (from *carnifex*) is a professional executioner.

There's no area of speech in which Cicero does not demonstrate a complete understanding of the expressive and—I emphasize—*psychological* potential. To use language well does not mean simply to give form to one's thoughts, but to *communicate them* to others. And when you're speaking to a public audience, efficiency is crucial: to say the right thing in the right way at the right time. You're not up there to bore or bludgeon the audience, but to engage and attract them—and only through this sort of intrigue will you get them to listen, will you move and persuade them with your words.

Oratory, for Cicero, is also an emotional science, an aesthetics of reception, a theory of *linguistic pleasure*. The end goal of all this grammatical acrobatics is not the discourse itself, not the artist's flash of glory on Mount Parnassus, but capturing another's attention. Take what Cicero says about metaphor, for example. I've already mentioned his distaste for excessive imagery (or metaphor), which can spoil the argument. This view, however, does not blind him from the usefulness of metaphor as a device much appreciated by the listener. Why, exactly? Because metaphors add variety; because, though they seem to distance us from the thing they describe, they in fact place it *before our eyes* in another form, thus stimulating our imagination and engaging—which is the point—our senses, particularly vision, our most active sense (*De oratore*, III.159–61). I also spoke of Cicero's lack of tolerance for obscurity. Nevertheless, irony (saying one thing and meaning another) and allusiveness (saying just enough so that the listener may fill in the rest) have much to offer, because, yet again, they give pleasure, and the more gratified the audience is, the more likely they are to listen (*De oratore*, III.202–3).[3]

Cicero's linguistic methodology has proved to be one of the most revolutionary and successful endeavors in European cultural history. He redefined prose both in theory and in practice. And even if the verbal arts have over the centuries developed in different directions, sometimes directly opposed to Ciceronian ideals— beginning in the imperial age, though citing more recent times one might point to the anti-Ciceronianism of Poliziano or Erasmus of Rotterdam, or, in the late nineteenth century, the opposition of a novelist such as Huysmans—Cicero's example served as an inevitable and sometimes even normative reference point long after the end of antiquity. Attention to form, semantic precision, correspondence between vocabulary and subject matter, the avoidance of terms that elicit surprise or disapproval from the reader, the pursuit of clarity and elegance, respect for grammar—all of this we have inherited from Cicero, whether directly or indirectly.

But Ciceronian Latin is not merely a linguistic artifice. It is also—and here's the source of its great worth—the means by which an entire value system was formed, a mode of reflecting on what it means to be human, and one so effective that it has echoed through the centuries. In Cicero's Latin, vice, virtue, and duty found their definitions, and—most critically—linguistic excellence came to be an expression of spiritual excellence. In practice, one cannot establish ethical superiority except through perfect speech. Cicero has Crassus affirm, in *De oratore*, that eloquence is one of the highest virtues: "Est enim eloquentia una quaedam de summis virtutibus" (III.55). For to speak well is a form of knowledge that produces not only beautiful speeches but the organization of civil society itself: customs, laws, governments. To speak well is a philosophy: it is the practice of justice and the creation of happiness. To speak (or write) well is to be good at heart; it is to defend the highest values of our shared existence;

it is freedom itself. And Cicero embodied this fact by placing his eloquence in the service of a society threatened by tyranny. Latin, it could be said, rose to its grammatical excellence in the actions and reflections of Cicero, sworn enemy of all despotism and heroic spokesman for the Senate, and therefore an instrument of liberty, *libertas*, one of the words he held most dear. Take for example this passage from his Third Philippic, one of the speeches he wrote opposing Mark Antony, where his ideological defense of liberty manifests itself in a sophisticated rhetorical-syntactic device:

> Hanc vero nactus facultatem nullum tempus, patres con-scripti, dimittam neque diurnum neque nocturnum, quin de libertate populi Romani et dignitate vestra, quod cog-itandum sit cogitem, quod agendum atque faciendum, id non modo non recusem, sed etiam appetam atque depos-cam. Hoc feci, dum licuit; intermisi, quoad non licuit. Iam non solum licet, sed etiam necesse est, nisi servire malu-mus quam, ne serviamus, armis animisque decernere. (*Philippicae*, III.33)

The first sentence of the passage is its most complex. The lines that follow are simpler, their word order being closer to that of modern languages. Even these, though, have their share of preci-sion and structural elegance: symmetry, repetition, and variation, in which the various inversions of meaning come to symbolize the spirit of protest and desire for retribution. In translation:

> But now with this opportunity [Cicero's chance to give ad-vice to the Senate, since he has not yet been executed by Mark Antony], O senators, I won't let a moment pass, day or night, without considering what must be considered for the freedom of the Roman people and for your dignity. And whatever must be planned or done [to this end] I will

not only not shrink from, but will take to with relish and eagerness. This was my response before, when it was in my power; and while it was not in my power [under Julius Caesar's dictatorship], I ceased temporarily. Now not only is it within my power but it is my duty, unless we prefer being slaves to wielding our weapons and souls in a fight against slavery.

Under Cicero's direction, Latin takes the stage as a language of truth and justice. The speaker is not a theater mask or the character from an epic but an actor in life: a man who fights, relying on his own intelligence and honesty, against the collapse of society and political corruption, and who sees himself and his neighbor first as citizens of the *Urbs*, as children of the greatest republic of all time. In the hands of such a civic-minded man, Latin is gradually refined and perfected by the meticulous search for the arguments and evidence that present "reality as it is" and help to identify any necessary solutions, to point out any crookedness and set it straight without ever losing sight of the ideal future—which, for Cicero (typical of Romans and of Westerners throughout the centuries), almost always took the form of an example of past excellence. In short: a continual, impassioned criticism of the present combined with a nostalgia for a fully realized, ideal antiquity. Between these two poles—criticism and nostalgia—and with Cicero as referee, Latin played its most glorious game. And the referee, of course, had a substantial role in the game, because thanks to him Latin became the language of a new subjectivity, the language of autobiography. Cicero's voice, in fact, paints for us a perfectly complete and defined historical individual, a man conscious of his own aims, who strives to forge a linguistic and rhetorical identity, and to come entirely alive through his words. Thus he manages to establish one of the most prevalent myths of Western society: the great man, the saintly layman, a mélange of disdain, modesty, linguistic expertise, rigor, resistance to evil, thirst for glory, self-promotion, audacity, vehemence, severity, moralism, horror in the face of historical decline.

Cicero's political engagement served as the principal source of Latin's formal development, through both his theoretical work and his numerous institutional roles. But one must also keep in mind the author's speculative engagement, his participation not only in political discussion and legal battles, but also in the realm of spiritual reflection. Cicero, it could be said, gave philosophy its Roman citizenship. His philosophical writings, which, not surprisingly, he composed only after his retirement from the public sphere, represent yet another important moment in the history of Latin and in the history of Western thought (one need only mention Voltaire's laudatory entry for Cicero in his *Dictionnaire philosophique* to prove his enduring influence). He broadens Latin vocabulary by turning to Greek sources (Platonism, Aristotelianism, Stoicism, Epicureanism), and by bringing new color to terms already in use. Most significantly, he sets new debates in motion, offering moral and spiritual models that will endure across centuries: on virtue, our intellectual faculties, happiness, the meaning of death, the value of life, the nature of the soul. In the above-mentioned *Tusculan Disputations*, Cicero's philosophical masterpiece (c. 45 B.C.E.), he lays out the properties of the mind in four infinitive verbs, properties he holds to be almost divine: "vigere, sapere, invenire, meminisse" (I.65). That is, "vigor, knowledge, discovery, memory." On the properties of memory, that mysterious and magnificent faculty, Cicero was already posing fascinating questions, paving the way for Saint Augustine's analysis. Interestingly, Augustine, in his *Confessions*—composed toward the end of the fourth century C.E.—will claim to have discovered philosophy through his reading of Cicero's *Hortensius*. But just witness this splendid ode to thought:

illa vis quae tandem est quae investigat occulta, quae
inventio atque excogitatio dicitur? ex hacne tibi terrena
mortalique natura et caduca concreta ea videtur? aut qui
primus, quod summae sapientiae Pythagorae visum est,
omnibus rebus imposuit nomina? aut qui dissipatos homines congregavit et ad societatem vitae convocavit, aut
qui sonos vocis, qui infiniti videbantur, paucis litterarum
notis terminavit, aut qui errantium stellarum cursus,
praegressiones, institutiones notavit? (*Tusculanae dispu-
tationes*, I.62)

what is that force which seeks out hidden things, which
we call invention and imagination? does it seem to you an
earthly substance, and therefore mortal and fleeting? who
was it then who first gave things their names—a task that
to Pythagoras seemed to require great intelligence? who
then gathered men from across the earth and called them
to social life? who, with a few alphabetical scrawlings,
defined the seemingly infinite sounds of the voice? who
was it to note the orbits, the wanderings, the stations of
the planets?

7

Ennius's Ghost

Say the word "Latin" and the first thing that comes to mind is a fixed number of texts and testimonies, a literature long since laid to rest, bound by strict grammatical rules and here forever in its changeless state. But this is not the case. What we call Latin is a collection of writings that have made miraculous escapes from destruction and dispersal, some of which came to light only after long eclipse, others irreparably defaced, none preserved in its original condition. Continuity is not a necessary requirement of what we call tradition. To transmit, or pass on, is far from a linear process and follows no fixed path or program. The Latin studied today in high schools or universities, to be clear, is the result of an endless process of reconstructing—a process reliant on the surviving materials and even speculation and conjecture. The beauty of Latin is the beauty of what's been salvaged and guarded from the flux of life. To study Latin—and we must always remember this—is also to come to terms with loss; to learn to enjoy the little (quite a lot, nonetheless) that fate has left us, to respect it, to care for it. As Boccaccio wrote in the preface to his *Genealogia deorum gentilium* (On the Genealogy of the Gods of the Gentiles), time eats away the stones: what would you have it do with books? And we're not speaking of minor scribblings, but of widely read and deeply influential works. I won't go listing all our great losses here (for that I suggest Henry Bardon's two-volume *La littérature latine inconnue*). One alone will suffice: the work of Ennius (239–169 B.C.E.), model to Virgil in the art of the epic, and much more. Ennius, in fact, tested his skills in an extraordinary variety of genres, from theater (comedy and tragedy, at which he excelled) to satire, from epigrams and epic prose to his *Annales* (in eighteen books), to which he dedicated the last years of his life. Of such a vast and influential body of work only a few crumbs remain. In literary surveys, he's remembered simply as a pioneer, renowned for his characteristic use of alliteration, a trait typical of archaic Latin in general, as well as of other languages, such as Old English. Still to this day, one can conveniently explain alliteration by this one line of Ennius's poetry: "O tite tute Tati tibi tanta tyranne tulisti," which means . . . well, no, it doesn't quite matter. Better left as is, intact with all its *t*'s—which for me, in my third year of high school, was the extent of its meaning anyway.

Born in the Messapian city of Rudiae (whose ruins lie a few miles from modern Lecce), Ennius came of age in the vibrant melting pot of Magna Graecia. As a young man in his early twenties, he fought in Sardinia against the Carthaginians, who threatened the survival of the Roman Empire. We find an engrossing account of this military adventure in the seventeen-book *Punica*, by Silius Italicus (XII, vv. 388ff.), a poet of the first century B.C.E.—a literary undertaking that itself owes much to Ennius. At age thirty-five he reached the capital, led by Cato the Elder. Future generations would consider this poet, who sang the glory of ancient Rome and the deeds of Scipio Africanus (destroyer of Hannibal at the Battle of Zama), the father of Latin literature. Indeed, *Pater*, "Father," is the honorific by which many later poets would refer to Ennius.[1] Lucretius attaches an affectionate *noster* to his name (*De rerum natura*, I.117). A millennium and a half later, Petrarch too evokes him, portraying him as his double in *Africa* (Book IX), the Latin epic poem that would help earn him eternal glory: Ennius speaks of the poetic laurels, recounting a dream in which Homer predicts the future of Latin poetry and the arrival of a great poet named Francesco. The *Annales* also opens with a dream—modeled after the dream that the Greek poet Hesiod describes in the opening pages of the *Theogony*: Homer appears to Ennius and reveals that, after a brief stage as a peacock, he's been reincarnated as him, as Ennius, opening the latter to the mysteries of the world. The same tale is recounted by Lucretius, in the passage cited earlier. And Cicero too will recall Ennius's dream, in Book VI of *De re publica*, where Scipio Aemilianus has his dream of Scipio Africanus.

Ennius played a crucial role in the development of a national consciousness, at the same time expressing full awareness of his literary mission. In doing so, he offered himself as a model to Lucretius and to Virgil, and as father of the epic genre. And still more: as the linguistic conscience of all Latin poetry to come.

In a fragment from Book VII (fr. 133) of the *Annales*, the poet declares the newness of his poetry in no uncertain terms, giving proof of the artistic awareness that sets him firmly apart from the mere Homeric impersonators who came before him:

Scripsere alii rem
vorsibus quos olim Faunei vatesque canebant,
quom neque Musarum scopulos
nec <docti> dicti studiosus quisquam erat ante hunc.[2]

Others wrote things
in verse the Fauns and the seers once sang,
since [none climbed] the hills of the Muses
nor did anybody before me care for learned words.

What we have here is a very direct, and a very proud, attack. His reference to *alii* is not as vague as it might seem. It alludes to a work by the poet Naevius (275–c. 201 B.C.E.)—of whose oeuvre only a few scraps remain—regarding the Second Punic War. The meter that Naevius uses is the ancient Saturnian verse, which Ennius replaces here with Greek hexameter—the same meter we find in the *Iliad* and the *Odyssey*. This is why Ennius—and not without a measure of scorn—speaks specifically of fauns, native woodland divinities, and seers, who deliver their oracles in poetic form. His decision to invoke the Muses, the Greek goddesses—rather than the Italic Camenae, as Naevius does—is an important mark of his Hellenism. The word "Muse" appears in the first line of the *Odyssey*, and is probably linked to the Greek word *menos*, meaning "vital force." We find it in another fragment of Ennius as well, in Book I of the *Annales* (fr. 1), which many scholars believe to be the opening verse:

Musae, quae pedibus pulsates Olumpum[3]

Muses, who strike Olympus with your feet

For Olympus we're perhaps to understand not the mountain in Greece but the heavens. The *scopuli*—a term that means principally "rocks"—are the Greek hills where the Muses reside, Parnassus and Helicon (though some have interpreted *scopuli* as a metaphor for difficulty, which it may well be). Another Hellenizing and revolutionary aspect is Ennius's declaration of a poetics: here, *for the first time*, we have Latin poetry that has been carefully weighed. The model he has in mind is the Alexandrian Callimachus, a poet who will have a substantial influence on later Latin poets as well (chief among them Catullus and Virgil, though also Propertius and others): a cultured and erudite poet, a lover of the the outlandish, of all things vagrant and valuable. The theme of dreams, so fundamental to the *Annales*, is not just Hesiodic, as suggested above, but also Callimachean: at the opening of his *Aetia* he dreams of being transported to the mountain of the Muses, where he learns of the myths he'll later recount in the poem. Also worth pointing out is the adjective *studiosus*, which derives from *studium* (hence the English "study"): passion, engagement, dedication. Two fragments from Book VII, which fall sequentially in the text (fr. 134–35), emphasize his superior poetic intelligence—which he acquired through Homer's revelation and not by study or experience—and the boldness of his undertaking:

> nec quisquam sopiam sapientia quae perhibetur
> in somnis vidit prius quam sam discere coepit.
> [. . .]
> Nos ausi reserare.

> nor has anyone, without learning of it first,
> seen the Sophia they call wisdom [among the Romans] in
>   his dreams
> [. . .]
> We dared open up.[4]

For Ennius, then, the reformation of the Latin language amounts to this: one must be initiated into a new poetic consciousness, and use language and the tools of expression according to the highest Hellenistic aesthetics. The poem's most substantial fragments make abundantly clear just how innovative his work was. I'd like to quote from two of them: one a psychological characterization (fr. 164), the other a physical description (fr. 332). Here we meet the man known as Servilius's friend (Servilius Geminus was consul in 217 B.C.E. and died in the Battle of Cannae a year later):

> Haece locutus vocat quocum bene saepe libenter
> mensam sermonesque suos rerumque suarum

comiter impertit, magnam cum lassus diei
partem trivisset de summis rebus regundis
consilio indu foro lato sanctoque senatu:
quoi res audacter magnas parvasque iocumque
eloqueretur cuncta <simul> malaque et bona dictu
evomeret si qui vellet tutoque locaret;
quocum multa volup <et> gaudia clamque palamque.
Ingenium quoi nulla malum sententia suadet
ut faceret facinus levis, aut malus; doctus, fidelis,
suavis homo, facundus, suo contentus, beatus,
scitus, secunda loquens in tempore, commodus, verbum
paucum, multa tenens antiqua sepulta vetustas
quae facit, et mores veteresque novosque tenentem
multorum veterum leges divumque hominumque,
prudentem qui dicta loquive tacereve possit:
hunc inter pugnas compellat Servilius sic.[5]

These things said, he calls [the man] with whom he often
and eagerly shares meals and conversation
and business matters, having spent himself
all day in the large forum and sacred senate
weighing the most urgent issues and giving counsel;
to whom he speaks boldly on matters large and small,
pretty and ugly, joking and venting his spleen
as he pleases and in good confidence, relaying
joys and pleasant affairs in public and private,
toward whom he holds no thoughts of ill intent,
or ever treats lightly; learned, faithful,
a mild, eloquent man, contented, blessed,
experienced, knows what to say and when, who's kind
and careful with words, knows many ancient things
buried by time, knows customs old and new,
the ancient laws of gods and men,

wise, who knows when to speak and to be silent.
So Servilius addresses this man in the midst of battles.

The unevenness of the syntax in these lines is evident, especially when compared to the classical fluidity of Virgil, Ennius's most famous heir. Even beneath this archaic exterior, however, the moral argument is vivid and complex. Here we have a lively sketch of one of the first great friend figures in Latin literature, prototype of the many excellent companions who populate the canon and who make friendship one of the cornerstones of Roman ethics: Catullus's poem 50 comes immediately to mind; or the friendship between Nisus and Euryalus in the *Aeneid*; or else Cicero's *De amicitia*, in which he indeed cites Ennius as the authority on the subject, though he quotes a different passage. Some have speculated that the good companion Ennius means to portray here is himself. He certainly gives us the portrait of an ideal man, the cultivated Roman, who is at once disciplined, moderate, trustworthy, pleasant, serious, spirited, and in possession of a deep knowledge of history and skill as an orator; an individual who is both the perfect friend in private and the perfect confidant and counselor to a political figure, a sort of "courtier" *ante litteram*. Note how frequently he turns to the theme of the word, because the word is at the foundation of civilization: the word as source of knowledge and reason. I'd also like to underline just how pregnant with meaning the adjective *facundus* is. This is formed from the root of the verb *fari*, "to say" (whose present participle, when used in the negative, gives us the word *infans*, a child who cannot yet speak, or "infant"), and from the suffix *-cundus*, meaning "able" (which we find in *fe-cundus*, *vere-cundus*, etc.). In Latin there also exists the noun *facundia*: Quintilian, for example, uses it to describe the historian Livy (*Institutio oratoria*, VIII.1). *Facundus* is a person who knows how to speak, not merely spout words. Quintilian also drew a distinction between *loquax* and *facundus* (IV.2).

And here's the second example:

Et tum sicut equos qui de praesepibus fartus
vincla suis magnis animis abrupit et inde
fert sese campi per caerula laetaque prata
celso pectore; saepe iubam quassat simul altam;
spiritus ex anima calida spumas agit albas.

And then, like a horse well nourished in the stalls
who snapped his bonds with the force of his soul, and
      from there
travels over the lush green fields of the plain,
breast held high, while tossing his long mane,
the breath from his hot spirit foaming white.

The simile here is typical of the epic genre. Ennius has modeled it—adding the fields and the foam—on a passage from Homer
(*Iliad*, VI.506s). In the source text, the comparison is made to
Paris as he advances toward the citadel of Troy. For Ennius, as
well, the subject of comparison in the original is likely a warrior.
Apart from its dependence on Homer, the passage is evidence of
his mastery of the descriptive art: he sets the scene with confidence and fixes it in a memorable image. Already we notice some
of the characteristics that will later define the *Aeneid*: a fluid narrative style, the semantic emphasis placed on the beginning of
each line, the sensory concreteness of the descriptive elements.
His use of alliteration is hard to miss: *fartus/fert*; *campi/caerula/
celso* (the *c* in Latin, remember, is always hard, pronounced like
a *k*); *prata/pectore*; *spiritus/spumas*. Ennius is renowned for his
droning alliteration, but here the sounds feel neither forced nor
mechanical; not only do they help to structure the poem, but they
reinforce the imagery, giving all a unified sense of musicality.

For anyone with an interest in semantics and etymology,

there's plenty to mine here. *Fartus* is the past participle of the verb *farcio*, "to fill." The compound *in-fartus* leads to the modern "infarct" and "infarction," which do, precisely, indicate a filling up, or occlusion. *Caerula* is a rather vaguely dark color, which varies from sky blue (it derives, after all, from *caelum*, "heaven," and gives us "cerulean") to sea blue, to green, and even to black. *Laeta* means "fertile," "lush": its root, for good reason, is also present in the word *laetamen*, "manure."

8

Caesar, or the Measures of Reality

Whenever our teacher gave us a passage to translate from Caesar (101 or 100–44 B.C.E.), the class broke into cheers. Caesar was a cakewalk, as far as we were concerned. And it's true, even the slackers could get by with only a few minor errors. Our teacher too, who took delight in labyrinthine complexity, branded less difficult passages as mere "Caesar league." No one suspected that in fact disguised beneath this apparent simplicity was the Latin language expressed in one of its highest, most perfect forms.

In his *De bello Gallico*, Caesar's best-preserved work, he recounts the conquest of Gaul (58–51 B.C.E.). Or more precisely, he recounts the intentions and results and last-minute solutions of his campaign. Each of his actions falls like a domino in a well-planned strategy, winning him one victory after another—victory being nothing other than the overcoming of various difficulties. The text is composed of a series of dispatches, all in the third person, that Caesar sent to the Senate to keep them informed of his military actions. It's possible that these dispatches were meant as a set of notes for a more polished story, to be written at the close of the war. I won't dwell here on the work's great ideological and propagandistic value, nor on the fact—both moving and disconcerting—that the man speaking to us is one of the most decorated in all of antiquity, describing one of the most consequential military campaigns in world history, one that would shift Rome's power from East to West. I'll add only this gem by Bertolt Brecht:

> He had inaugurated a new era. Before him Rome had been a city with a few scattered colonies. He was the one who founded the empire. He codified the law, reformed the currency, and even modified the calendar on the basis of scientific knowledge. His Gallic campaigns, which had taken the Roman flag as far as Britain, had opened up a new continent to trade and civilization. His statue had its place with those of the gods, he had given his name to cities as well as a month in the calendar, and the monarchs attached his illustrious name to their own. The history of Rome had found its Alexander. It was already apparent that he would become the unattainable model for every dictator.[1]

What I'd like to focus on here is what the Latin language itself was able to accomplish through the work of Caesar. I should say right off that Caesar was not only a great writer but also an important linguistic theorist. We know from various sources that he composed a treatise entitled *De analogia*, though only a few fragments remain. Its dedicatee was none other than Cicero. We can get an idea of its contents: it must have offered a defense of proper Latin and in particular of the correct usage of morphology. "Analogy" is a Greek term and in ancient treatises on language it points to strict grammar, uniformity, and morphological coherence, standing in contrast to the term "anomaly," which indicates a multitude and variety of forms. The guiding principle of analogists is simplification: no more variations, no more archaisms, no more alternating inflections. Caesar, as Brecht reminds us, altered even the Roman calendar, ridding the timekeeping method of uncertainties and imprecisions (the Julian calendar was used up until 1582, when it was substituted by the even more accurate Gregorian calendar). It can be said that he took a similarly rational approach when it came to language, with an analogous desire for containment and measure. Geography, not surprisingly, was one of his chief interests. We know from later sources that at a certain point he hired four Greeks to explore the *oikumene*—that is, the entire inhabited world. Clearly such an interest is also linked to his pragmatism as a military man.

Rationalism and pragmatism rear their heads in his surviving work as well. Everything has its explanation, *everything can be broken down into parts and primary elements*, as if the obscurity and vagueness of our deeper motives had no place here, or worse, as if they didn't exist at all (for these one must turn to Livy and Tacitus, as we'll see). The first sentence of the work is itself an example of disassembling: "Gallia est omnis divisa in partes tres . . . ," "The whole of Gaul is divided into three parts . . ." To disassemble is to calculate: hence his use of numbers and measurements. Distance, breadth, depth, and all variety of record keeping—of space and time alike—are distinctive traits throughout the work.

After all, *De bello Gallico* is the adventure of a language trying to re-create the world mathematically and geometrically, its sentences organized according to precise cause-and-effect relationships and set in a clearly defined time period. The theme of ends and consequences also plays a dominant role, for that which has no aim or provokes no change is not worth mentioning.

Language, then, for Caesar, is an account of something that occurs in a particular moment, for a particular reason, in view of a particular aim, and with particular consequences. Here's a characteristic passage:

His rebus gestis, Labieno in continenti cum tribus legionibus et equitum milibus duobus relicto, ut portus tuere-
tur et rem frumentariam provideret, quaeque in Gallia
gererentur cognosceret consiliumque pro tempore et pro
re caperet, ipse cum quinque legionibus et pari numero
equitum, quem in continenti reliquerat, ad solis occasum
naves solvit . . . (*De bello Gallico*, V.8)

With these things done, and having left Labenius behind
on land—with three legions and two thousand horses,
to guard the ports and restock the granaries, and to
familiarize himself with the situation in Gaul and make
decisions according to need and occasion—he [Caesar],
with five legions and as many horses, which he'd left on
land, set sail toward the west . . .

This passage is a perfect ensemble, seasoned with precision
and arithmetic; one might even call it a true work of grammatical
architecture. That Caesar holds a passion for the art of construction is no surprise, and it's precisely in those passages where he's
describing certain structures that he achieves his highest mastery
of Latin prose: the bridge over the Rhine (IV.17), erected in just
ten days (efficiency is one of Caesar's foremost talents), which allowed the Roman troops to cross from Gaul into Germany, only
to be dismantled eighteen days later when Caesar marched back
into Gaul (VII.23); and Venetian ships (III.13). Numbers abound
in these passages: distances and dimensions. His is a language
under pressure: in the fewest words possible he must lay out how
the structure develops, how its various parts interact, and how
they correspond to form a whole.

Let's look now at his description of the bridge over the Rhine,
a particularly illuminating passage in that it describes not a com-

plete work but one in progress, as demonstrated by the many verbs in the imperfect:

> Rationem pontis hanc instituit. Tigna bina sesquipedalia
> paulum ab imo praeacuta dimensa ad altitudinem flu-
> minis intervallo pedum duorum inter se iungebat. Haec
> cum machinationibus immissa in flumen defixerat fistu-
> cisque adegerat, non sublicae modo derecte ad perpen-
> diculum, sed prone ac fastigate, ut secundum naturam
> fluminis procumberent, iis item contraria duo ad eundem
> modum iuncta intervallo pedum quadragenum ab infe-
> riore parte contra vim atque impetum fluminis conversa
> statuebat. Haec utraque insuper bipedalibus trabibus
> immissis, quantum eorum tignorum iunctura distabat, bi-
> nis utrimque fibulis ab extrema parte distinebantur; qui-
> bus disclusis atque in contrariam partem revinctis, tanta
> erat operis firmitudo atque ea rerum natura ut, quo maior
> vis aquae se incitavisset, hoc artius inligata tenerentur . . .
> (*De bello Gallico*, IV.17)

Here was his plan for the bridge. First he took pairs of one-and-a-half-foot pilings, cut to equal length—to match the depth of the river—and tapered to a point, and trellised them together, setting a pair every two feet along the waterline. Having stood the pilings in the river with an engine, he rammed them into the riverbed—not upright like posts, but leaning slightly into the current; about forty feet downstream, he drove in more of these same pilings, doubled up in the same way, but stood them leaning upstream, against the current. Between each pair he wedged two-foot-wide girders (to span the distance between the double timber pilings), and trussed them up at either end with pairs of braces. With the pilings thus linked and held apart, and leaning in toward one another, the structure was so strong, and the interplay between its parts so balanced, that the greater the force of the water beating against it, the greater the system's resilience.

The passage opens, we notice, with the term *ratio* (from which we get the English "reason"): plane, form, rule. Then comes the parade of technical terms, which occupies the remainder of the paragraph.

What renders such a passage extraordinary is not simply that it describes the engineering with exactitude and concision, but that it puts the labor of language itself on display: the process of linking one piece to another to form a solid, enduring structure. Language, Caesar shows us, is a bridge, a wall, a ship: it conjoins, contains, transports. It is, in other words, syntax: a group of necessary components assembled according to a given function, which, for Caesar, in this particular case, is to inform and explain, surveying and conquering every inch of the expressible.

9

The Power of Clarity: Lucretius

There's something sacred about discovering Lucretius; it feels like stepping into heaven.

His *De rerum natura* reveals the atomic structure of the universe in six books, taking its cues from the philosophy of Epicurus. It seeks to lift the shade of ignorance from our minds, to free our hearts from a false belief in the gods and from the fear of death, to teach the truth and the joy of living. Of its author, Lucretius, we know very little, and with little certainty. Primo Levi, who included a passage from *De rerum natura* in his anthology *La ricerca delle radici* (*The Search for Roots*), writes, "There has always been a whiff of impiety about his verses. For this reason, at the end of antiquity a cloak of silence was wrapped around him and today almost nothing is known of this extraordinary man."[1]

To such impiety we owe one of the greatest tributes to life of all time, found right at the poem's beginning: a celebration of the world's generative power, embodied in the traditional figure of Venus, the goddess of love, beauty, spring, the renewing force of all creation, and a source of peace.

Lucretius, as Ennius before him, declares himself a great

innovator (I.921–50 and, in the same words, IV.1–25). He affirms his love for the Muses and poetry and is convinced not only that he's bringing new truths to light, but that he's doing so with elegance and care, and that he should be crowned for his achievements:

> avia Pieridum peragro loca nullius ante
> trita solo. Iuvat integros accedere fontis
> atque haurire, iuvatque novos decerpere flores
> insignemque meo capiti petere inde coronam
> unde prius nulli velarint tempra Musae . . .
>   (I.926–30 and IV.1–5)

> I roam those lands of the Pierides
> where none before has stepped. I thrill to touch,
> to drink from pristine fountains, pluck new flowers,
> and make myself a beautiful crown with which the
>   Muses
> have dressed the temples of no other man before . . .

The Pierides are the Muses themselves, so named for their home in Pieria, a region of Macedonia. Also of interest are the lines preceding these (921–25), in which the poet declares that a type of Bacchic inspiration lies at the root of his love for poetry. In the case of the atheist Lucretius, of course, it's clear that we're dealing with a stock image, not a contradiction: poetry, as much as it proposes itself to be a scientific endeavor, is a state of feverish and irrepressible exaltation, a reinvigoration of the mental capacities: *mente vigenti*, where *vigenti* is the participle, in the ablative, of the verb *vigeo*, meaning "to flower," the root of which gives us "vigor" and "vigilant." And *vigere*, as you'll remember, is one of Cicero's four properties of the mind.

When your aim is the reeducation of mankind, you have no choice but to produce syntax that unfolds in smooth paragraphs, crisp sentences, sharp imagery. Because he's working in verse— that is, in a structure regulated by metrical rules—it might seem that Lucretius's style tends toward a certain rigidness, and at times that is indeed the case. The guiding principle of Lucretius's work, in fact, is the systematic search for order and clarity. This becomes most apparent when observing his use of terms that emphasize logical relationships of cause and effect, such as *quoniam* (since), *praeterea* (furthermore), *sic . . . ut* (so that), and *primum . . . deinde* (first off . . . then). What looks like syntactic rigidity is argumentative rigor, and the examples he proposes are the proof.

His lexicon, no less than his syntax, responds brilliantly to the innovative nature of his project. Lexicon is without doubt the principal element of Lucretius's modernism, starting with the title of the work itself. Taken literally, it means "on the nature of things." *Rerum* is the genitive plural of *res*, a much-used and long-lived word, which absorbs meaning from its context (our "reality" comes from there!). Originally it stood for a "material good," a "possession." It can also indicate an action: *res gestae* are "military actions" (things done); or else "circumstances," "situations," which are either *malae* (*adversae*) or *bonae* (*secundae*), "unfavorable" or "favorable." Virgil uses the expression—now famous (and considered by many to be incomprehensible)—*sunt lacrimae rerum*, in the passage in which Aeneas, while in Carthage, reflects on a painting of the battle of Troy (*Aeneid*, I.462): among the various scenes depicted is "the people's lament for the present tragedy." Followed by the adjective *publica*, *res* comes to mean the "state," and in particular that form of state whose principal institution is the Senate: that is, the "republic."

Lucretius certainly laid his claim to the word *res*. *Res* is matter, substance, the very heart of what it is to be an object. Consider the following passage, where his concern is not physical but moral:

> Quo magis in dubiis hominem spectare periclis
> convenit adversisque in *rebus* noscere qui sit;
> nam verae voces tum demum pectore ab imo
> eliciuntur et eripitur persona, manet *res*.
>   (III.55–58; emphasis mine)

> One should measure a man when thrown in peril
> and get to know him in adversity;
> only then will his voice rise truly from within his soul,
> and his mask dissolve—leaving only essence.

These four lines make for an excellent example of just how attentive Lucretius is to vocabulary: the word *res* appears not once but twice: the first time in a circumlocution (*adversae res*), the second in a unique contrast to the word *persona*, meaning "mask."

Lucretius defines and delimits his meanings with stark precision, avoiding all sense of vagueness or inertia. In this aspect alone, one can see just how fundamental a contribution he made to the development of Latin.

Let's turn to another example of his way with vocabulary: the word *pietas*. It expresses a highly important concept in Roman culture, also a distinctive characteristic of Virgil's Aeneas (later carried over into Christianity, which intensified and specialized the term). *Pietas* is respect for the gods, for one's parents, and for one's country; it is the highest form of love: participation, devotion, commitment, trust. It can, therefore, when dealing with the metaphysical, be translated as "religion." *Religio* does exist in Latin with the meaning "religion." However, Lucretius uses the term only to mean "superstition," leaning heavily on its etymological root, *lig-* (if that is indeed its root), meaning "to bind," as survives in the English word "ligament." *Religio*, therefore, is a chain, a knot from which one must free oneself (*De rerum natura*, I.931–32 and, again, IV.6–7). Lucretius wholeheartedly contests the existence of the gods and, as a consequence, all faith in them, whether superstitious or not. Observe the skill with which he gives new meaning to the word *pietas*:

> nec pietas ullast velatum saepe videri
> vertier ad lapidem atque omnis accedere ad aras,
> nec procumbere humi prostratum et pandere palmas
> ante deum delubra nec aras sanguine multo
> spargere quadrupedum, nec votis nectere vota,
> sed mage pacata posse omnia mente tueri.
>   (V.1197–1202)

> Nor does piety mean to be frequently spotted
> in a veil, addressing this stone, approaching that altar,
> nor to fling oneself on the ground with palms upturned
> before the shrines of gods, or drench their altars
> in quadrupeds' blood, nor to loop your vows with vows.
> But rather, to contemplate everything with peace of mind.

Pietas, then, is devotion to intellectual clarity, to responsible judgment, to assured intuition, not the practice of bloody or theatrical ceremonies. Ritual violence against animals stands in direct contrast to such a concept. One of the most beautiful and moving passages of *De rerum natura* is when Lucretius describes the plaint of a cow as its calf is sacrificed:

> nam saepe ante deum vitulus delubra decora
> turicremas propter mactatus concidit aras,

sanguinis expirans calidum de pectore flumen;
at mater viridis saltus orbata peragrans
novit humi pedibus vestigia pressa bisulcis,
omnia convisens oculis loca si queat usquam
conspicere amissum fetum, completque querellis
frondiferum nemus adsistens et crebra revisit
ad stabulum desiderio perfixa iuvenci;
nec tenerae salices atque herbae rore vigentes
fluminaque illa queunt summis labentia ripis
oblectare animum subitamque avertere curam,
nec vitulorum aliae species per pabula laeta
derivare queunt animum curaque levare:
usque adeo quiddam proprium notumque requirit.
    (II.352–66)

thus often does a calf, before the gods' rich temples,
fall slain at incense-burning altars,
exhaling a stream of warm blood from its chest;
meanwhile, the bereft mother, ranging through green
    valleys,
recognizes the prints left by its cloven hooves,
sending her eyes to every piece of land, hoping to catch
a glimpse of her lost child, and pausing now
she fills the verdant forest with her moans, again and
    again
returning to the stalls, tortured by the absence of the calf.
Nor can the slender willows, nor the grass revived with dew,
the river gliding full between the banks,
bring comfort to her heart or dull her pain;
nor can the sight of other calves at pasture
distract her heart or lighten her dismay:
so keenly does she search for what she knows, and is
    her own.

Of particular interest here is that Lucretius describes the poor mother's pursuit of her calf in the very same terms that, elsewhere, he uses to describe the pursuit of knowledge. The action verb that he employs for her search through the green valleys is *peragrans*, the present participle of *peragro*, the same verb that Lucretius uses—as we saw above—to proclaim the newness of his poetic journey. Then follows a series of verbs, many of which related to sight, that further suggest a process of investigation and reason: *convisens, conspicere, revisit, requirit.* The cow's method, like the author's, is nothing short of the scientific method, or that of a modern sleuth: she gathers clues, follows footprints (*vestigia*).[2] The absence, conjured up by the word *desiderium*, literally "nostalgia" (and, in a different sense, the English "desire," or the longing for something *that one no longer has*), invokes a hoped-for rediscovery, a reuniting with what's been lost. It's that very same condition we recognize in those who are oblivious and uncertain, deprived of all sense of truth, and who race about aimlessly. It's no surprise, then, that Lucretius will be the first to portray dissatisfaction, or anguish—and he links it directly to the absence of intellectual clarity. Here's his portrait of the anguished man:

exit saepe foras magnis ex aedibus ille,
esse domi quem pertaesumst, subitoque revertit,
quippe foris nihilo melius qui sentiat esse.
Currit agens mannos ad villam praecipitanter,
auxilium tectis quasi ferre ardentibus instans;
oscitat extemplo, tetigit cum limina villae,
aut abit in somnum gravis atque oblivia quaerit,
aut etiam properans urbem petit atque revisit.
Hoc se quisque modo fugit, at quem scilicet, ut fit,
effugere haut potis est: ingratius haeret et odit,
propterea morbi quia causam non tenet aeger . . .
    (III.1060–70)

he will often leave his big house,
tired of sitting indoors, and will quickly come back,
knowing it's no better out than in.
He runs home like a madman, spurring his horses,
as if he meant to bring help to the burning place;
but then, not even through the doorway, he'll be yawning
and collapse in sleep, evading consciousness,
or even hurrying back to see the city.
In this way all men flee themselves—though, as it
        happens,
he who cannot flee, clings to, and hates, himself,
because, while ill, he cannot grasp the cause of his
        disease . . .

Here we encounter two verbs associated with the mother cow, *quaerit* and *revisit*. But here again, though for different reasons, the search comes to nothing. This theme will resurface in Horace (*Odes*, II.16, 22), and the word for dissatisfaction, for ennui, will in his case be *cura*, the same word Lucretius uses to describe the cow's painful and fruitless search.

But let's pause for a minute and look at this fine Latin word *cura*. The most ancient words in our language are like haunted houses. Try as the owner might to avoid going up to the attic (or down to the basement), to keep that one door shut and the lights on at night, the whispers of the previous occupants slip through the walls; no number of lamps can dispel their shadows. Or else they're like magicians' hats: Take it off, nothing. Put it back on, remove it again, and voilà!, a dove flies out with its characteristic flutter.

Cura, as we've seen, doesn't quite mean in Latin what "cure" tends to mean today in English—that is, "remedy," especially in the medical sense. *Cura* instead means "preoccupation," "mental fixation," "anguish," "obsession." Even "remorse" or "regret." In

Virgil's portrayal of the afterlife we encounter a personification of the word, along with personifications of other discomforts such as hunger and poverty (*Aeneid*, VI.274).

Looked at from a different perspective, the word "cure" can indicate mental engagement of an entirely positive sort—nearing even the idea of love. And so it has come to mean "concern," "thoughtfulness," "dedication." "To do something with care"; "to take care of yourself"; "to care for someone else." We even have the "curate" (an assistant to the parish priest in English, though *curato* in Italian refers directly to the priest): an individual who tends to the spiritual well-being of others, a guide for souls. And we have "curious." A curious person is just that, a person who has *cura*—that is, someone who "cares," whose thought is guided by enthusiasm (perhaps at times excessive). It's true, things often end poorly for the curious. Take for example Apuleius's Lucius, who, eager to learn more magic, uses the wrong ointment and ends up turning into an ass. In any case, better to be curious than careless.

But what about medical cures? This sense arises, as expected, from the word's connotations of "thoughtfulness" or "attention." Medical cures are the practical application of what was initially only a mental engagement. In the context of medicine, hospitals, and pharmacies, the word's original negative connotation vanishes: this care is restorative, not destructive. It gets you back on your feet. And yet . . . that root meaning of anguish, that nagging feeling that keeps the heroes of ancient epics up at night, must not be forgotten: not so that we can label this word a paradox (or an oxymoron), but to understand its richness, to respect its full potential; so that we can dig deeper without fear of the darker corners, knowing that a word's meaning—even words we use every day—is history itself, and that now it's our responsibility and our privilege to live it.

But let's get back to the theme of our chapter.

Lucretius, with his faith in words, tries and succeeds in representing reality in its most varied forms, letting his capacity for description fan out in all directions: the material world and emotions, the microscopic and the macroscopic, the imaginary and the real, animal behavior and human conduct, the history of civilization and the plague that struck Athens in the fifth century. He's an observer, one who's always on the lookout, describing what he sees, with a profound love for the perceptible world—as when he relates the pleasure of stretching out in the grass on a sunny day (II.29–33), or points out the iridescent reflections in the feathers of a dove or a peacock (I.800–808). With Lucretius, even thoughts and speculations are perceptible events. He turns often to the everyday world to illustrate a physical theory or hypothesis, those things which are not immediately demonstrable. For example, when he declares that human language has its origins in nature, and was not the invention or imposition of an individual (V.1028–90), he bases his argument on animal calls, between dogs and birds: they too produce different sounds depending on the circumstance.

Lucretius openly admits that Latin, unlike Greek, has a dearth of vocabulary (I.832). Therefore, to wage certain arguments, he often finds himself in need of new terms, which he must invent for himself, using Greek, perhaps, as a model. Lucretius's preferred solution, however, is to extend the meaning of a term that already exists in Latin. His methods are "semantic saturation" and "metaphorization." The poem deals specifically with atomism, and yet the Greek word *atomos* never appears. In its place, and with the same meaning, we find *semen* (seed), *corpus* (body), and *primordium* (beginning)—all three semantic extensions of words already in use with a different meaning, and all three metaphors. Some adjectives end up as nouns or technical terms (using the saturation method mentioned above): *inane* (the void), *imum* (the depths), *immensum* (the infinite). Then there are his famous coinages such as *clinamen*, which has become something of a Lucretian trademark (formed from the root of a verb, *clino*, which occurs only as the past participle *clinatus*, and from the suffix -*men*, which we find in other common words such as *semen* or *nomen*): it refers to the sudden and unpredictable swerve of atoms—a symbol of free will itself—which determines the formation of complex organisms. Where the metaphorization of a single term won't suffice, he fuses multiple terms into a complex metaphor: *moenia mundi*, "the walls of the universe" (II.1045), or *materiae pelagus*, "the sea of matter" (II.550). And he's capable of stretching his metaphorical language much further, establishing powerful links between dimensions—and arriving at true interpretive paradigms. Such as when he compares the way in which common atoms combine into different life-forms (human and vegetable, for instance) to the way in which the same set of letters in the alphabet combine to form an endless variety of words—just as they do in the poem we now hold in our hands, Lucretius reminds us (II.687–99). Life therefore organizes itself in the universe—and here's the interpretive paradigm—just as language organizes itself on the page. The creation is writing, and writing the creation. The poem itself is a small-scale image of the universe! It goes without saying that such an intuition ranks among the most sublime, not only in *De rerum natura* but in all of Latin poetry.

10

The Meaning of Sex:
Back to Catullus

Now, as promised, let's talk profanity.

I mentioned the abundance of swear words in Catullus—and how eager we students were to learn them. Profanity goes hand in hand with teenagers' awkward sense of sexuality, their love of freedom and rule breaking: because curse words shock, they uncover what's hidden, they threaten social hierarchies, they're funny, raucous, subversive. Moreover, these words seem in and of themselves to erase the gap between past and present; there's something eternally "in the moment" about them: of course, they regard the body, the very foundation of our reality.

In truth, profanity too is subject to the laws of time, as well as to those of geography. It may be that the anatomy from which this language spawns (the reproductive organs and our backsides) remains the same over the centuries, but the metaphors and symbolic representations that we associate with them are in constant flux. Unfortunately, such nuance escaped our high school minds. We were too busy pursuing instant gratification to consider the cultural differences and the anthropological complexity that suffuse even our basest words, particularly in the case of literature.

Let's look then at how the cogs of obscenity turn in Catullus, beginning with a rundown of sexual vocabulary.

Parts of the body: *mentula* ("dick"); *cunnus* ("pussy"); *culus* ("ass"). Verbs: *futuo* ("to fuck") and its relatives—*confutuo, ecfutua, defututa, diffututa*; one also comes across the noun *fututio* ("a fuck"); *pedico* ("to sodomize"); *irrumo* ("to force to perform oral sex"); *glubo* ("to peel," "to shuck," a metaphor for being "sexually spent"); *fello* ("to suck"); *perdepso* ("to knead," a metaphor for "possessing someone sexually"); *voro* ("to devour," that is, "to receive in the mouth or in the ass"); there are even cases of the adjective *vorax* ("voracious"). Other nouns: *scortum* ("slut"); *scortillum* ("little slut"); *pathicus* ("passive male sexual partner"); *cinaedus* ("passive male sexual partner").

Catullus's profanity is limited to the first and third parts of his book—to the more "autobiographical" sections, those that pulse with passion and resentment. The mythological and learned poems, which occupy the middle section of the book, bear no trace of indecency. The lexical equivalent of the ever-popular "dick," *mentula* appears just twice in the literal sense. Small beans. The female counterpart meanwhile appears only once. While we are here, let me propose an etymology for *mentula*. The origin of this word is apparently still obscure. To me, it's quite clear that it's linked to *mentum*, "chin," and to *mons, montis*, "mountain," giving it the meaning of something like "protrusion." Anyway . . .

Catullus's true passion lies not with the nouns, or body parts, but with the verbs—with the sexual act and the roles we play in it. The Catullus we know through his use of profanity asserts his status as a free man, in other words as a male who always takes an active role in sex and therefore affirms his social dignity, both with women and with men. To enter a man's mouth or ass does not in fact imply homosexuality (a notion unknown to Latin) but is a demonstration of power and superiority; it carries a sociopolitical meaning. It was something you did to slaves and to the young, your subordinates—which isn't to say that genuine emotions never played a role—or something you threatened to do to your personal enemies. Any free adult male who assumes a passive role in sex, indicated by the two Greek terms *pathicus* and *cinaedus* (whose principal meaning is "male dancer"), is disgraceful, an image of utter humiliation, a man unworthy of his freedom.

It's also important to note that Catullus purposefully avoids profanity when speaking purely of desire, erotic instinct, or physical attraction. Even when he speaks of his own erection, he avoids the word *mentula* (Catullus 56). In those cases where he does let a swear word or two fly, as in the playful carmen 32, he does his best to compensate with a few romantic and tender expressions, drawn from a more sentimental, introspective register:

Amabo, mea dulcis Ipsitilla,
meae deliciae, mei lepores,
iube ad te veniam meridiatum.
Et si iusseris, illud adiuvato,
ne quis liminis obseret tabellam,
neu tibi lubeat foras abire,
sed domi maneas paresque nobis
novem continuas fututiones.
Verum si quid ages, statim iubeto:
nam pransus iaceo et satur supinus
pertundo tunicamque palliumque.

Please, my sweet Ipsitilla,
my joy, my honey,
call me over this afternoon.
And if you agree, make sure
that no one bolts the door.
And don't get any ideas of going out.
Just stay home, and save me

a string of nine straight fucks.
If you'd like, you can have me this instant:
I'm right here lying back with a full stomach,
already poking through my cloak and tunic.

Right away, among other examples, we notice his use of *Amabo*, the future tense of the verb *amo*. Literally it means "I will love," but colloquially, as here, it is understood as "Please." Its literal meaning, however, is not lost; it's there, implied, instilling in the reader a tenderness that even the blunt *fututiones* cannot erase.

Another essential fact about Catullus is that he avoids double entendre, and only rarely uses metaphor to stretch the meaning of a word. It's true that the sparrow in his two famed poems can be taken as a metaphor for the poet's penis, but it's just as true that the poems are free of obscenities and nevertheless work perfectly well if understood at face value (the lament for the death of an animal was in fact a subgenre of Hellenistic poetry). The principal function of Catullus's profanity is as an instrument of social protest. It is a "rhetoric"—that of a free man opposed to historical chaos, to political corruption, and to all deviation from one's proper place in society. His respect for sexual roles stands as both a real and a symbolic respect for social order; it is even a form of religiosity. In sexual conduct, just as in social relations, one must know one's proper place. To act otherwise would be the end of civil life, a complete social breakdown, as evinced even in the poems of his that don't resort to profanity. For two elegant examples we might look at poems 61 and 63. These works are among the learned poems that I referred to earlier. The language here is far different from that of his bawdy epigrams, though the ideological thrust is the same that drives all of Catullus's poetry: the horrifying prospect of society's breakdown. In Catullus 61, an epithalamium—or a poem in celebration of marriage—the poet invites the groom to bring his bride home and set happily about perpetuating the family name. To do so, however, he must renounce his life as a bachelor. Meaning he must go so far as to relinquish his concubine, the little slave boy he's been amusing himself with up until that very day. And the slave too will have to say his goodbyes, bid farewell to their days together, cut his hair short, and find a girl of his own to settle down with. As you can see, sex is a matter of status, not of taste, and the chains of marriage are there to ensure that each and every person, free or slave, male or female, behaves within the confines of his or her social position. In carmen 63, the young Attis, gripped by holy fervor, unmans himself. Lacking his penis (not *penis* or *mentula* in this poem, but instead *pondera ili*, "the groin's burden"), he lacks the clearest indicator of *social* identity: social, I insist, not sexual. The castrated Attis no longer belongs to the city he lives in: he is an exile, a pariah, an utter failure, a slave—and worse, a female slave (*famula*). His plaint is charged with nostalgia not only for who he was, but also for the reality to which he can no longer belong.

I've mentioned the carnivalesque character of profanity. And yet in Catullus's baser lines there's no hint of the carnivalesque, no sense of subversive comedy. To the contrary: he uses profanity in the service of a proud impulse to conserve. There's nothing plebeian about it (though we find *mentula* even among the graffiti at Pompeii), nothing grotesque or pornographic. In the work of Catullus, swear words are anything but expressions of vulgarity or raw emotion. They belong to a strict moral code, one in defense of justice, personal dignity, and proper custom. It seems a paradox, but in the case of Catullus, profanity flows from a pious mouth.

11

Syntactic Goose Bumps,
or Virgil's Shivering Sentences

In the event of a global catastrophe, the book to salvage would be the *Aeneid*. Not only is it the precursor of numerous other works, it is also a condensation of the *Iliad* and the *Odyssey*, the oldest books in Western civilization. When Saint Augustine, in his *De civitate Dei*, was looking for ways to affirm the superiority of the new Christian religion, it was to the *Aeneid* that he turned for examples to discredit paganism, because the *Aeneid* was the written evidence of an entire civilization—nothing short of a new Gospel. Plato too, in order to promote his philosophy, had no choice but to begin with the dismantling of Homer. It goes without saying, of course, that both Augustine and Plato were enamored of their antagonists; that their battle was first and foremost an assault on their own hearts.

Extinction, in any case, has never been a real threat to the *Aeneid*. Or at least not since Virgil himself, on his deathbed, unable to put the finishing touches on his work, asked his friends to burn it. This dramatic scene is reenacted in the Austrian writer Hermann Broch's great novel *The Death of Virgil*, begun in a Nazi prison and published in 1945. If Virgil's friends had obeyed, the Western tradition would have taken a very different course. Luckily, they ignored him, and of all the ancient classics—the classic par excellence according to T. S. Eliot—the *Aeneid* is the one that has enjoyed the longest and most consistent readership. No era has gone without its *Aeneid*, in the original or in translation—and some translations of the poem have become classics themselves, such as Annibal Caro's or John Dryden's. Never has there been a need to rediscover it, as eras rediscovered Lucretius, Catullus, and so many others. Not even the fierce opposition of Christianity, which buried so many other texts, could suppress it. The work sailed safely into the age of the quintessential Christian poet, Dante Alighieri, who adopted Virgil as his master, no less. And later, Petrarch, the other pillar of Western literature—he too a Christian—formed a personal cult around the Latin poet. His Virgilian codex, which has fortunately survived (a magnificent manuscript, illuminated by Simone Martini and now housed at the Biblioteca Ambrosiana in Milan, for which reason it is known also as the *Virgilio Ambrosiano*), stands as evidence of his complete devotion to Virgil, as a poet and as a man; his love for this *corpus* is love in the truest sense, an unquenchable need to grow nearer his subject, not unlike his obsession with Laura.

Nor in my life as a student were there periods in which the *Aeneid* didn't figure. I initially read it in its entirety during my first year of high school, in Rosa Calzecchi Onesti's celebrated and still unsurpassed translation, a real literary achievement in its own right. Then I read it in Latin while in college. And I've been rereading it ever since, in whole or in part, for my own pleasure or whenever I've taught the text in class. I'm constantly turning back to it, if only through other texts. Studying the *Divine Comedy*? High time to reread the *Aeneid*. Analyzing a passage from Ariosto's *Orlando furioso*? Some detail calls me back to the *Aeneid*. Diving into Tasso's *Jerusalem Delivered*? The *Aeneid* serves as the perfect companion text. Because the *Aeneid* is everywhere: in a Robert Lowell poem, or alluded to in one by Ungaretti.

Virgil's enduring success is owed first of all to the beauty of his language. No other poet of antiquity, not even the masterful Horace, is his equal. No one puts it the way he puts it; no one convinces as he convinces; no one portrays as he portrays; no one moves the reader as he does. In the history of Latin literature, Virgil is to poetry what Cicero is to prose. This comparison is one of the basic myths of humanism, but it reflects a historical truth. Virgil reestablished the poetic language of Rome and left an insurmountable legacy. That he now and then nods to his predecessors (Ennius, Lucretius, Catullus)—in his vocabulary and in certain imagery—is indisputable, but Virgil's Latin exists outside traditional constraints. It assimilates and rearranges; it does not obey.

While Lucretius's greatness lies in his lexical innovation, Virgil's lies in the way he restructures syntax: both in so-called *iuncturae* (adjective + noun, for instance) and in complete sentences, and in the dialectical relationship he establishes between sentence and line. No trace of formulaic sentences or stock phrases. Lucretius demonstrates and defines; Virgil dramatizes and sets in motion. Lucretius tends to express a complete syntactical unit on a single line; Virgil, though his line breaks do coincide at times with complete thoughts, typically stretches his phrases over several lines. This is determined, of course, by the nature of the narrative, and even the emotional weight of the scene, not by the poem's didactic aim. Enjambment turns out to be the single most distinctive trait of Virgil's language—and, I would go further to say, the most profound structure in his vast repertoire. I'd like to look carefully at this aspect, which I find to be an inexhaustible source of pleasure and admiration, an unfailing means of reigniting one's sense of wonder—which is what sets us reading in the first place.

It happens quite often in the *Aeneid* that the first word of a line is the verb of the sentence that started in the preceding line. It's a shock, this jutting verb. And because it arrives at a critical moment in the metrical structure of the line—the beginning—this delayed verb gives a special charge to its sentence: just as it's ending, it seems to start again. Whatever sense of inertia there may have been is dispelled. Below are just two of the many possible examples, here translated into something like Yoda's English, to better illustrate Virgil's device:

> Improvisum aspris veluti qui sentibus anguem
> *pressit* . . . (II.379–80)

> Like he who, among thick brambles, on a serpent
> *has suddenly stepped* . . .

> adversi rupto ceu quondam turbine venti
> *confligunt* . . . (II.416–17)

> as when, amid a storm, the rival winds
> *do battle*

Other common occurrences in Virgil are cases when verbs appearing at the beginning of two consecutive lines create a chiasmus—an inverted structure with an ABBA pattern—with the subjects and objects to which they're linked: meaning that the verbs are both in the same metrical position—again, at the beginning of the line—but that the first verb comes after its subject (still up on the line above), while the second comes before it. And so we have two syntactic elements that occupy the same position in the line, but that occupy two different, even contrary, positions within the sentence. Once again, all sense of inertia is dispelled. What looks like repetition is really a shift in momentum. Take the following example, drawn from one of the poem's most memorable moments, the night of queen Dido's suicide:

> At non infelix animi Phoenissa neque umquam
> *solvitur* in somnos oculisve aut pectore noctem
> *accipit.* (IV.529–31)

> But the unhappy Phoenician queen never
> *sinks* <u>into sleep</u>, nor into <u>her eyes or heart the night</u>
> *she welcomes.*

Or this one, from Aeneas's musings at sea:

> hinc <u>altas cautes proiectaque saxa</u> Pachyni
> *radimus*, et fatis numquam concessa moveri
> *apparet* <u>Camerina procul campique Geloi</u> . . .
>   (III.699–701)

> next <u>the high cliffs and long reefs</u> of Pachynus
> *we skirt*, and, forbidden by fate to move,
> *appears* <u>Camerina in the distance and the Geloan</u>
>   <u>plains</u> . . .

We also find cases of chiasmus within a single line (and with the same purpose). Here's how Virgil opens the second book, as the refugee Aeneas prepares to recount his tale to Dido and her company:

> *Conticuere* <u>omnes</u> <u>intenti</u>que ora *tenebant.* (II.1)

> *They quieted* <u>all</u>, <u>attentive</u> their faces *they kept.*

And later:

Iungimus hospitio <u>dextras</u> et <u>tecta</u> *subimus.* (III.83)

We clasp <u>hands</u> in welcome and <u>the houses</u> *we enter.*

In the first example (II.1) we find yet another typically Virgilian device (rare in Lucretius): enallage. Enallage, in this case, is when an adjective is linked not to the noun one would logically expect, but to another element in the sentence: their attentiveness here is a characteristic of their "faces," and thus the object of the verb "to keep," not its subject. Metrical constraints demand the use of *intenti* rather than *intenta*: the ending *-i* of *intenti* is a long vowel—and this is what the hexameter needs in that position, a long vowel—while the ending *-a* of *intenta* is short. However, as Gian Biagio Conte demonstrates in a superb essay, it is not merely a question of satisfying the meter: the enallage acts as an inconsistency, an estrangement, one that jolts us into a new appreciation of the words and their relationships, allowing for new resonances to arise and interact. This in turn lends the text a renewed poignancy and urgency: "Its principal function is to create a language parallel to everyday language, one similar enough but also substantially more intense. It's up to the reader to take note of the inconsistencies."[1]

The enjambed word, of course, can also be an adjective, an adverb, or any other part of speech. And even in these cases—where the word left hanging is other than a verb—the meaning of that word intensifies. A goose bump, of sorts, runs along the skin of the sentence. Here, for example, is an adjective of uncommon power:

Hoc dicens ferrum adverso sub pectore condit
fervidus . . . (XII.950–51)

Saying this, he plunges his sword into his chest
violent . . .

We're at the end of the poem. Aeneas slays his enemy, Turnus, who in the following verse flies off among the shadows (*umbras*, indeed, is the book's final word—and we'll come back to this marvelous term later).

Virgil's semantic strength, what charges the lines of his poem, derives not from the preassigned meanings of the words he uses—as is the case with the meticulous lexicographer and coiner of new terms, Lucretius—but from the *place* each word occupies in the sentence. He is a true master of the *ordo verborum*. Reading the *Aeneid*, one senses a certain freedom, a fluidity not found in Lucretius. Along with this freedom, however, comes an exactitude, a complete control over every cog in the mechanism. And each cog, though operating on its own, is in truth working for the whole: to maintain the system's equilibrium and, at the same time, to ensure that the euphonic fluidity driving the system forward, and carrying all in its path, does not prevent the appearance of the occasional aberration, like a peak in the frequency.

Let's take a look at a lengthier example:

> [. . .] hasta volans noctis diverberat umbras
> et venit aversi in tergum Sulmonis ibique
> frangitur, ac fisso transit praecordia lingo.
> Volvitur ille vomens calidum de pectore flumen
> frigidus et longis singultibus ilia pulsat. (IX.411–15)

> [. . .] the spear cuts soaring through the shades of night
> and comes into the back of opposed Sulmo, and there
> it snaps, his stomach punctured by the splintered wood.
> He writhes, vomiting a hot stream from his chest,
> cold, and his body jerks with long seizures.

Here we're in the midst of the Nisus and Euryalus episode, where they lead a midnight raid on the enemy camp, slaughtering many but losing their own lives in the exchange (a scene cherished by readers throughout the centuries, and imitated by numerous writers, including Ariosto in his *Orlando furioso*). Again we find an example of chiasmus ("hasta [. . .] frangitur [. . .] / Volvitur ille"). We can also sense how lithely Virgil's syntax moves from verse to verse, snaking down from *hasta* to *lingo*. But which are those moments when Virgil, as compared to Lucretius, is truly Virgilian? The phrase *calidum de pectore flumen*, in fact, is lifted virtually wholesale from a passage in *De rerum natura*—the very passage we encountered above, in which the cow grieves for her calf. Here again are the relevant lines:

> nam saepe ante deum vitulus delubra decora
> turicremas propter mactatus concidit aras,
> sanguinis expirans calidum de pectore flumen . . .
>   (II.352–54)

> thus often does a calf, before the gods' rich temples,
> fall slain at incense-burning altars,
> exhaling a stream of warm blood from its chest . . .

So what has Virgil done with respect to Lucretius? He's intensified the river metaphor, eliminating *sanguinis*, "[of] blood" (a word that Lucretius maintains for clarity); he's made effective use of enjambment, allowing the line, though it comes to a brief stop with the definite-sounding *flumen*, to wind forward with *frigidus*; and from that adjective is born a brilliant oxymoron: blood is warm, but Sulmo is already cold. Life and death brush paths, are united for an instant, in a poignant tangle of pathos. Oxymoron too is a typically Virgilian device, which comes as no surprise among such "theatrical" language. There's no time to go making a list here, but one oxymoron in particular is well worth mentioning: when Euryalus's mother receives her son's defeated body, she bursts into hysterical sobbing. And here's the oxymoron: *incendentem luctus* (IX.500), "which ignited her tears." We've already arrived at the height of the Baroque!

But what purpose does metaphor serve for Virgil? Lucretius gives new meaning to an old word (*semen*, normally "seed," comes to mean "atom"), though without drawing attention to the metaphor: the new term solidifies on contact. With Virgil, on the other hand, his analogies have a life beyond their metaphorical usage (that *flumen* is not just a stream of blood; it remains, nonetheless, a river). We never lose sight of its "figurative" sense, of his effort to make language do and say more. And this extra jolt he gives to language is not something conceived of a priori, like a drawing that precedes a painting, but something that happens in the very act of description and representation. His meanings, like his syntax, are guided by "dramatic" thrust. They arise on the spot, in the midst of the scene—and that's where they stay.

We learn two things from this last example: that Virgil's literary memory is very much engaged and that it's far from derivative or mechanical. Virgil, in any case, was no exception, for all his genius. In ancient Rome, poetry formed the bedrock of education. It was regularized and codified and, as such, developed through the perpetuation of different styles, mannerisms, and images, at times quoting directly from past texts or else alluding to them in ways more or less apparent.[2] The essence of literature, indeed, is tradition. Literature is a handing-down, a reservoir of memory, a genealogical system; in a word, *imitatio*, a cornerstone of aesthetics in the ancient world.[3] Imitation does not prohibit or exclude innovation. The poet-creator's so-called originality is in truth a myth of the Romantic age, and perhaps only the myth of a myth: even the most trailblazing avant-gardist must face the past in one way or another. Leopardi, one of the major figures of Romanticism in

Europe, fed himself on classical literature. So did Shelley, Keats, and even Wordsworth (who—speaking of Virgil—translated a few passages of the *Aeneid*). And to cite an example on the other end of the spectrum, the futurist Filippo Tommaso Marinetti couldn't resist the temptation of translating Tacitus's *Germania*. He even declared his intention—though he never followed through—to translate the *Historiae*.

Imitation implies a respect for one's predecessors. It serves to "classicize" innovation, to stamp experimentation with the seal of a certain *auctoritas*, to make a phrase memorable. But even the most profound respect, even the most fervent desire to mirror the past, brings with it variation and critique. A poet who adopts another's words is by no means saying the same thing, nor would it be possible. Imitation, though it may seem to produce something similar in the modern text, alters the ancient text in an essential way, stripping it of its function as the "origin" and rendering it a model. Using another's words shows a desire for convergence, not merely to repeat, casting an aura of continuity around the relationship between ancient and modern. Intentional continuity, in fact, is exactly what we're dealing with here: the view that books, even those that are vastly different, are all foundational elements of a single culture, and that literary writing has the task of propagating identities and forms of knowledge. There's something sacred about the sense of language and words that gives rise to such great responsibility. The systematic reuse of certain expressions, terms, or rhythms occurs because certain expressions, terms, and rhythms appear to be excellent, perfect, even absolute, and can therefore carry significance far outside of the context in which they were created, no matter which new meaning they take on.

Let's look at a renowned example: the scene in which Aeneas encounters Dido in the afterlife, in Book VI of the *Aeneid*. The queen, out of love for Aeneas, took her own life at the end of Book IV, and now he has the chance to explain himself, to console. His excuse is that it was *not by his own will* that he left Carthage, but that the gods commanded him . . . and here's how he puts it:

invitus, regina, tuo de litore cessi. (VI.460)

against my will, O queen, I left your shores.

Or in Seamus Heaney's beautiful rendition:

I embarked from your shore, my queen, unwillingly . . .[4]

Here, the emphasis on Aeneas's involuntary departure is effectively expressed at the end of the line.

As has often been noted, this memorable passage of *Aeneid* VI strikingly rephrases a passage in one of Catullus's learned poems:[5]

invita, o regina, tuo de vertice cessi . . . (Catullus
     66.39–40)

against my will, O queen, I left your head . . .

The two contexts are quite different, however. In Catullus, the line is pronounced not by a heartbroken and apologetic hero, but by Queen Berenice's hair, which, detached from her head, has become a constellation. Virgil's recontextualization, then, would appear to have its share of irony. Indeed, why else set Aeneas on par with a mop of hair? Others, however, contend that Virgil gave his own stamp of seriousness to the joke. I see neither irony nor its opposite. My view is that the source itself, Catullus's text, is a serious poem. Her hair *really does* suffer over its detachment, and not even its new existence as a constellation can console it for the loss of its owner. We must understand that the theme of separation is a primary source for Catullus's poetry, to which he turns time and again for various motives, even to express death. Once we understand this, we can understand that Catullus, even in his poem on Berenice's hair, where his tone seems playful, aims to present a defining emblem, a totem of sorts, and not only that but a totem quite important in and of itself, insofar as it's a synecdoche of royalty and divinity. Furthermore, if we look more closely, we find that Catullus's elegy, like the sixth book of the *Aeneid*, is set in a supernatural realm.[6] The complexity and emotional depth of Catullus's elegy were not lost on Virgil (just as the striking pathos of the Lucretian calf's sacrifice was not lost on him). In the elegy of Berenice's hair, Virgil found a dramatic archetype, a matrix of his own feelings. It's no coincidence that this verse of Catullus's appears in yet another passage of the *Aeneid*, toward the end of the poem, and therefore at a moment of great importance in the text. Jupiter is speaking to Juno, guardian of Turnus and the Latins. He asks her to cease opposing the victory of Aeneas and his men. In the end, Juno bows her head and pronounces the following words:

Iuppiter, et Turnum et terras invita reliqui . . . (XII.809)

Jupiter, I've abandoned Turnus and the earth against my will . . .

Invita is back, though almost unrecognizable in its new position, and *cessi* has become *reliqui*. Are we yet again left with too little evidence to claim a direct link to Catullus? No—not if we compare the larger context in which these two lines appear. And here there's no need even to translate, the coincidences in vocabulary are evidence enough on their own:

invita, o regina, tuo de vertice *cessi*,
invita: *adiuro* teque tuumque *caput*,
digna ferat quod si quis inaniter adiurarit:
sed qui se ferro postulet esse parem?
Ille quoque eversus mons est, quem maximum in oris
progenies Thiae clara supervehitur,
cum Medi peperere novum mare, cumque iuventus
per medium classi barbara navit Athon.
Quid facient crines, cum ferro talia cedant?
Iuppiter, ut Chalybon omne genus pereat,
et qui principio sub terra quaerere venas
institit ac ferri stringere duritiem! (Catullus 66.39–50)

ista quidem quia nota mihi tua, magne, voluntas,
Iuppiter, et Turnum et terras *invita* reliqui;
nec tu me aeria solam nunc sede videres
digna indigna pati, sed flammis cincta sub ipsa
starem acie traheremque inimica in proelia Teucros.
Iuturnam misero [fateor] succurrere fratri
suasi et pro vita maiora audere probavi,
non ut tela tamen, non ut contenderet arcum;
adiuro Stygii *caput* implacabile fontis,
una superstitio superis quae reddita divis.
Et nunc *cedo* equidem pugnasque exosa relinquo.
        (*Aeneid*, XII.808–18)

It's startling to see just how many traces of Catullus's elegy show up in Virgil's passage. Given the very different placement of the elements they share in common, it's clear that the references were not intentional. This does nothing to deprive it, however, of its allusive force. The trauma depicted by Catullus in the hair's detachment is one shared by Virgil. The *Aeneid* itself is one long series of detachments and departures: from his wife,

Creusa, to his father, Anchises; from Dido to his friend Palinurus, and his wet nurse Caieta. And think of Virgil's first eclogue: there too we find detachment, a painful departure, the abandonment of one's beloved countryside, exile. Even Juno's detachment from Turnus is a traumatic experience. Which is why we see this archetype of trauma resurfacing, why Virgil lets the voice of detachment have its say—because in Virgil's imagination detachment and the elegy of Berenice's hair are one and the same.

Memory is the fabric of the *Aeneid*. Aeneas remembers, Dido remembers. The soul of everyone and everything brims with the past. Long before Proust, Virgil has given us a *recherche du temps perdu*. Others will argue that the *Odyssey* did it first. But the *Odyssey*, in truth, is a song of return. Odysseus remembers his homeland, and that's precisely where he ends up. The time regained in the *Aeneid*, however, is not a return but an illusion, a vicarious recovery, because it happens elsewhere: in Latium—which is by no means Troy (already in ruins). The story, therefore, has a sense of mournfulness: it is indistinguishable from the thought of irrevocable loss.

And Virgil is so nostalgic, so fixated on memory, that he not only gives us characters who in their remembering lose the will to act, but basks in sustained epiphanies about how things age, shed their original meaning, and even become symbols and instruments of death. So many objects in the *Aeneid* remind us that an age, a world, has ended. The moment just before Dido's suicide is a remarkably apt example:

> at trepida et coeptis immanibus effera Dido
> sanguineam volvens aciem, maculisque trementis
> interfusa genas et pallida morte futura,

interiora domus inrumpit limina et altos
conscendit furibunda rogos ensemque recludit
Dardanium, non hos quaesitum munus in usus.
    (IV.642–47)

But Dido, shuddering, fierce with terrible purpose,
her rolling eyes shot through with blood, her mottled
        cheeks
quivering, pale already with future death,
rushed into the palace's center, climbed the tall
pyre, crazed, unsheathed the Dardanian sword,
the gift she'd begged from him—oh, not for this!

The narrator emphasizes that the sword is a gift from the
Trojan Aeneas (*dardanio* meaning a descendant of Dardanus, the
founder of Troy). Actually, it's not the narrator: the observation occurs in the mind of Dido herself. It is free indirect discourse. The
bloodied sword is, literally, a "memory." The grammar itself, in
the course of a single sentence, stages a convergence of the past,
present, and future with its three participles: *coeptis* (the action
just now conceived), *futura* (the imminent conclusion), *quaesitum*
(the original cause, her request of the gift/pledge). "Future death,"
a cruel oxymoron, ups the ante: the happening and not yet happened are made to concur ("future" being, after all, the feminine
future participle of the verb *sum*).
    Another example, another sword:

Transiit et parmam mucro, levia arma minacis,
et tunicam molli mater quam neverat auro,
implevitque sinum sanguis; tum vita per auras
concessit maesta ad Manis corpusque reliquit.
    (X.817–20)

The point passed through his shield, too light a weapon
    for threat,
and the tunic his mother wove with golden thread,
and blood ran through the folds; life then in the air
fled sorrowfully to the dead, and left his body.

This is the fall of Lausus, son of Mezentius—at the hands of Aeneas. The narrator includes the detail of the mother's embroidery, imbuing the battle scene with tenderness, carrying us back to another time, another place, a kind of affection he'll never recover. Even Aeneas feels compunction in the face of his own triumph, showing a regard for the young warrior that he hasn't yet shown to other combatants. And again in the following book, at the funeral of Pallas—another young soldier fallen in battle—we encounter an object-memory. Here too it's a work of embroidery: none other than the gold-and-purple cloak that Dido made *suis manibus*, "with her own hands," for Aeneas (XI.74). Now it covers the face of the lifeless boy, with whose body it will burn.

12

The Master of Diffraction, Tacitus, and Sallust's Brevity

In chapter XXIX of *The Red and the Black*, Julien Sorel encounters the Bishop, proves to him his mastery of Latin, and departs with a precious gift: the complete works of Tacitus in eight volumes. A truly rare gift for a seminary student, as made clear by the others' envy.

But why Tacitus and not, say, Saint Augustine? Because Tacitus teaches the mechanics of power, and the Bishop is convinced that Julien has a brilliant career before him in the church, if he can learn to conduct himself properly.

Tacitus (c. 56–after 117 C.E.) is my preferred Latin prose writer as well, despite my visceral repulsion to all political careerism. To me, Tacitus is the very essence of Latin, the fullest and most conscious expression of its most original characteristics: brevity, efficacy, richness, chiaroscuro (intended also as mystery and elusiveness). Gone is all excess; gone, even, is the essential, if it can be inferred from other, more necessary components of the sentence. Latin, in the workshop of Tacitus, resembles that gooey substance left in the jar of paintbrushes after all the turpentine has evaporated.

Unlike Julien, I was not given the works of Tacitus. Instead I bought them with my savings, in an edition published by Les Belles Lettres, on my first trip to Paris. I was seventeen at the time and paid what struck me as an exorbitant price. It was, however, a necessary purchase. I'd never read Tacitus, either in Latin or in translation. All I knew was that he was difficult, and that if he ever came up in class, then good luck and godspeed. In my case, he came up during high school exit exams. That year, 1984, Latin turned out to be the topic for the written portion, and someone on the exam committee had chosen a passage from the *Annales*. The opening words are engraved in my memory: "Laeti neque procul Germani agitabant . . ." (The Germans lived happily and not far off . . .)—the beginning of chapter 50, Book I.

At university, we were expected to be able to translate Tacitus on the spot. Professor Grilli would open the *Annales* or the *Historiae* at random and ask us to read a passage—that is, to give it back in Italian without pausing too long to think about it, lest he send you home (a rather common occurrence).

It's true that Tacitus is harder to grasp than other authors. The difficulty of his phrasing rests in its rapidity, its surprise; his tools of choice are allusion, the omission of linguistic components (verbs and prepositions), brevity, and what is known as *variatio*, or the juxtaposition of elements linked by meaning but not by syntax: the above-cited *laeti neque procul* (an adjective coupled with an adverb) is one example.[1] Here's another:

> [. . .] palam laudares, secreta male audiebant. (*Historiae*, I.10)

Before diving into the joys of this brief sentence, I should say that the passage is taken from the description of one Licinius Mucianus, the governor of Syria. His portrait is a litany of contradictions and ambivalences. A friend of the powerful, though disliked by the emperor Claudius, he winds up in the far reaches of Asia. He's a zealous weakling, a likable snoot, a debauchee who yet can give a hand should any emergency arise. He is, in other words, a walking oxymoron. And the sentence above captures him with memorable precision. I here give a literal translation:

> [. . .] publicly you'd praise [him], [but] in private life he was poorly regarded.

The adversative conjunction between the first and second parts of the sentence is absent; absent too is the direct object, the pronoun "him." A typically Tacitian trick. The "but" must be supplied by the reader because, on a logical plane, it occurs subsequently; it forms part of a judgment, a reflective phase that comes only after the facts are presented. Tacitus never pronounces this or any such judgment himself, but leaves the pronouncing to us. As for the implied direct object, that arises naturally enough from the context. And this ellipsis serves to strengthen the opposition between the two concepts: the governor's good reputation and the reprehensible behavior of his private life. The *variatio* adds further tension to the clash, by juxtaposing an adverb (*palam*) and a neutral plural (*secreta*), the second-person singular of an imperfect subjunctive verb (*laudares*) and an imperfect indicative in the third-person plural (*audiebant*). All asymmetrical and yet constrained to make symmetry: and this symmetry arises not from a preestablished order, not as a preventative technique, as something a priori to equivalent grammatical forms, but from the conclusions drawn by the reader. In a sentence characteristic of Tacitus, it's as if the discourse acquires a first level of truth from the semantics of the individual words, but only in a second stage, thanks to the intervention of the reader, does it reveal the corresponding relationships between these words. The semantics of each individual word—in this method, so common in Tacitus, of diffracting the discourse—plays a fundamental role: because each word, while having distinct meaning in itself, maintains a certain vagueness, a phosphorescence of sorts. *Palam* here means "publicly." Tacitus applies it to the verb *laudares*; in reality, for logical purposes, the adverb refers to the behavior of Licinius Mucianus, to his role in society: that is to say, the praise reserved for Licinius Mucianus is public because his public profile is perceived as praiseworthy. What's at play is a sort of hypallage, an exchange of elements (as we saw in Virgil): a characteristic of the implied object (Licinius Mucianus) finds its way over to the subject. *Secreta* is the plural of *secretum*, which besides "secret" can mean "mystery," or even "hidden place." It's clear in this case that Tacitus is skewing the word's meaning toward the antithesis of *palam*—therefore "secret" comes to indicate the hidden life of Licinius Mucianus, which one might translate, as I have, to "private life." *Audiebant* comes from *audio* (infinitive *audire*), which means "I hear," "I listen." With the adverbs *male* (badly) and *bene* (well), *audio* takes on the intransitive meaning of "I have a bad or good reputation." Nothing out of the ordinary here, we find this usage in other writers. Tacitus, though, goes a step further, playing confidently, and ironically, with the contrast or concurrence between *laudo* (I praise), which is a verb related to speech, and *audio* (I hear) understood in its most basic sense, "I perceive with my ears."

Tacitus is a follower of Sallust (c. 86–36 B.C.E.). Sallust, a contemporary of Cicero, used an utterly personal language, clearly distinguishable from Ciceronian grammar and style. Take for example *The Conspiracy of Catiline*, his masterpiece, which paved the way for a new classical historiography. In his syntax, which takes its cue from the Greek of Thucydides (known and notorious for his sublime abruptness), he avoids all complexity: his lines move block by paratactic block, in lists; conjunctions are sparse; he favors the *variatio*, or the juxtaposition of incongruous elements, not balance or symmetry; he detests rhythmic figures. His vocabulary abounds with antiquated terms; even his gerunds have a mustiness about them, ending as they do with *-undus* rather than *-endus*. The same goes for certain adjectives (e.g., *pessuma* instead of *pessima*, *divorsa* and not *diversa*). His prose gives one the sense of a nervous dryness, a purposeful standoffishness, though not without its attraction and its own arid innate beauty.[2] The Sallustian style, no surprise, became an educational cornerstone—and not only for Tacitus (Seneca derides his imitators in letter 114 to Lucilius). Proof enough is the praise Nietzsche reserves for him in *Twilight of the Idols* (1888):

> My sense of style, of the epigram as style, was awoken almost instantaneously on coming into contact with Sallust [. . .] Compact, severe, with as much substance as possible, a cold malice towards "fine words," also towards "fine feelings"—in that I knew myself. One will recognize in my writings, even in my *Zarathustra*, a very serious ambition for *Roman* style . . .[3]

At the height of humanism, Poliziano adopted this style to great success in his account of the Pazzi conspiracy—one of the most admirable works of Neo-Latin literature. And the playwright Vittorio Alfieri (1749–1803), to speak of another modern, even took it upon himself to translate *The Conspiracy of Catiline*, calling its author "divine" in the preface to his Italian version and describing his style as one marked by "clarity, brevity, and energy."

Witness the death of Catiline, for example:

> Catilina postquam fusas copias seque cum paucis relicuom videt, memor generis atque pristinae suae dignitatis, in confertissumos hostis incurrit ibique pugnans confoditur. (LX)

Catiline, having seen his troops disband and himself now left with but a few supporters, in memory both of his family and of his own previous dignity, charges into the thickest ranks of the enemy and is slain there in battle.

The story's apex is reduced to this fleeting instance, couched mainly in the historical present. For good measure, he sprinkles the passage with a few archaisms (*relicuom* for *reliquum*, *confertissumos* for *confertissimos*, *hostis* for *hostes*). The narrator spares a few more lines for Catiline a bit later—though no less brief—portraying him in agony among the other corpses, still gripped by indomitable pride. For Sallust, however, we know that moral characterization, as brief and summary as it may be, is far more important than the dramatization of events. A good example of this would be his multilayered sketch of Sempronia, Catiline's ally: a woman of her own will, a talented singer with an ear for languages, an unabashed pleasure-seeker with a criminal streak, brimming with bold spirit (*The Conspiracy of Catiline*, XXV).

Tacitus thrives on brevity and the *variatio*, and indeed any device least associated with Cicero. His central argument migrates into the periphery, while in Cicero it rests in a single buttressing sentence, from which all the lesser elements of his rigorous logic descend; allusion and implication throw long, flickering shadows over his meanings, which can be grasped only through meticulous interpretation and an intuition for filling in the gaps. Yet it would be limiting to say that the Latin of Tacitus's historical works is merely a development of Sallust's. Latin, in Tacitus, reaches remarkable new heights, because Tacitus, of the two, has the superior mind, his art deriving from a far more complex and critical sensibility. We cannot forget that languages—and Latin is a prime example—are only as refined as the intellect and passion of the individual employing them. Their growth and change and evolution depend on us. Of course, we all use and study languages, but nuanced invention, an individual's will to push a language into completely new territory, is another matter. Let's keep to our theme of violent death and look at the murder of Agrippina, Nero's mother, in Tacitus's *Annales*:

> Anicetus villam statione circumdat refractaque ianua obvios servorum abripit, donec ad fores cubiculi veniret; cui pauci adstabant, ceteris terrore inrumpentium exterritis. Cubiculo modicum lumen inerat et ancillarum una, magis ac magis anxia Agrippina, quod nemo a filio ac ne Agermus quidem: aliam fore laetae rei faciem; nunc solitudinem ac repentinos strepitus et extremi mali indicia. Abeunte dehinc ancilla, "tu quoque me deseris?" prolocuta respicit Anicetum, trierarcho Herculeio et Obarito centurione classiario comitatum: ac si ad visendum venisset, refotam nuntiaret, sin facinus patraturus, nihil se de filio credere; non imperatum parricidium. Circumsistunt lectum percussores et prior trierarchus fusti caput eius adflixit. Iam in mortem centurioni ferrum destringenti protendens uterum "ventrem feri" exclamavit multisque vulneribus confecta est. (XIV.8)

> Anicetus surrounded the house with guards and, having broken the gates, dragged off any servants who confronted him, till he arrived at her chamber door. Only a few servants remained in front of it, all the others having fled in fear of the intruders. In the room was a dim light and a single maiden, [and] Agrippina, growing ever more anxious, since still no messenger had come from her son, not even Agermus: a happy ending [she thought] would have a different appearance; now [instead], only solitude and sudden loud noises and signs of a terrible catastrophe. As the maid stepped out, she called, "You too are abandoning

me?" And, having thus spoken, she turned to Anicetus, accompanied by the trireme captain, Herculeius, and the naval centurion, Obarito. If he'd come to see her, [she said], then he should send word that she's recovered; if instead [he'd come] to commit a crime, she'd never believe that her son had a hand in it; he would not have ordered his mother's death. The assassins closed in around her bed and first the trireme captain struck her over the head with his club; then, as the centurion clutched his sword and made ready to kill her, she offered her uterus and shouted, "Strike my womb." And she was slain with many wounds.

Here we're in the mind of Agrippina, the evil mother who succumbs to her evil son. It's not only the grammar (the indirect discourse) letting us know that these are her thoughts, but the setting itself speaks on her behalf. The pale light symbolizes her life, soon to be extinguished; the departure of the last maiden tells of just how desolate an end it will be. Then there's her internal drama—the undying disbelief of a mother who refuses to accept that her own son wishes her dead; and, with that disbelief, her deepest sense of foreboding; and her theatrical posturing.

Sallust recounts a conspiracy of his time, a failed governmental coup (we're in 63 B.C.E.), reducing all to a simple lesson, one underlying motive: rampant corruption. No political analysis, no psychological examination. Catiline looms large, but he's an obelisk, he's criminality itself, not a particular type of criminal. Nor are his companions depicted with any greater depth. They are evil, pure and simple, even if lightened now and then by flashes of intelligence. The others, their conquerors, are an embodiment of good. Tacitus too speaks of matters close to his heart, he too is quick to condemn and summarize, offering his moralistic view of events. But what charge he gives his words! Every observation is worth two, because lurking behind what little he tells us is a broader discourse, a hidden commentary on the complexity and ultimate unfathomability of human reasons and purposes. With Sallust, on the other hand, narration and commentary are one and the same: his brevity conceals no abundance but exhausts the subject then and there. And his judgment—which, in any case, he's already made in advance—infuses every word. His protest is a protest, nothing more.

13

Ovid, or the End of Identity

Any Italian who's studied Ovid (43 B.C.E.–17 or 18 C.E.) in school will have encountered him first in Dante. Indeed, the *Divine Comedy* plucks at will from Ovid's masterwork, the *Metamorphoses*. In one particular case, the transformation of thieves (Canto XXV of the *Inferno*), Dante openly challenges the skill of his predecessor, awarding himself the victory palm in a much-celebrated passage: "Let Ovid be silent [. . .] I envy him not" (vv. 97–99).

While Dante's rewriting of Ovid has without doubt contributed to the long success of the *Metamorphoses*, it has also led us, rather blindly, to consider the poem as nothing more than a source text, an archive of myths, a warehouse from which to take what we want when we want it. What was once a magnificent fresco that stretched across fifteen books—the history of the universe itself, written against the backdrop of the Roman Empire in a period of turbulent change—has cracked into colored panels, episodic fragments: Narcissus becoming a flower, Echo fading into a voice, here a sex change, there a shapeshifting into a bat or a bird or a cow . . . The rest, doomed by its own complicit structure, has been reduced to a framework, a scaffolding.

Our schools, meanwhile, haven't done much for Ovid's reputation. The image they've perpetuated is one of a futile and in-consistent poet, as fickle as the physical appearance of one of his characters: a worldly man who mines the store of Greek mythology and gives it back to us in his own style, with irony, yes, but without depth: an assortment of precooked microwaved foods, in a way; a false epic that, because of its falseness, never quite gets off the ground. Too talented, too simple: a bit superficial, Ovid, a bit of a gossip.

Nor has he benefited much from comparisons to Virgil, his contemporary for a quarter century. This comparison, however, was never quite enough to relegate him to obscurity—in fact, in some ways it even added to his glow, like the glimmer of a few distant fireworks. Virgil went down in history as the *poet of Rome*; Ovid as an *artist of certain merit*, a writer too conscious of his gifts and, therefore, in the end, cold, smug, ornamental, fatuous. He was taken for a peacock and a panderer. Even someone as astute as Leopardi found the *Metamorphoses* to be nothing more than a string of images and gratuitous descriptions, lacking urgency:

> The poet has to show that he has a far more serious pur-pose than to awaken images and make descriptions . . . to describe and introduce images with gravity, with serious-ness, with no show of taking pleasure in them or having studied them deliberately, or having given thought to and taken care over them, or intending the reader to dwell on them. That is what Homer, Virgil, and Dante do, who de-spite being absolutely full of the most vivid images and descriptions, give no sign that they are aware of this, but allow people to think that they have a much more serious purpose instead which is all they are concerned with . . . *Whereas Ovid does the opposite* [emphasis mine]. He does not disguise, let alone conceal, but displays and, so to say, proclaims what he is, that is, that he has no greater or more serious intention, indeed that he aims at nothing

other than to describe and to inspire and disseminate images and sketches, and to figure and represent the whole time. (*Zibaldone*, 3479–80, September 20, 1823)[1]

Here Leopardi presents the most essential merits of Ovid's style as mere defects. It's true: Ovid is always carrying on, describing, illustrating, trying to squeeze everything into one scene. A little succinctness would go a long way. Part of his power, however, rests in how easily words flow from his pen, in the aggregation of details, in opening one drawer after another, and hidden drawers within the drawers, inciting the reader's thirst for discovery. Taking the opening lines of the *Metamorphoses* as a telling instance of the poet's manner, Robert Lowell noted: "The word placing gives almost the impression of a child waking up and talking. Though meticulously ordered, the words seem to drop where they will in their hurry to announce themselves."[2] And Italo Calvino thus described his characteristic abundance: "Ovid's instinct is always to add, never to cut; to go further into detail, never to languish in vagueness. Such a process produces different effects depending on the tone—now subdued and suited to minor matters, now agitated and impatient to saturate the tale's miraculous events with objective observations of real world phenomena."[3]

Here's one example:

extenuant vigiles corpus miserabile curae,
adducitque cutem macies, et in aera sucus
corporis omnis abit; vox tantum atque ossa supersunt:
vox manet; ossa ferunt lapidis traxisse figuram.
    (*Metamorphoses*, III.396–99)

The nymph Echo has fallen in love with Narcissus, who will have none of it. In her desperate need to speak his name, she's reduced to just a voice:

sleepless anguish consumes her pitiful body,
her skin folds up, and all her body's fluid
goes into thin air; just voice and bones remain:
then only voice; her bones, they say, took on the shape of
    stones.

It's a sequence of snapshots, one still frame after another.
Leopardi is right: the images pile on. Virgil is theater, opera, and
every moment in his story is a simultaneity of events. He gives us
a complete portrait, contained entirely on the stage. Ovid, on the
other hand, is film—one thing at a time, a frame-by-frame unfold-
ing of events and details. In Ovid, narrative prevails over drama.
Again, I cite Leopardi: "The spirit is led to see objects little by
little through their parts" (*Zibaldone*, 895). Alliteration (all those
c's, several *s*'s, a few *t*'s, the two final *f*'s) and the repetition of certain words (*corpus/corporis*, *vox/vox*, *ossa/ossa*)—stylistic echoes,
that is to say—help to forge a chain from the separate links. And
it's the unexpected reference to an external viewpoint—*ferunt*, or
"they say"—that determines where the chain ends, launching the
event, which has otherwise been narrated in the present, into the
past; historicizing it, in the true sense of the word, as is suggested
by the use of the perfect infinitive, *traxisse*. What we're left with is
the final residue, the chemical precipitate of a life.

I didn't really start reading Ovid until after college. Rather than
start right in on the *Metamorphoses*, I began with the *Heroides*,
a collection of imaginary letters written by mythological women,
and historical Sappho, all addressed to their distant lovers; an
exquisite work, which has had its share of success in modern literature and which presents us with an utterly Ovidian characteristic:
the desire to understand emotion—the pain of separation, in this
case—and to express it in the most memorable form, blending

passion and intelligence. While in the United States, between courses for my doctorate, I translated these letters. I'm not really sure why, or perhaps for reasons I've long ignored—I too was an emigrant at the time, and, as someone who'd been writing useless love letters since my childhood, I identified with these heroines.

Some years later, I translated the works of Ovid "the exile" (*Tristia* and *Epistulae ex ponto*), the fallen poet, banished by the very same Augustus whom he praised in the last book of his *Metamorphoses*. The reasons behind such an unexpected punishment are still vague. That Augustus was serious about the sentence, however, is clear: Ovid would never return to Rome, and for all his pleading with the prince and the trust he placed in his wife and few friends remaining in the capital to intercede on his behalf, he died right there where Augustus's anger had landed him, on the coast of the Black Sea, in a place that went by the macabre name of Tomi, plagued by the memory of the example Medea had made there of her brother (*tom-* is the root of the Greek verb *temno*, meaning "to cut"). Apart from the human story behind them, Ovid's exile poems are the least stimulating of his oeuvre, especially for someone trying to translate them. Ovid is far more successful when the suffering is merely imagined, as in the *Heroides*. When the pain is real, the work turns whiny and repetitive, and the poetry shies away from all commitment with polish and finish, as the poet himself is ready to admit.[4] Seneca is definitely superior when speaking of his own exile. The emperor Claudius wanted to remove him from the opposition and therefore banished him to the rugged island of Corsica. During his exile, which lasted from 41 to 49 C.E., Seneca wrote his mother, Elvia, some of the most profound pages of Latin in the history of the language (*Consolatio ad Helviam*). While Ovid does nothing but feel sorry for himself and exaggerate the remoteness and ugliness of his new home, Seneca, with the explicit intention of consoling his addressee, denies outright that there's even such a thing as exile. Movement, as he sees it, is a fact of life. The entire universe (*mundus*) is ceaselessly shifting its position, all is in motion; even the minds of men are constantly exploring and pressing new boundaries, because the mind itself is made of the stuff of the stars and heavenly bodies, which never stand still. It's in reading such reflections that one again understands how unique and necessary Latin literature is: in its ability to link the smallest occurrence, a personal story or a blip on a timeline, to the cosmic order, which transcends all but which also invests all with a dignity and profundity that stretch beyond the terrestrial. Even Rome—Seneca argues—was begun by a refugee, Aeneas. And the Romans established colonies in every corner. And before them the Greeks spread throughout the Mediterranean. Entire populations relocate—and here Seneca, referring to what were ancient times even in his day, seems to be speaking of the present moment. If emigration ("populorum transportationes," *Consolatio ad Helviam*, VII.5) is exile, then we must speak of a collective exile ("publica exilia," ibid.). Why suffer, then, at being far from Rome? Why should a mother go weeping with nostalgia as if her child were dead? And why, then, believe that exile is a loss of public esteem? Are not fallen temples ("aedium sacrarum ruinae") honored as if they were still standing (XIII.8)?

To dispel any lingering sense of negativity attached to his estrangement, there's one other argument Seneca makes use of—and through which his discourse reaches new heights: man is everywhere at home, because what truly matters, what's truly sublime, holds the same value from every point on earth. There's no such thing as rugged and inhospitable Corsica, there's no ground below at all, only the heavenly vault above, where bodies of varying brightness rise and set and trace their orbits and flash and, by all appearances, fall from the sky, leaving brilliant trails of light in their wake, ennobling the minds of all who look up by their mere existence (VIII).

Nevertheless, though there's far more poetry in the *Consolatio ad Helviam* than in *Tristia* and *Epistulae ex ponto* (texts that would have been known to Seneca), in the modern age we associate exile not with Seneca but with Ovid. For the Frenchman du Bellay, "exiled" in Rome in the mid-sixteenth century (precisely where Ovid would have loved to have returned), it was the *Tristia* that gave him the inspiration and imagery to produce some of his best work in the vernacular and in Latin. Ovid the exile has become an archetype in the modern and postmodern imagination, which places great insistence—also for historically verifiable reasons—on the figure of the *déraciné*, excluded poet, the victim of one colonialist or dictatorial act or another. At least two fine novels from the end of the last century that take Ovid as their protagonist come to mind: *An Imaginary Life* (1978) by the Australian writer David Malouf— a most remarkable piece of prose—and *The Last World* (1988) by the Austrian writer Christoph Ransmayr.

It wasn't until 2000 that I read all of the *Metamorphoses* in Latin. I was thirty-five years old and happened once again to be living in New York. At last I understood it for what it is: a journey into the vital forces of creation, not some giant warehouse of Graeco-Roman mythology, not just channel flipping through calamitous cartoons. At last I realized that it is a tragic tale, one in which the narrative itself undergoes its own subtle metamorphosis, and episodes are linked reciprocally by often extremely tenuous threads. In its course, it covers everything from the life-threatening chaos that surrounds us to the most hidden cells in our body; the absurd that becomes reality; the disintegration of the self; the endless variety of existence. There's one rhetorical device in particular that Ovid seems to favor—and that we've already seen in the excerpt above with Echo: the repetition or variation of a word within the space of a few lines, and sometimes in the very same line. We find evidence of this preference more or less throughout the work, though especially in those cases in which Ovid is describing a transformation. Here the language becomes something other than itself;

through repetition—varying the grammatical case or verb tense, or passing from a verb to its corresponding noun—he most patently enacts the collapse of identity. Below are just a few examples:

*venatrix*que metu *venantum* territa fugit! (II.492)
and the huntress flees in fear of the hunters.

[. . .] quique a me *morte revelli*
heu sola *poteras, poteris* nec *morte revelli.* (IV.152–53)
[. . .] and you, whom death alone could steal
from me, you can be stolen not even by death.

Quae quia mendaci *parientem* iuverat *ore,*
ore parit [. . .] (IX.322–23)
Because with her deceitful mouth she had helped a
    woman give birth,
she gives birth from the mouth [. . .]

[. . .] *Lugebere* nobis,
*lugebis*que alios [. . .] (X.141–42)
[. . .] You will be mourned by us,
you'll mourn for others [. . .]

[. . .] *amat* et non sentit *amorem.* (X.637)
[. . .] she loves and does not recognize her love.

[. . .] aliisque *dolens* fit causa *dolendi.* (XI.345)
[. . .] and while suffering, causes others to suffer.

[. . .] *decepta*que *decipit* omnes. (XIV.81)
[. . .] having been deceived, she deceives all.

The list could go on for pages.

Transformation is a violent process, a "death in life," and its occurrence gives rise to a stream of bloody, disturbing images. It is, of course, a direct assault on the stability of the material world. Crucially, however, it is also a means of homeopathy, of justice: universal, divine justice, which restores equilibrium and assigns each individual to their rightful place within the cosmos. After finishing the poem over ten or so days—during which time I'd filled an entire notebook with my thoughts—one thing was clear above all else: the *Metamorphoses* is a poem about justice! Which is precisely how Dante must have seen it: as a punitive system. To become *other* is in itself a form of retribution, some kind of *poena* (punishment): "versae poena figurae," or "the penalty of transformation" (X.234; the word *poena*, by my count, appears more than seventy times in the poem). Already in Ovid, we find, the transformation fits the transformed, or is its antithesis. The root of Dante's *contrapasso*, therefore, should be traced back to Ovid's *Metamorphoses*, not to medieval theologians. Observe how the goddess Latona handles this group of farmers who've blocked her from quenching her thirst at a small lake, hurling insults and stirring up the water:

> "Aeternum stagno" dixit "vivatis in isto!"
> Eveniunt optata deae: iuvat esse sub undis
> et modo tota cava submergere membra palude,
> nunc proferre caput, summo modo gurgite nare,
> saepe super ripam stagni consistere, saepe
> in gelidos resilire lacus, sed nunc quoque turpes
> litibus exercent linguas pulsoque pudore,
> quamvis sint sub aqua, sub aqua maledicere temptant.
> Vox quoque iam rauca est, inflataque colla tumescunt,
> ipsaque dilatant patulos convicia rictus.
> Terga caput tangunt, colla intercepta videntur,
> spina viret, venter, pars maxima corporis, albet,
> limosoque novae saliunt in gurgite ranae. (VI.369–81)

"Then wallow," she said, "in your pond eternally!"
And the goddess's wish comes true. They take delight
    underwater
now submerging entirely their limbs in the hollow mire,
now peeking their heads, now swimming along the
    surface,
squatting often along the banks, and often
diving back in the water's cool; and all the while
wagging their filthy tongues in shameless spats,
even underwater, hurling underwater abuse.
Their voices are harsh now, throats swell tumid,
wide mouths stretching wider with their scorn,
shoulders are leveled with head, necks shrink,
their backs go green, their bellies (now their bodies)
    white—
they ply their muddy pool as new-made frogs.

Likewise, when Orpheus is killed by the women of Thrace, Bacchus "did not let their crime go unpunished," but transformed them all into trees with gnarled roots. And again with Minerva, after she's lost to Arachne in a weaving contest. When Arachne hangs herself in pride—having seen her beautiful work destroyed and suffered a beating from the goddess—Minerva prevents her from dying and transforms her into a spider. In this way, though she's been transformed, she can continue to weave—in other words, to be exactly who she always was, in fact becoming even more herself through the metamorphosis. So Dante will treat the souls he meets in hell, doling out punishments that perpetuate their essence for all eternity.[5]

14

Breathing and Creaking: Reflections on Livy

The Paduan Titus Livius (59 B.C.E.–17 C.E.) wrote a monumental history of Rome, spanning from its foundation (753 B.C.E.) to the events of his present day (9 C.E.). He himself felt overwhelmed by the vastness of the project. In the introduction to Book XXXI of the *Ab urbe condita*, he confesses that the further he gets in his narrative, the further it seems he's descending into an underwater abyss, the project growing rather than shrinking the more he completes.

Only 35 of the original 142 books survive: I–X and XXI–XLV—an enormous and irreplaceable loss, which Petrarch mourned in a letter addressed to Livy himself (*Familiares*, XXIV.8).

This foundational work is the saga of a slow collapse: it celebrates the tumultuous creation of the empire, heralding a new cast of national heroes, and criticizes the mounting corruption, the abandonment of customs, the present degeneration. Livy is a historian of nostalgia—a theme that pervades all Western historical thought and gives it much of its character. A prime example is Edward Gibbon's principal work, *The History of the Decline and Fall of the Roman Empire*, which appeared between 1776 and 1788. Livy makes it very clear in his preface that writing about antiquity brings him more pleasure than writing about the present, because it allows him to avert his gaze from the dismaying world around him. Petrarch too, in the above-mentioned letter, following Livy's example, attributes his deep engagement with Livy's works to that same desire to forget the present moment. And it's no coincidence, of course, that the books to survive are precisely those that celebrate the foundational years of the Roman Empire.

This stump, just more than a quarter of the original whole, has been enough to keep the memory of Livy alive and to inform us of essential events in Rome's history, a tale as fascinating as myth. And that's not all. Symbolically, in the posthumous fortune of Livy's work one can recognize the essence of early humanism, its true spirit, the drive to rediscover, to reexamine those ancient texts, whether Latin or Greek, that contributed largely to the formation of the literary and cultural identity of modern Europe. A priceless work was dropped in the street, its pages scattered—and then, after a millennium of neglect, philology stepped in, putting a halt to the disaster. First came Petrarch, who gathered all of the fragments and assembled the first complete manuscript of Livy's available books.[1] Machiavelli, almost two centuries later, took Livy as his model and wrote an important political treatise, far more important than *The Prince*—his *Discourses on the First Ten Books of Titus Livy*.

Livy's history of Rome is the sole remnant in prose of the Augustan age. Livy is a self-professed Ciceronian, decidedly anti-Sallustian. In the course of his lengthy account, he puts all of Latin's capabilities on display: ample, articulate sentence structures; a wealth of syntactical and narrative approaches (including first-person narration and dialogue), in which he demonstrates his mastery of the complex verbal system used for indirect discourse (lots of infinitives, lots of subjunctives); regular forms; a vocabulary suited to all manner of situations; and here and there a flight into poetic diction. Cicero's firmly structured syntax provides Livy—beyond the comfort and confidence of a linguistic norm—with a means of forming a complex and detailed narrative, through which he's able to mount a so-to-speak novelesque examination of events, behaviors, and emotional states. Something that Sallust's terseness—deprived of the tragic leavening of someone like Tacitus—could never achieve.

Learning from Cicero, Livy becomes an artist of *episodes*. He stacks one on top of another: the details mount and take on metaphorical resonances; events are relayed in sequences, with a crescendo and a climax. They even explore the psychological effects of those who were present at the time to witness it. An event, in Livy, is never reduced to an objective occurrence, as we saw in Sallust or, though in a different manner, in Caesar: rather, it is the sum of various elements, circumstances, and emotions, all of which possess their own complexity; it is always something sensational, which elicits astonishment, admiration, and bewilderment in whoever was there to experience it, long before the writer or reader. When the event he's recounting is an ancient one, he goes a step further, adding the burnishing of memory, through which the event is filtered before reaching the historian. And so Livy gives his account as the story of a story, filling his syntax with echoes of the "original." Here's a brief example:

Eo tempore in regia prodigium visu eventuque mirabile fuit. Puero dormienti, cui Servio Tullio fuit nomen, caput arsisse ferunt multorum in conspectu; plurimo igitur clamore inde ad tantae rei miraculum orto excitos reges, et cum quidam familiarium aquam ad restinguendum ferret, ab regina retentum, sedatoque eam tumultu moveri vetuisse puerum donec sua sponte experrectus esset; mox cum somno et flammam abisse. (*Ab urbe condita*, I.39)

What's taking place here? The soon-to-be sixth king of Rome, Servius Tullius, is still a child. The Roman people believe him to be the son of slaves. A miraculous omen, however, proves that he's freeborn and destined to lead the city (a very similar omen is to be found in the *Aeneid*, II.679–91, in regard to Aeneas's young son, Ascanius). This passage is a gem of grammatical precision, variety, lexical force, musicality, narrative vivacity, and roundedness. Here is my translation:

> There occurred at this time in the royal palace an omen remarkable in both its manifestation and its meaning. It's told that while the child known as Servius Tullius was sleeping, his head burst into flames in the presence of many. So great was the outcry at such a miracle the king and queen were alarmed (or awoken). When a servant arrived with water to quench the flames, the queen stopped him, quieting the uproar and demanding that no one touch the boy until he awoke on his own. Soon afterward sleep left him, and with it went the flames.

In his telling of the Lucretia episode (I.57–59), Livy weaves together drama and syntax in a stunningly powerful crescendo. Sextus Tarquinius, the king's son, catches sight of Lucretia, the most virtuous of the matrons, and is gripped with desire. A few days later, he bursts into her room, threatens her with his sword, and rapes her. Livy is able to mimic the words of the rapist—a brusque and simple utterance, declaring the vile reasons behind his action:

> "Tace, Lucretia," inquit; "Sex. Tarquinius sum; ferrum in manu est; moriere, si emiseris vocem." (I.58.2)

> "Silence, Lucretia," he said. "I am Sextus Tarquinius; my sword is in hand; any noise, and you'll be dead."

Lucretia resists at first. But then, after Sextus Tarquinius declares his intention to kill her and, to sully her honor, set her body in the embrace of a dead servant, she gives in. Immediately she summons her father back from Rome and her husband from Ardea and tells them of what happened, referring to the violence she suffered as "pestiferum [. . .] gaudium" (I.58.9), "destructive pleasure." The language of Lucretia and her family is lucid and elegant, in sharp contrast to the boorish rhetoric of her violator. No false sentimentality, no garbled anger. Lucretia is after justice. Her family promises her she'll have it. They console her, even, entering into subtle but substantial distinctions between each person's responsibility:

> consolantur aegram animi avertendo noxam ab coacta in auctorem delicti: mentem peccare, non corpus, et unde consilium afuerit culpam abesse. (I.58.10)

> they console the distraught woman by shifting the blame from her, who was forced, to him who committed the sin. It is the mind that errs, not the body, they maintain, and where there is no intention there is no guilt.

Lucretia, however, has her own idea of justice; she thinks not only of her own good name, but of that of all women. And in this way, through Livy's words, she becomes one of the most celebrated female icons of all time, both in literature and in art history:

> ego me etsi peccato absolvo, supplicio non libero; nec ulla deinde impudica Lucretiae exemplo vivet. (I.58.11)

> even if I absolve myself of guilt, I do not excuse myself the punishment; no more will women live defiled, with Lucretia as their example.

Her use of juridical vocabulary is of particular interest here: the verb *absolvo* and the noun *peccatum*. Interestingly, this very terminology will be picked up by Christian authors in strictly religious meaning. In the end, bringing her reasoning to its logical extreme, Lucretia takes her own life:

Cultrum, quem sub veste abditum habebat, eum in corde defigit, prolapsaque in vulnus moribunda cecidit. (I.58.12)

She plunged into her heart the knife she kept hidden beneath her garments, and, bent over the wound, collapsed dying.

The scene is reminiscent of Dido's suicide, even in minute elements of its vocabulary (to this day, in truth, we have no verification of any direct relationship between Livy and Virgil, nor can we say—despite examples like this one—whether it was Virgil who borrowed from Livy or vice versa): *moribunda* is the same adjective that the queen of Carthage uses to refer to herself (*Aeneid*, IV.323); *prolapsa* harks back to the *Aeneid*'s *conlapsam* (IV.664); Livy's "defigit [. . .] vulnus" is Virgil's "infixum [. . .] vulnus," (*Aeneid*, IV.689). I'd also point out that the expression "aegram animi" echoes the "infelix animi" of Dido (*Aeneid*, IV.529), and that Dido herself is twice defined as *aegra* in Book IV (lines 35 and 389). Even the reaction of those who witness the event is similar in the two authors: "Conclamat vir paterque" in Livy (I.58.12), "it clamor ad alta / atria" in Virgil (IV.665–66).

There is, however, a fundamental difference between the deaths of the two women: Dido's suicide is one of passion (even if it does mark the beginning of an age of discord between the two peoples—the Carthaginians and the Romans who descend from Aeneas), one caused by desperation, by rage at having been abandoned; Lucretia's is a political suicide, which her gesture makes very clear. That it brings about the fall of monarchy in Rome is no mere accident: so disgusted are the Romans by the actions of the king's son that it throws into question the entire regime, under which Rome has lived for centuries.

I've made the claim that, in his language, Livy seeks to express the psychological and emotional resonances of an event. An excellent example of this is a passage from the fifth book, in which the Gauls infiltrate Rome and make ready to conquer it. It would have been enough to simply report the facts, the military actions. Livy, instead, dives into each unique event, into its singular pathos and paradigm, drawing out its dramatic effects. The Gauls, he recounts, find themselves in a deserted city. The old warriors have retreated indoors, dressed in the insignia of their onetime rank, awaiting their deaths on ivory thrones. An ominous air envelops all, becoming one with the invading army:

> in forum *perveniunt*, <u>circumferentes</u> oculos ad templa deum arcemque solam belli speciem <u>tenentem</u>. Inde, modico <u>relicto</u> praesidio ne quis in dissipatos ex arce aut Capitolio impetus fieret, <u>dilapsi</u> ad praedam vacuis occursu hominum viis, pars in proxima quaeque tectorum agmine *ruunt*, pars ultima, velut ea demum intacta et referta praeda, *petunt*; inde rursus ipsa solitudine <u>absterriti</u>, ne qua fraus hostilis vagos exciperet, in forum ac propinqua foro loca conglobati *redibant*; ubi eos, plebis aedificiis <u>obseratis,</u> <u>patentibus</u> atriis principum, maior prope cunctatio *tenebat* aperta quam clausa invadendi . . . (V.41.4–8; emphasis mine)

It's a gorgeous sentence—not exactly brief, but not as complicated as it might seem at first glance. Only a few principal verbs (which I've set off in italics) support its structure, all of them verbs of movement except the last, whose precise purpose is to bring the movement to a halt, to signal a frightful hesitation; in between are a variety of secondary clauses, which expand the semantic range of the primary actions, mostly through the use of participles (which I've underlined), like the ripples around a stone tossed in a pond, or the shadows thrown from a body under crisscrossing lights. The Gauls, in this way, flit here and there, looting, until at last they pause before the sight of the austere old men, sitting and waiting:

> they came to the forum, gazing around at the temples of the gods and at the Citadel, which alone wore any appearance of war. Then, leaving a small unit to guard against an attack from the Citadel or the Capitol while their men are scattered, they took to the empty streets in search of loot, some filing in to the nearby houses, others making for those farther off, believing these to be still untouched and filled with treasures; then, once again, spooked by their own solitude that they might be walking into a trap, they returned en masse to the forum and its surrounding areas; where, being that the shades of the plebeians' dwellings were shut, while those at the palaces of the ruling class were open, they were almost more reluctant to enter the open homes than the closed ones . . .

Though the action occurs at various times and in various places, what we have here is, essentially, a single scene: the Gauls' disorientation. Were it a scene in a film, the music would cut. We'd hear only the actors' breathing, a creaking here and there, and nothing else. The entire episode, in fact, is a means of buying time, a lead-up to the final massacre—which, as it must, arrives, throwing the cast into a frenzy of violent gestures. This gory spectacle, with its string of close-ups, is shot in the wide frame of a

single sentence: three simple narrative, infinitive verbs (which
function here like verbs in the past progressive), all three of which
are passive, fired in rapid succession. The style hints already at
Tacitus:

> post principum caedem nulli deinde mortalium *parci,
> diripi* tecta, exhaustis *inici* ignes. (V.41.10)

> after the massacre of the city leaders, no man was spared,
> the houses were sacked, and fire was set to all that was
> left.

The tale of Lucretia can be regarded as a short story: indeed,
it gives us the essential facts, in the necessary order, with dramatic force and a moral lesson. In other moments in Livy's history,
the narrative is truly novelesque. I'm thinking in particular of the
sections in Book XL (5–6; 21–24; 56–57) that recount the rivalry
between Perseus and Demetrius, the two sons of Philip V of Macedonia. Like a novel, it has a buildup, emotional and psychological
complexity (hatred, betrayal, regret, pain at injustice, etc.), a variety of rhetorical devices, and catastrophe. Perseus despises his
younger brother and, though he's destined for the throne by right
of birth, wants him dead nevertheless. So he accuses him, before
their father, of an attempted fratricide—distorting a whole series
of insignificant events—and of being too friendly with the Romans
(that Demetrius was a friend of the Romans cannot be denied,
given that his own father had sent him to Rome as an ambassa-
dor). Though taken by surprise, Demetrius overcomes his distress
and responds to this quite convincing accusation with his own ex-
pertly crafted counterargument, dismantling Perseus's points of
evidence one by one (in their two speeches, Livy demonstrates
himself an excellent student of Cicero's forensic art). Shortly after,
we watch as Perseus strikes again and Demetrius is murdered at

the order of his own father. Finally, at the height of desperation, Philip realizes that he's just killed his innocent son and let the wicked one live. In a last-ditch effort, he attempts to name Antigonid as his heir, but his sudden death leaves Perseus with the clear advantage. Here is the scene of Demetrius's death, in which he's poisoned by Didas, one of King Philip's men:

> Poculo epoto extemplo *sensit*, et mox coortis doloribus, relicto convivio cum in cubiculum recepisset sese, crudelitatem patris conquerens, parricidium fratris ac Didae scelus incusans *torquebatur*. Intromissi deinde Thyrsis quidam Stuberraeus et Beroeaeus Alexander, iniectis tapetibus in caput faucesque, spiritum *intercluserunt*. Ita innoxius adulescens, cum in eo ne simplici quidem genere mortis contenti inimici fuissent, *interficitur*. (XL.24.6–8; emphasis mine)

As is typical of Livy's Latin, of the many verbs used here only a very few are principal verbs (which I've set off in italics): four out of twelve. We should also note that these principal verbs come always at the end of the sentence or clause, lending it a sense of surprise and finality. Here's my translation:

> As soon as he'd drained his cup, he understood; and, the pain having struck him immediately, he left the banquet and returned to his room; and, bemoaning the cruelty of his father, and stewing in accusations of his brother's crime and Didas's wickedness, was tortured by suffering. Then through the door came a certain Thyrsis from Stuberra and Alexander from Beroea, who wrapped his head and mouth in a rug to cut off his breathing. So it was that this innocent young man, for whose enemies one method of death alone would not suffice, came to be murdered.

So ends the chapter, all the more poignantly and piteously for the judgment decreed by the omniscient narrator, who proclaims Demetrius the innocent party and accuses his enemies of the most complacent act of violence.

Have a look, as well, at the death of Philip, which comes several chapters later:

[. . .] cum Amphipolim venisset, gravi morbo est implicitus. Sed animo tamen aegrum magis fuisse quam corpore constat; curisque et vigiliis, cum identidem species et umbrae insontis interempti filii agitarent, cum diris exstinctum esse exsecrationibus alterius. (XL.56.8–9)

[. . .] having reached Amphipolis, he was seized by a severe illness. Though it was known to be an illness more of the soul than of the body; and in anguish and in sleeplessness, haunted by visions and the ghost of his innocent, murdered son, he died, with a curse for his other son on his lips.

Here again, the ax falls in just a few quick lines. But look what force is contained in those two words, *species* and *umbrae*, the appearance of the bitter ghost (*species* is akin to the noun *spectaculum*, both sharing the root of the verb *specio*, "to see")! We began with two long speeches, one of accusation and one of defense, with a tense opposition between two brothers, and here that opposition is revived and inverted in the dying words of a father come to his senses far too late, in a revelation that is merely a denouncement of the wrongdoing. End of novel.

15

The Word *Umbra*: Virgil's *Eclogues*

One morning in my junior year of high school, just before she began her lecture, our professor was summoned to the front office. "Nicola," she ordered, stepping down from the podium, "you come do the reading and translation, from the first line." So it was that I, standing before the class, began interpreting one of the most enduring opening passages in all of literature:

> Tityre, tu patulae recubans sub tegmine fagi
> silvestrem tenui Musam meditaris avena;
> nos patriae finis et dulcia linquimus arva,
> nos patriam fugimus; tu, Tityre, lentus in umbra
> formosam resonare doces Amaryllida silvas.
> (*Eclogues*, I.1–5)

I don't think I could fully describe the marvel I felt at encountering these words—an experience that struck me all the more forcefully, given that I was standing at the podium in place of my professor, completely unprepared. It was an experience that, in all likelihood, at last solidified my nebulous interest in a teaching career. I can, however, affirm beyond doubt that this sense of marvel has never faded, for all the times in my life I've returned to Virgil's *Eclogues*. These opening lines of the *Eclogues*—and I say this without fear of exaggerating—have been a guide for me, a source of comfort and clarity, a place where I'll always be young, always hungry for the future. After finishing my doctorate in the United States, I left to start a new life back in Italy, and when I wasn't busy trying to figure out what the next step was, I set about translating the first eclogue. My aim, in truth, was to translate them all, but I got distracted—my eyes were then still bigger than my stomach. For which reason I never made it past the second eclogue. Nevertheless, I won't rule out the possibility that one day or another I'll dive back in again and start from zero—from *Tityre*.

Admittedly, as anyone with a solid foundation in the language can see—and as even I noticed immediately—the Latin of Virgil's *Eclogues* is rather "basic." His sentences—excepting the line breaks that come with poetic writing—are linear, and tend toward aphorism; his vocabulary free of archaisms. Which is why, in the *Eclogues*, we find some of the clearest and most memorable expressions in all of Latin:

[. . .] quis enim modus adsit amori? (II.68)
[. . .] what measure could there be for love?

iam redit et Virgo [. . .] (IV.6)
now the Virgin too returns [Astrea, goddess of justice,
        transformed into the constellation Virgo]

incipe, parve puer, risu cognoscere matrem (IV.60)
child, begin to recognize your mother by her smile

Pastores, hedera nascentem ornate poetam (VII.25)
Shepherds, adorn your newborn poet with ivy

omnia nunc rident [. . .] (VII.55)
all is laughing now [. . .]

[. . .] fors omnia versat (IX.5)
[. . .] Chance reshuffles all

omnia vincit Amor [. . .] (X.69)
Love conquers all [. . .]

There is, however, even among such plainness and clarity, something that remains ungraspable, indefinable, that escapes even the most scrupulous translator; each word, though tied musically to those around it, possesses its own absoluteness, its own inexhaustible semantic complexity, which—like the golden branch in the *Aeneid* (VI.140–48 and 183–211)—regenerates just in that moment you think you've captured its meaning. Look back to the opening lines: *patulae*; *recubans*; *tegmine*; *meditaris*; *linquimus*; *resonare* . . . These words, clear and simple, are the components of a magic spell; saturated with meaning, they're precise and metaphorical at once. In fact, in some cases, it's through metaphor that the words arrive at their precision, hedging in or stretching out an initial meaning. *Musam* does not mean "Muse" but "poetic song"; *meditaris* does not mean "to reflect [upon]" but refers to the result of reflection, therefore "you compose" (the entire second verse reappears in a different order in VI.8: "agrestem tenui meditabor harundine Musam"); *tenui* refers to the small size of the reed pipe, but also to the low register of the style. I'll try to translate:

Tityrus, stretched in the ample shade of a beech
composing a sylvan song on your slight reeds;
we abandon our native land and these sweet fields,
we flee our home; you, Tityrus, at ease in the shade,
teach the woods to sound of the fair Amaryllis.

As you'll notice, I've chosen to translate *Musam* as "song," following in line with a long tradition. The word *Musam*, with such strong connotations, has a double effect in the context of a pastoral poem: it lowers all godly sense to the reality of shepherds; at the same time, though, it raises the poetry to sacred art. In this semantic ambivalence, which traps the macro and the micro in an infinite circle, we have one of the most characteristic virtues of Virgil's Latin.

The shepherd who's speaking here, Meliboeus, has been stripped of his lands. This sad situation reflects historical truth: Augustus decided to repay his veterans through the heavy-handed method of expropriation; Virgil too saw his lands taken from him. Conversely, Tityrus is permitted to stay, to continue leading his goats to pasture, basking in nature and singing his love songs. His is the true bucolic world. Nature is protected and protective, emotional, animate, involved in the fates of men and saddened at their deaths. The shepherds are concerned only with eros, friendship, and poetry, of which the *Eclogues* are an intermittent celebration. Poetry (*carmen*, or "song") represents the human word in its most powerful form; something even supernatural, as in Eclogue VIII, where a smitten sorceress plies the stubborn heart of her beloved with magic spells. It is comfort, and consolation:

Tale tuum carmen nobis, divine poeta,
quale sopor fessis in gramine, quale per aestum
dulcis aquae saliente sitim restinguere rivo. (V.45–47)

To us, divine poet, your song is like sleep
on the grass to the weary, like slaking one's thirst
by the churning shore of a freshwater stream.

We're quite clearly in a utopia here, or better yet an ideal of suspended happiness, removed from history, cities, buildings, politics, and death (see Daphne's beautiful lines on death in Eclogue V). The bucolic utopia is one of the most enduring myths (and literary archetypes) of Western culture. We run into it everywhere: in the Latin pastoral poetry of humanism and in the vernacular of Jacopo Sannazaro's *Arcadia*; but also in Ariosto's *Orlando furioso* and Torquato Tasso's *Aminta* and *Jerusalem Delivered*; in Philip Sidney's *Arcadia*; in Shakespeare's *As You Like It*; in the melodramatic tradition; in the modern lyrical tradition; and so on. For all its variations, however much it oscillates between disengagement and a critique of the system, between complete obliviousness of events and the anguish felt at their threat, it is always a song of nostalgia.

This is not the place to dive into the specifics of the bucolic genre, which Virgil imported to Rome from Greece, nor to explore the principal characteristics of Virgil's poem, whose ideological and literary complexity, even in relation to its Greek antecedents, merits our undivided attention. What I do want to point out here, however, is that in the simple and linear Latin of early Virgil we find two archetypes of Western culture: first, the primordial landscape, which Virgil re-creates by incorporating the countryside of his native Mantova; and second, the dream of renewal. To return to the *Eclogues* is to return to the fountainhead of thousand-year-old thoughts and images.

Close-ups of the natural world abound. Let's have a look at the most exemplary:

Fortunate senex, hic inter flumina nota
et fontis sacros frigus captabis opacum;
hinc tibi, quae semper, vicino ab limite saepes
Hyblaeis apibus florem depasta salicti,
saepe levi somnum suadebit inire susurro;
hinc alta sub rupe canet frondator ad auras,
nec tamen interea raucae, tua cura, palumbes
nec gemere aeria cessabit turtur ab ulmo. (I.51–58)

Blessed old man, here by familiar streams
and sacred fountains, you'll find a place to cool;
here, by its boundary, the usual hedge,
where Hybla's bees sip from the willow blossoms,
will lull you to sleep with its low buzzing;
here under the cliff, the woodsman will sing to the breeze,
and neither the doves their throaty song, your love,
nor the turtledoves in the elms, will cease their moaning.

Here Meliboeus is speaking to Tityrus. Giacomo Leopardi must have been thinking of line 53—which contains the adverb "always" (*semper*) and the noun "hedge" (*saepes*), and which expresses a similar sentiment—when he composed the opening lines of his *Infinito*:

This lonely hill was always dear to me,
and this hedgerow, which cuts off the view
of so much of the last horizon.
But sitting here and gazing, I can see
beyond, in my mind's eye, unending spaces,
and superhuman silences, and depthless calm . . .[1]

The same idea of a "limit," which Leopardi examined repeatedly in his writing, and from which he derives his own idea of the infinite, is here before us quite literally, in the ablative form of the noun *limes*—that is, *limite*.

In this second example, below, Daphne addresses Meliboeus:

huc ades, o Meliboee; caper tibi salvus et haedi;
et, si quid cessare potes, requiesce sub umbra.
Huc ipsi potum venient per prata iuvenci,
hic viridis tenera praetexit harundine ripas
Mincius, eque sacra resonant examina quercu. (VII.9–13)

come, Meliboeus; your goat and kids are safe;
and, if you can linger a bit, lie back in the shade.
The calves will cross the meadows to drink here on
    their own,
here Mincius drapes his shores in tender reeds,
and high in the sacred oak the swarms resound.

In the following lines, sung by Moeris and Lycidas, Virgil sets
the countryside in clear contrast with the seascape, realm of the
nymph Galatea:

Hic ades, o Galatea; quis est nam ludus in undis?
hic ver purpureum, varios hic flumina circum
fundit humus flores, hic candida populous antro
imminet et lentae texunt umbracula vites.
Huc ades; insani feriant sine litora fluctus. (IX.39–43)

Come, Galatea; what pleasure is there on the waves?
here spring blushes; here the earth pours flowers
in all their colors by the river; here a white poplar leans
from a cave, and the vines braid softly into arbors.
Come; let the waves crash, foolish, on the shore.

As can in part be seen from these excerpts, Virgil captures
the flora and fauna of the pastoral landscape—the first great
European landscape, we might say—in precise detail. We have
bushes (*arbusta*), viburnums (*viburna*), hazels (*coryli*), oaks (*quer-
cus*), marshmallow (*hibiscus* or *hibiscum*). We have roe deer (*capre-
oli*), bees (*apes*), oxen (*boves*), cicadas (*cicadae*). A surrounding of
springs (*fontes*), rivers (*flumina*), mountains (*montes*), caves (*antra*),
woods (*silvae*). We even get a sampling of the bucolic diet: apples
(*poma*), chestnuts (*castaneae*), milk (*lac*), plums (*pruna*). These
lists, of course, are not exhaustive. But rather than enumerate

every last item, I'd like to note one element of the landscape in particular—one that appears generic enough and unquantifiable, but that has its own special force, even a rhythmic and structural function: *umbra*, "shadow" or "shade" (a distinction other modern languages—Italian included—don't make). For Virgil, even this vague little word becomes something personal, a calling card of sorts. In the *Aeneid* too, he manages to employ it to memorable effect again and again. And again in the *Georgics*. It is with *umbra*, as we've seen, that his first eclogue opens, and with *umbra* that it closes:

maioresque cadunt altis de montibus umbrae. (I.83)

longer shadows fall from high in the mountains.

Umbra—the word is repeated no fewer than three times—concludes the tenth and final eclogue:

Surgamus; solet esse gravis cantantibus umbra,
iuniperi gravis umbra; nocent et frugibus umbrae.
Ite domum saturate, venit Hesperus, ite capellae.
   (X.75–77)

Let's rise; shade is harmful to singers,
harmful is the shade cast by the juniper; shade damages
   crops.
Go home well fed, for Hesperus comes, my goats.

Umbras, as we've seen, will also appear as the final word of the *Aeneid*. There, though, it refers to the kingdom of the dead.

Umbra, for me, is one of the most beautiful words in the Latin language. Its meaning is captured in its brevity, as it passes from the dark of its initial vowel to the light of its final one, via a con-certino of no less than three consonants—the nasal *m* (which prolongs the impression of darkness) and the midrange (or sonorous) labial pair *b* + the liquid dental *r* (which press us gently toward the light). Etymologically, *umbra* is related to *imber*, "rain" (*ombros* in Greek): both words, in fact, point to a scarcity of light. And it would seem that Virgil too was aware of this fascinating etymological bond, if it's not by coincidence that the two words appear together—and in the same position—in the following passage:

> Aret ager; vitio moriens sitit aeris herba;
> Liber pampineas invidit collibus umbras:
> Phyllidis adventu nostrae nemus omne virebit,
> Iuppiter et laeto descendet plurimus imbri. (VII.57–60)

We're in the midst of Eclogue VII, which depicts a singing contest between the shepherds Corydon and Thyrsis. These lines are sung by Thyrsis. Below is my translation, though inevitably I've lost the play on *umbras/imbri*:

> The fields dry out; the grass in the stale air dies.
> Bacchus begrudges the hills the shade of the vines:
> but the woods will bloom again when my Phyllis arrives,
> and Jove will descend with tides of fertile rain.

The presence of so many shadows—apart from their usual boon as relief from the heat—suggests that for Virgil there's a world untouched by the sun's long rays. Shadows are an unseen existence, the souls of the dead themselves, as we witness in masterful form in Book VI of the *Aeneid*, and in the poem's final line recalled above. Shade is refuge from a swelter, a place to cool off (if not always pleasant, as in the poem's finale), the opposite of love's fire, which burns at all hours of the day (*Eclogues*, II.67–68). But it's also mystery, the occult, a presage of the beyond, or even the invasion of the beyond into the here and now, ritualized every day with the fall of evening. In the shadow, the semantic and emotive ambivalence of Virgil's Latin finds its most eloquent symbol.

I briefly mentioned the dream of renewal, which nourished even Christianity in important ways and would eventually erupt into the humanistic culture of the fourteenth and fifteenth centuries, later deemed by nineteenth-century historians as a rebirth, or renaissance.[2] Virgil, turning to Greek philosophy and poetry, spoke in Eclogue IV of a return to the mythical golden age (Christians will read this as a messianic prophesy), a primitive, prehistoric age, prior to any decline, when mankind knew no toil or suffering and found in nature all that was needed to survive. In truth, we can look at the entire bucolic world as a golden age of sorts; because all of the eclogues, as I noted above, are a utopia, and what is a golden age but a perfection of the bucolic ideal? It is precisely through this attempt to depict utopia—and thanks to the efforts of young Virgil—that Latin breaks completely new ground metaphorically and reaches the height of its expression. The task, after all, is not to represent something simply imaginary, but something impossible, something that cannot be confirmed by experience or memory, but that is in fact counterintuitive and paradoxical. Here is just a brief example:

> Ipsae lacte domum referent distenta capellae
> ubera, nec magnos metuent armenta leones;
> occidet et serpens et fallax herba veneni
> occidet; Assyrium vulgo nascetur amomum.
> At simul heroum laudes et facta parentis
> iam legere et quae sit poteris cognoscere virtus,
> molli paulatim flavescet campus arista
> incultisque rubens pendebit sentibus uva
> et durae quercus sudabunt roscida mella. (IV.21–30)

The goats will make their own way home, their udders swollen with milk, and the cattle will fear no lions;

and snakes will die, and deceitful, poisonous herbs
will die; the fields will flow with Assyrian spices.
Once you've read of the heroes' glories and the deeds
of your father, you'll know what virtue is, and the fields
will slowly turn to gold with tender wheat,
and from the wild briars, grapes will hang,
and the hardest oaks will ooze fresh honey.

In essence, this is a list of *adynata*, or logical impossibilities: goats don't come home if not led; cattle will always be terrified of lions; snakes will never just vanish from the face of the earth, nor will poison. And yet here he's saying otherwise, and he's doing so out of the same radical loyalty to ambivalence that I spoke of earlier: the ability to say more than can be said at one time, uniting light and dark without contradiction; giving primacy to *umbra*.

16

Seneca, or the Serenity
of Saying It All

Of all the ancient authors, Seneca is the one who's taught me most
how to live. Virgil moves me; Tacitus leaves me aghast at cruelty;
Lucretius sends me whirling and drifting and sinking; Cicero
has me dreaming of perfection in all—thought, speech, behavior.
Seneca teaches me happiness.

And he's by no means a difficult teacher. No need, with him,
to go hunting for answers. Happiness is not something imagined,
desired, or envied: it's right here, within our grasp. It belongs not
to the future but to the present. It has nothing to do with hope
(*spes*), which Seneca contests openly (*Letters to Lucilius*, 5.7–8)
and which will be viewed, instead, as one of the principal virtues of Christianity. To hope is to postpone; to welcome fear, un-
certainty, frustration. To hope is to waste time, our most precious
resource. Happy are those who have a clear understanding of
their own interior state, who know exactly what they need, who
can distinguish between the essential and the vain; those who
know, when left alone, how to keep themselves company. Happy
are those who avoid dissatisfaction, inconclusiveness, incon-
stancy, disappointment, waste, emptiness, boredom, nausea (a

Greek word derived from *naus*, "ship," referring to seasickness, which we find as early as Cicero and which Seneca infused with psychological implications to mean "sick of life," as he does in letter 24 to Lucilius); those who know their own capacities and never yearn for more than they can gain, who obtain all that they need by their own efforts, so that nothing can be taken from them, even if stripped of house and home. Happy are those who feel no fear, who place no trust in popular opinion, who don't get mired in mere hypotheses—protecting themselves from wholly imaginary dangers—who are unfazed by external events, who remain independent. Happy are those who judge with confidence, who go their own way and trust in their own intelligence; those who respect their teachers but are never slave to them, knowing that *patet omnibus veritas*, "the truth is open to all" (*Letters to Lucilius*, 33.11). Happy are those who never let others steal their time; who look within and find themselves in tune with their own being.

Seneca lived and died a philosopher. He witnessed the sordidness and misery of others and suffered them himself; and yet he defended the divine nature of mankind:

> Totum hoc quo continemur et unum est et deus; et socii sumus eius et membra. Capax est noster animus, perfertur illo si vitia non deprimant. (*Letters to Lucilius*, 92.30)

> All we are surrounded by is one and it is god; and we are its allies and its limbs. Great is our mind; it's taken up there, if vices don't take it down.

His creed was Stoicism, though he never discounted the teachings of other doctrines, including those of his most spirited rival, Epicurus (Lucretius's master). From counseling, teaching, and consoling he forged his profession. And he too, like Cicero, was a victim of politics; of brutal power, with which he was per-

sonally acquainted (an act for which Petrarch will hold him ac-
countable thirteen centuries later, in his *Familiares*, XXIV.6); a
perfect symbol of the utterly Roman conflict between participation in public life (*negotium*)—traditionally the most respected
lifestyle—and taking refuge in one's study (*otium*). Unlike Cicero,
however, he took his end into his own hands, before the emperor
Nero—his former student, already stained with matricide—could
strike again. (If some people just don't learn, it's not necessarily the fault of their teachers.) His death, thanks to its depiction
in Tacitus (*Annals*, XV.62–63), is one of the most famous in the
ancient world, along with that of Socrates. Many modern painters
have taken up the subject, including Rubens. Monteverdi adapted
the scene in *The Coronation of Poppea* (1643), one of the first
lyric operas based on a historical subject.[1] Slitting the veins in his
wrists and legs, so the blood would drain out slowly, he began dic-
tating several pages of philosophy. He then took poison, but even
that was not enough to stop his heart. Only later, in a bath of warm
water, did he breathe his last.

Seneca's Latin is a direct reflection of his clarity of mind and
penchant for synthesis: he slashes and chisels, going straight to the
heart of the matter, no complications, no hollering, no displays of
resentment. Annaeus Serenus, his somewhat clueless and insuf-
ferable friend, lays out a linguistic ideal at the beginning of his *De
tranquillitate animi* that might as well be Seneca's own:

> In studiis puto mehercules melius esse res ipsas intueri
> et harum causa loqui, ceterum verba rebus permittere, ut
> qua duxerint, hac inelaborata sequitur oratio [. . .] aliquid
> *simplici stilo* [emphasis mine] scribe: minore labore opus
> est studentibus in diem. (1.14)

> In literary studies I indeed hold that it's best to address
> things directly and to speak on their behalf, to let things

dictate words, so that the discourse follows spontaneously where they lead [. . .] write in *a simple style* [emphasis mine]: he who writes day by day has less need for elaboration.

Stilus means first and foremost "stylus," the tool used for writing on wax tablets. But in Seneca, as in other authors of the period, the word has already taken on its vernacular meaning as "a manner of writing." *Simplex* is a curious adjective. The root *sim* indicates unity. We find it in the time-related adverbs *semper* (always) and *semel* (once). Seneca also makes use of the noun *simplicitas*, meaning a quality that we might liken to our concept of "sincerity" or "loyalty" (see for example *De tranquillitate animi*, 15.1 and 17.2). This "simple style" is an ideal of primary importance for Seneca; it's not merely a rhetorical principle (he speaks of it in *Letters to Lucilius* as well, 40.4: "oratio incomposita esse debet et simplex," "a speech's form must be natural and simple"). It rests at the very foundation of his philosophy, the aim of which is the listener's moral betterment. It is a mode of thought before a mode of speech; a search for mental more than verbal clarity. Philosophers who waste their time on literature are deserving of reproach (*Letters to Lucilius*, 88.42). On a purely operative level, simple style means avoiding risky metaphors and relying on similes—a practice already embraced by ancient writers, as Seneca reminds us:

> illi, qui *simpliciter* [emphasis mine] et demonstrandae rei causa eloquebantur, parabolis referti sunt, quas existimo necessarias, non ex eadem causa qua poetis, sed ut imbecillitatis nostrae adminicula sint, ut et dicentem et audientem in rem praesentem adducant. (*Letters to Lucilius*, 59.6)

> those who spoke *simply* [emphasis mine] and demonstratively, were full of similes, which I see as necessary, not

in the same way that it is to poets, but insofar as similes shore up our [intellectual] shortcomings, helping to focus the attention of both the speaker and the listener on the object in question.

The Latin word for "simile" here is *parabola* (from the Greek *parabolé*), a word we typically associate with the Gospels. As the apostle Mark says, "[Jesus] docebat eos in parabolis multa," "Jesus taught them many things by parables." This convergence point between the rhetoric of Jesus and that of a pagan philosopher like Seneca should not be overlooked.

Seneca's Latin cultivates spontaneity, intentionally lacks polish, and considers *concinnitas* (that is, the refined and studied elegance of Cicero's writing) to be a sign of effeminacy (*Letters to Lucilius*, 115.2). It is not the Latin of a man who's spouting his thoughts for posterity but of a meditative thinker, or better yet: a man who forms and adapts his ideas as life dictates. Which is how, in time, his Latin became the strongest adversary of Ciceronian Latin—its opposite, we might say, or its negative, to use a metaphor from photography. No rounded wholeness here, no abundance, but in their place a clean linearity, lacking in conjunctions, more sententious than argumentative; the use of repetitive structures ("non . . . non . . . non . . ."; "alius . . . alius . . . alius") or the condensing of a thought into comparisons and contrasts. Here's a typical sentence:

Non exiguum temporis habemus, sed multum perdidimus. (*De brevitate vitae*, 1.3)

Our time is not brief, but we've lost a great deal.

Just farther down the page, the same juxtaposing, repetitive structure—and twice, no less:

[. . .] non accipimus brevem vitam sed fecimus, nec inopes eius sed prodigi sumus. (1.4)

[. . .] the life we're given is not brief, but [brief] we've made it, nor are we lacking of it, but we squander it.

He then has the ability to crystallize a thought in a proverbial phrase, as in these few examples from *De vita beata*:

Nemo sibi tantummodo errat . . . (1.4)

No one errs for himself alone . . . [that is, one man's error envelops others]

[. . .] argumentum pessimi turba est. (2.1)

[. . .] crowds are proof of shoddiness. [that is, if everyone likes it, it can't be valuable]

[. . .] omnis ex infirmitate feritas est. (3.4)

[. . .] all cruelty is born from weakness.

We must remember, however, that Seneca holds no preconceived bias toward Cicero. On occasion he even praises him, recognizing in Cicero's prose something perfectly compatible with his own ideals. More than that, he considers it to be the very essence of Roman, as opposed to Greek, oratory (*Letters to Lucilius*, 40.11): a well-articulated and well-ordered speech, which gives the listener time to absorb the message. Quite the opposite of haste and impetuosity:

Cicero quoque noster, a quo Romana eloquentia exiluit, gradarius fuit. (*Letters to Lucilius*, 40.11)

Even our beloved Cicero, fount of Roman eloquence, took one step at a time.

Lege Ciceronem: compositio eius una est, pedem curvat lenta et sine infamia mollis. (*Letters to Lucilius*, 100.7)

Read Cicero: his composition is unified, advances slowly and is refined without excess.

In this last excerpt, the adjective *una* (unifies), which describes *compositio*, is a synonym for *simplex*.

Seneca's writing is a process of clarifying, simplifying, dismantling appearances, examining from all sides, upending perspectives to the point of paradox. Death, for example, is not ahead of us but behind us:

In hoc enim fallimur, quod morten prospicimus: magna pars eius iam praeterit; quidquid aetatis retro est mors tenet. (*Letters to Lucilius*, 1.2)

In this we fool ourselves, thinking that death is in our future: already she's mostly behind us; death dwells in all the hours at our backs.

Or elsewhere, we believe that what's in the past is no longer ours; but rather, it's what is not present that can't be taken from us:

Mihi crede, magna pars ex iis quos amavimus, licet ipsos casus abstulerit, apud nos manet; nostrum est quod praeterit tempus nec quicquam est loco tutiore quam quod fuit. (*Letters to Lucilius*, 99.4)

Trust me, the greater part of those we've loved, though chance stole them away, stays with us; time passed is ours, and nothing stands on surer footing than that which once was.

Seneca is not prescriptive but open-ended. He doesn't impose models; he deconstructs appearances:

rebus persona demenda est . . . (*Letters to Lucilius*, 24.13)

one must lift the mask from things . . .

Whether writing to Lucilius—to whom he sends one masterful letter after another—or to any of the other addressees of his treatises, he tells them not what they must be but what *they truly are* in the light of rationality. And the truth is often the opposite of what we thought: goodness is in what we commonly hold to be evil; and evil rests in the illusions of goodness with which we sedate ourselves—luxury, the company of others, fine cuisine. We've already seen the example of exile. Why consider it a disgrace, when every living form, including entire populations, including the stars, including our thoughts, is in a constant state of flux? With a little analysis, all can be transformed. Here are a few lines from *De tranquillitate animi*:

Adhibe rationem difficultatibus: possunt et dura molliri et angusta laxari et gravia scite ferentes minus premere. (10.4)

Apply reason to difficulties: what's hard can be softened and what's narrow widened, what's heavy weighs on him less who bears it ably.

Quintilian, a staunch Ciceronian, was concerned at how strongly young writers were drawn to Seneca. He therefore accused him of anticonformism, of being stuck in his own head, of cramming his thoughts into overly compact sentences—while nonetheless appreciating his encyclopedic mind, his prolificacy, his wit, and his aversion to all vice (*Institutio oratoria*, X.1.125–31). In the end, the Ciceronian school won out and established a long tradition. We cannot forget, however, that up until the threshold of the modern era Seneca too had his followers. Think only of Petrarch and the already much-cited *Familiares*, which, despite its critique of Seneca's dealings with the enemy, owes much to the model of his *Letters to Lucilius*. Or else of Montaigne, who is constantly imitating and quoting him in his *Essais*.

In 2003 my friend Julio Anguita Parrado, on assignment for the Spanish newspaper *El Mundo*, was killed in Iraq. He was thirty-three years old. To his grieving partner I gave a copy of the *Consolatio ad Marciam*. I had no doubt that in that moment Seneca's words would be far more precise and worthy than anything I could say or put to paper. Some would argue that in the face of death, especially violent death, no words exist: that words *must not* exist. I admit, words are not the only way of expressing our emotions. But I'm still convinced of one thing: that we all have the right to count on words, at any time in life, even the most difficult; that it's right to put our faith in words; and that, when they come to us, we should never be embarrassed to use them. Our linguistic inadequacy might lead others to feel uncomfortable; but it must never lead us to relinquish our words in preemptive fear. If we can't find them in ourselves, we must look for them in others. When they strike us as true, they are without owner; they belong to all of us. Through Seneca, therefore, I was able to *speak*, because not only had Seneca spoken well, but—and this is the point I want to emphasize—he showed no fear in speaking, not even when faced with the greatest of losses, the death of a loved one. And in truth, why be silent before death? Why pretend that only sobbing and silence are worthy? Words are life, and we the living must counter death with life at every occasion, in every form, including language.

Marcia has lost her son. And here Seneca reminds her that we were never meant to last. What is a man? he asks, and immediately provides his own answer: "imbecillum corpus et fragile, suapte natura inerme . . ." (11.3), "a weak and fragile body, defenseless by its very nature." And later, "[o]mnia humana brevia et caduca sunt" (21.1), "all things human are brief and fleeting"; in the great span of time, human life is no more than a blip: even if you manage to increase your days by some fraction, what do you really gain (21.2)? Taken on their own, these reflections are evidence enough of a concept that rests at the heart of Latin literature, and that remains one of its most durable and irreplaceable lessons: the concept of finitude. In this technological age of ours, apart from a few religious reflections, which branch of knowledge—humanistic or scientific—is capable of confronting finitude with as much wisdom and as much courage? Which would even want to give it a shot?

The most powerful argument of the *Consolatio ad Marciam* comes when Seneca depicts Marcia's son ascending to the stars. There he dwells among the happy souls of the dead and is able to reconnect with his brave grandfather, Cremutius Cordus, Marcia's father (forced to commit suicide by Sejanus, a prefect of the Praetorian Guard under Tiberius). Cremutius gladly gives his grandson a tour of the firmament, unveiling nature's secrets (25.1–3). This passage recounting the heavenly fate of Marcia's son (which should also be read in relation to Cicero's *Somnium Scipionis*) is the apex of the *Consolatio*. When I gave the book to Julio's partner, it was with this particular passage in mind. It ends with the following words:

Sic itaque te, Marcia, gere, tamquam sub oculis patris filique posita, non illorum, quos noveras, sed tanto excel-

siorum et in summo locatorum; erubesce quicquam hu-
mile aut vulgare cogitare et mutatos in melius tuos flere.
Aeternarum rerum per libera et vasta spatia dimissi sunt;
non illos interfusa maria discludunt nec altitudo montium
aut inviae valles aut incertarum vada Syrtium: omnia ibi
plana et ex facili mobiles et expediti et in vicem pervii
sunt intermixtique sideribus. (25.3)

Therefore bear yourself, Marcia, as if under the watch of
your father and son—not as you knew them, but far loftier
beings, stationed in a higher sphere; blush to have any low
and vulgar thoughts and to weep for those who have been
changed for the better. They have now been released into
the free and vast spaces of eternity; no dividing seas stand
between them, nor towering mountains, nor impassable
valleys, nor the treacherous flats of the Syrtes: the path
before them now is level, and they move swiftly and without
obstacle, in a reciprocal coexistence with the stars.

In the final lines of the *Consolatio* (26.2–7), Seneca returns
to the story of Cremutius Cordus, recounting his life among the
stars, how tiny and pitiful mankind appears from such a distance:
nothing but violence, deception, and discord. Poor humans, so
convinced of their immortality, when it is age (*vetustas*, 26.6) that
always has the last word, as the dead know well: the mountains
will crumble, the seas dry up, and all traces of men dissolve, their
cities swallowed in an immense abyss, all engulfed in a universal fire (the periodic conflagration of Stoic physics), including even
those happy, eternal souls. Because at some point, when the gods
see fit, they start again from scratch.[2]

17

Deviances and Dental Care:
Apuleius and Petronius

In the genre of the novel, Latin is at its most strikingly anticlassical, demonstrating a remarkable capacity for improvisation and inclusion. Following the model of the Greeks, their largely adventurous plotlines are filled with voyages, setbacks, ambiguities, and confusion. And this adventurousness seems to seep even into the language itself, restricting (and tempting) the author to produce a virtually infinite series of plot reversals and upheavals.

Let's look here at the two great surviving Latin novels, the *Satyricon* by Petronius (27–66 C.E.), of which we have only fragments, and *The Golden Ass* by Apuleius (c. 125–170 C.E.), known also as the *Metamorphoses*, which by great fortune we have in its entirety. The first of these I read in an Italian translation as a high school senior, at the recommendation of a particularly precocious friend. I remember being struck by the story's inconclusiveness, and disappointed by its representation of sex—as well as by the taste of my recommender. Even after that bitter first encounter, however, something powerful and disquieting lingered in my thoughts, like the flickering of a distant fire, a sense of morbid comedy, a grotesque fear—a feeling that still crops up every time

I hear the title *Satyricon*. I reread it in Latin the summer after I graduated, with a far different sense of satisfaction. This then spurred me to read Apuleius's novel in Latin—a book I would find a year later on the reading list, among other of his works, for my first Latin exam in college. Apuleius I took to immediately. Not only did I identify more with his character Lucius than I did with Petronius's Encolpius, but the narrative itself was more to my taste, with its tangle of magic and passion. I also saw how much the two novels resemble each other; and so my love for Apuleius only increased my affection for Petronius. It was as if I'd finally grasped their full historical significance—and therefore their originality.

In both novels, excepting the stylistic differences between the two authors, eclecticism and imagination rule the day, especially when it comes to the vocabulary. Other than its close similarities to later, even modern, authors (Joyce included), the language of Petronius and Apuleius never gave rise to a tradition: too inventive, too "Dantesque," too open to surprise, to the strange and the patched-together, soaked in an excess of the carnivalesque, the clownish, the subversive. And yet we do find a resurgence of Apuleius's style—an antidote to the widespread Ciceronianism, marked by a verbal ecumenism and the revival of obsolete vocabulary—toward the end of the fifteenth century, when *The Golden Ass*, already rediscovered by Boccaccio and translated by Boiardo, came out in an edition with commentary by the Bolognese humanist Filippo Beroaldo: a few sparse lines of text surrounded by a thick frame of annotations.[1] Though echoes of Apuleius resound even in the work of *Madame Bovary*'s author, Gustave Flaubert—who declared *The Golden Ass* a masterpiece, a dazzling blend of incense and urine, of brutality and mysticism.[2] Echoes that can still be heard in the late 1800s, as revealed by Walter Pater's novel-manifesto, *Marius the Epicurean* (1885), set in Rome in the second century C.E.:

Others might brutalize or neglect the native speech, that true "open field" for charm and sway over men. He [Flavian, who sets himself a literary healing program] would make of it a serious study, weighing the precise power of every phrase and word, as though it were precious metal, disentangling the later associations and going back to the original and native sense of each,—restoring to full significance all its wealth of latent figurative expression, reviving or replacing its outworn or tarnished images. Latin literature and the Latin tongue were dying of routine and languor; and what was necessary, first of all, was to reestablish the natural and direct relationship between thought and expression, between the sensation and the term; and restore to words their primitive power.

For words, after all, words manipulated with all his delicate force, were to be the apparatus of a war for himself. To be forcibly impressed, in the first place; and in the next, to find means of making visible to others that which was vividly apparent, delightful, of lively interest to himself, to the exclusion of all that was but middling, tame, or only half-true even to him—this scrupulousness of literary art actually awoke in Flavian, for the first time, a sort of chivalrous conscience. What care for style! what patience of execution! what research for the significant tones of ancient idiom—*sonantia verba et antiqua!*[3]

This passage, without question, ranks among the most beautiful tributes to the Latin language in post-Renaissance literature. One year earlier, in 1884, Joris-Karl Huysmans paid wondrous tribute to Apuleius and Petronius in his famous novel, *À rebours*— still recognized as one of the most eloquent portrayals of European decadentism. Its protagonist, des Esseintes, enemy of all things stale and fusty, naturally detested "classicism." Virgil, Horace, and

Cicero make him wince, and he accuses the Christians of padding the language to uselessness with abstractions and invented structures. But he does admit his fascination with the Christian author Tertullian, who preaches chastity and material simplicity under an emperor as sex-crazed and driven to excess as Heliogabalus. And in the figure of Claudian he recognizes the last great pagan poet. The portrait des Esseintes gives us of Petronius, in particular, is one of extraordinary power and skill, revealing Huysmans's rare gifts as a critic.[4] Then, of course, it's thought that Oscar Wilde himself produced a translation of the *Satyricon* (1902)—a fact significant enough on its own, even if the authorship of the version in question, published under the pseudonym Sebastian Melmoth, remains uncertain. When contrasted with such alternative views, Pater's passage appears all the more meaningful and powerful.

Lowly or coarse vocabulary, colloquialisms, neologisms, archaisms, poeticisms, Graecisms, and a general tendency toward contorted forms, contaminated registers, caricature, parody, and expressive excess all combine to form rich, glimmering prose—which one might call baroque or "decadent," a term used to describe Apuleius in particular. Which is to say, the exact opposite of Cicero and his love for playing by the rules. Petronius, meanwhile, in the first lines of what survives of the *Satyricon*, laments the downfall of great oratory (an argument also taken up by Tacitus in his *Dialogus de oratoribus*, "the admirable dialogue," as Coleridge called it in his *Biographia Literaria*), denouncing the latest Greek-inspired trend—promoted by a bad school system and irresponsible parents—of valuing ornamentation over substance. His own novel, set in the time of Nero, in a city in Campania (either Naples, Cuma, or Pozzuoli), aims to give voice to such grotesque vacuousness, to depict a world of incoherent words, detached from the truth and direct experience: hot air, in short. At the dinner of the freedman Trimalchio—the tale's most extensive, famous, and influential episode (*Trimalchio*, recall, was F. Scott

Fitzgerald's original title for *The Great Gatsby*)—hot air plays at least as central a role as the food, which is piled endlessly on the plates of his infinite guests, in spectacular portions and preparations. The servers, who can't keep a tune, are constantly singing, and the discussions we hear snatches of are utter nonsense, starting with those of the master of the house. A revolting, gloating parvenu, distinguished by his phony magnanimity, Trimalchio at one point sets about defending—of all topics—public flatulence:

> Nemo nostrum solide natus est. Ego nullum puto tam magnum tormentum esse quam continere. Hoc solum vetare ne Iovis potest. Rides, Fortunata, quae soles me nocte desomnem facere? Nec tamen in triclinio ullum vetuo facere quod se iuvet, et medici vetant continere. Vel si quid plus venit, omnia foras parata sunt: aqua, lasani et cetera minutalia. Credite mihi, anathymiasis si in cerebrum it, et in toto corpore fluctum facit. (*Satyricon*, 47)

> None of us here was born solid. I can think of no greater torment than holding it in. It's the one thing not even Jupiter himself can prevent. Do I hear you laughing, there, Fortunata, you who keep me awake all night? Even in my dining room my guests are free to do as they please, and doctors warn against holding it in. Or if nature really comes calling, everything's here at hand: water, bowls, whatever else you might need. Believe me when I tell you, if you let anathymiasis go to the brain, your whole body bubbles over.

His use of the Greek word *anathymiasis*, meaning exhalation, and the "scientific" tone, hardly succeed in elevating the discourse. In fact, things descend rather rapidly when Trimalchio brings up Fortunata and her nightly intestinal troubles. Even the other characters, after thanking him for his openness, are forced to shield their laughter behind their glasses. Meanwhile, Trimalchio's declarations, beyond their lack of elegance and coherence, are also ungrammatical, or at best colloquial: *Iovis* stands in for the commonly used noun *Iuppiter* (*Iovis* is the genitive form), *vetuo* for *veto* (*vetuo* is an anomaly), the adjective *ullum* for the pronoun *quemquam*, *foras* in place of *foris*, the masculine *lasani* in place of the neuter *lasana* (a Graecism). Then there's *desomnem*, which we find in no other text but this one.

Apuleius's Latin, though mindful of Petronius's precedent, seems less concerned with social criticism than it is with diving happily into the roots of language. Reading him, one senses the end of a tradition, or of a series of traditions. This ultimately philosophical (Platonic) novel reads like a collection of the rarest or most valuable lexical items. It reminds one of a museum display case or, better yet, of a flea market. Let's look, for example, at the crucial passage in which the protagonist Lucius turns himself into an ass. But first a little context. Lucius, an enterprising and rather curious young man, finds himself at the home of a witch in Thessaly. After watching her transform herself into a bird with a special ointment, he decides he'd like to try it for himself. However, the young girl assisting him—his lover—brings him the wrong ointment. His life as an ass is filled with danger and humiliation. But in the end, after a difficult journey of purification and expiation, absolving himself of the sin of curiosity, Lucius is restored to his human form through the intervention of the goddess Isis, to whom he becomes a devoted follower (nearly three centuries later, Saint Augustine will speak of *venenum curiositatis*, "the poison of curiosity," which destroys the soul: *Confessions*, XIII.21.30).

Here's the scene of Lucius's metamorphosis:

nec ullae plumulae nec usquam pinnulae, sed plane pili
mei crassantur in saetas et cutis tenella duratur in corium

et in extimis palmulis perdito numero toti digiti cogun-
tur in singulas ungulas et de spinae meae termino gran-
dis cauda procedit. Iam facies enormis et os prolixum et
nares hiantes et labiae pendulae; sic et aures immodi-
cis horripilant auctibus. Nec ullum miserae reformatio-
nis video solacium, nisi quod mihi iam nequeunti tenere
Photidem natura crescebat. (*The Golden Ass*, III.24)

no plumage appears, not a single feather. Instead my
hair thickens into bristles and my soft skin hardens to a
hide. On the tips of my palms, my fingers and toes fuse
into hulking hooves, their digits abolished, and a big tail
sprouts from the end of my spine. I now have a giant face,
a protruding mouth, gaping nostrils, and drooping lips;
my ears too grow out of all proportion and are covered in
hair. The only consolation I can see from this wretched
transformation is that, though I can no longer hug Photis,
at least my member has been growing.

Like Ovid, Apuleius too gives us highly precise details, using
the word *iam*, "now," to express the ongoing event of his trans-
formations. What we're witnessing here is extraordinary, and the
narrator is eager to let us know. One aspect, regrettably, cannot be
expressed in the English translation: the diminutives (*plumulae,
pinnulae, tenella, palmulis, ungulas*), which serve a purely emotional purpose, just like in Catullus. But it's important to note that
such stylistic figures had a life beyond the page—that is, they
were present in spoken language. Evidence of this are the many
words in Italian that derive from Latin diminutives used in regular
speech: *fratello* ("brother," from *fraterculus*, diminutive of *frater*),
unghia ("nail," from *ungula*, diminutive of *unguis*), *vecchio*
("old," from *vetulus*, diminutive of *vetus*), *orecchio* ("ear," from *au-
ricula*, diminutive of *auris*), and the list goes on. In forming their

linguistic style, then, Latin novelists not only borrowed elements from previous literature, they also drew on colloquial speech, furnishing us with interesting examples of Latin's evolution into the vernacular. This evolution, however, cannot be easily traced from point A to point B. How do we make sense, for example, of certain terms that were drawn from archaic sources but then later made their way into Italian? Were they already colloquialisms in their archaic source? Or did they only become such in the time and under the circumstances in which Apuleius revived them? Or, as could also be the case, did they enter spoken language through literature? For example, *exoticus* (stranger), a calque of the Greek *exoticós*—source of the English "exotic." It appears in Plautus (*Mostellaria*, 1.1.41), and Apuleius uses it in the opening lines of his novel, when Lucius declares that Latin is a foreign language for him (his mother tongue being Greek).

Let's look now at an excerpt from the fable of Amor and Psyche, the novel's glowing core, both for its central location and its highly symbolic value. Much like Lucius, Psyche ("soul" in Greek) is a victim of curiosity, and only after undergoing a series of difficult, nearly impossible trials can she rise to the heights of the divine. Here is the moment when, in her sleep, she discovers the features of her mysterious husband and rids her heart of all murderous designs:

Videt capitis aurei genialem caesariem ambrosia temulentam, cervices lacteas genasque purpureas pererrantes crinium globos decoriter impeditos, alios antependulos, alios retropendulos, quorum splendore nimio fulgurante iam et ipsum lumen lucernae vacillabat; per umeros volatalis dei pinnae roscidae micanti flore candicant et quamvis alis quiescentibus extimae plumulae tenellae ac delicatae tremule resultantes inquieta lasciviunt; ceterum corpus glabellum atque luculentum et quale peperisse

Venerem non paeniteret. Ante lectuli pedes iacebat ar-
cus et pharetra et sagittae, magni dei propitia tela. (*The
Golden Ass*, V.22–23)

She sees the golden head's marital mane drunk with
ambrosia, his graciously gathered ringlets flowing over
his milk-white neck and rosy cheeks, some falling in
front and others behind, the light of the oil lamp itself
quivering in their powerful, lustrous splendor; over the
winged god's shoulders, his dew-wet plumage glimmers
white with flowers, and, though his wings are still, the
soft and delicate little outer feathers leap and flutter in
tireless play; the rest of his body so smooth and gleaming
that Venus would be proud to have borne him. At the foot
of his little bed lie his bow and quiver and arrows, the
great god's trusted weapons.

Again we run into a few of the words we encountered earlier,
in the scene of Lucius's metamorphosis, though used here with
different connotations: *plumulae: plumulae*; *tenella: tenellae*; *extimis: extimae*; *pendulae: (ante)pendulos/(retro)pendulos*. The over-
abundance, or rather redundancy, of the passage is immediately
evident. Apuleius avoids all simplicity, taking every occasion
he can to embellish his prose: diminutives; hypallage (using
"marital" to describe his hair and not his head, then "golden" to
describe his head and not his hair; an instance of double hypallage, and even double chiasmus, conceptually and syntactically);
simple metaphor (his hair drunk with ambrosia, his flowering
wings); extended metaphor (the god's hair as the heavens, since
"splendor" stretches the figurate meaning of *globos*, which, beyond simply indicating a circular shape, can be used to mean celestial bodies); neologisms (*decoriter*, *antependulos*, *retropendulos*);
etymological wordplay (*lumen/lucerna*); animating the inanimate

(*lumen . . . vacillabat*, a device we encounter in an earlier passage, where the knife, fearful of committing sacrilege, slips from Psyche's hand—not that a god could ever be killed!); forced syntax (*inquieta lasciviunt*, where the intransitive verb *lascivio*, "I provoke" or "I play," takes on a direct object, the neuter plural *inquieta*, "restless/tireless"); alliteration (*capitis: caesariem: cervices*; *tenellae: tremule*; *peperisse: paeniteret*).

Who were they, Petronius and Apuleius?

Antiquity has very little to say about the life of the former. Only Tacitus speaks of a certain Petronius, in his *Annales* (XVI.18–19). But given the vagueness of the biographical details he provides, and that he makes no mention at all of the *Satyricon*, we can't be sure that this is our man. However, the psychological portrayal of this Petronius—an outstanding example of Tacitus's Latin—accords with the image of the author that we can infer from his novel. And so, relying on Tacitus's account, we have it that Petronius held important political positions (proconsul, and later consul, in Bithynia, we don't know in what years), but that his chief distinction was as a man of pleasure and refined manners, without sinking to ostentation. Nero elected him as a model of good manners (*elegantiae arbiter*) and Tigellinus, a favored prefect of Nero's, jealously accused him of being friends with Scevinus, an accomplice in Gaius Calpurnius Piso's plot to overthrow the emperor. Rather than sit around waiting to be tortured, Petronius took death into his own hands, just as the philosopher Seneca did, though his would be a different end. Unlike Seneca, Petronius did not embark on long philosophical discourses, but instead chatted about frivolities, wanting only to hear songs and light verse, while he opened and closed the slits in his wrists as he pleased. He then wrote a letter against Nero, sent it to him, and destroyed his personal seal so that it could not be used to make forgeries. Then, at last, he went to sleep, thinking it the most natural segue to death.

It's the opposite case with the life of Apuleius, who even left us an autobiographical account. Born in the province of Africa, in Madaura (close to the present-day M'Daourouch, in Algeria), he studied in Carthage and Athens and traveled far and wide throughout the empire, building a career as a brilliant lecturer and garnering fame as a philosopher. He excelled in both Greek and Latin (though only a few of his Latin works survive), cultivating himself as a writer of great variety and virtuosity. At thirty, he married the forty-year-old Pudentilla, a rich widow and the mother to two sons. When the younger son died, her relatives dragged Apuleius to court, accusing him of having wooed her with a love potion. In his defense, Apuleius mounted a pyrotechnic counterargument, filled with humor and narcissism—hardly cast in the tone and formality of judicial proceedings. Known as *De magia*, the speech puts the Philistinism of his contemporaries on full display, in all of its obscene vulgarity. His first point, aimed at those who condemn his beautiful visage, is that beauty is a gift of the gods, and that Pythagoras himself, the first philosopher, was the most beautiful man of his day. And besides, he continues, what he possesses is not indeed beauty. Haven't they seen his hair? Rumpled, uncombed, all tangled (*inenodabilis*, 4). And what harm is there in being eloquent? Of course he's eloquent; he's dedicated his entire life to becoming so. There's nothing that lies beyond his powers of expression, and that he can't repeat in public (5).

But then, how to explain the toothpaste (*dentifricium*)? . . . As proof against Apuleius, Pudentilla's relatives bring up a gift he'd once given her: a few lines of poetry, accompanied by a certain powder. So what!—Apuleius objects. Would they have her wash her teeth with urine, as the Celtiberians did (according to Catullus)?[5] Would they rather she have a dirty mouth? The mouth, of all places, the most visible and noble part of the human body?

Just read how boldly he sings the mouth's praises in the passage below. As with all of Apuelius's Latin, it's marked by his extraordinary wit, hovering somewhere between mockery and humanism:

> Crimen haud contemnendum philosopho, nihil in se sordidum sinere, nihil uspiam corporis apertum immundum pati ac fetulentum, praesertim os, cuius in propatulo et conspicuo usus homini creberrimus, sive ille cuipiam osculum ferat seu cum quicquam sermocinetur sive in auditorio dissertet sive in templo preces alleget. Omnem quippe hominis actum sermo praeit, qui, ut ait poeta praecipuus, dentium muro proficiscitur. Dares nunc aliquem similiter grandiloquum: diceret suo more cum primis cui ulla fandi cura sit impensius cetero corpore os colendum, quod esset animi vestibulum et orationis ianua et cogitationum comitium. Ego certe pro meo captu dixerim nihil minus quam oris illuviem libero et liberali viro competere. Est enim ea pars hominis loco celsa, visu prompta, usu facunda. Nam quidem feris et pecudibus os humile et deorsum ad pedes deiectum, vestigio et pabulo proximum; nunquam ferme nisi mortuis aut ad morsum exasperatis conspicitur. Hominis vero nihil prius tacentis, nihil saepius loquentis contemplere. (7)

Such a charge is worthy of a philosopher, to allow no dirt on oneself, to tolerate no filthiness or stink on any part of the exposed body, especially around the mouth, which man uses so frequently and in plain view, whether giving a kiss, or holding discourse, speaking in public, or praying in a temple. In fact, all men's actions are preceded by words, which, as the supreme poet [Homer] says, pass through the wall of our teeth. Now imagine someone with such a high command of language: in his own words he'd say along with the most authoritative men that those who take care in their speech must protect their mouths above all other parts of the body, since the mouth is the antechamber of the soul, the doorway to speech, and a gathering place for thoughts. I for my own part can say with certainty that there's nothing less seemly for a freeborn and free-minded man than an unclean mouth. Indeed, the mouth occupies a high position on the human body, is the first thing one sees, and is a vehicle for eloquence. You'll notice that the mouths of wild beasts and animals are positioned low and face the ground, down by their hooves, among grass and footprints, never to be seen except at death or when they're driven to bite. With a silent man, however, it's the first thing you notice, and there's nothing you notice more when he starts to speak.

18

Brambles, Chasms, and Memories: Augustine's Linguistic Reformation

In high school, we hardly touched on Christian Latin—too late in the game, too bland. And yet, in the right hands, it too can be beautiful. Certain passages of the Gospels and of the *Confessions*, St. Augustine's autobiography, I read on my own, in preparation for my exit exams, though also to see how the story of Latin came to a close.

With the arrival of Christianity, Latin did certainly undergo an immense and turbulent transformation. The radical reforming of values that accompanies the rise of a new sense of individuality and a new religion—at the cost of the centuries-old institution of the empire and the ideal of the *civis Romanus*—cannot but bring substantial and far-reaching change to all fields of expression. Which explains why Augustine (354–430 C.E.), at the beginning of the *Confessions* (a necessary companion to anyone who studies literature, whether ancient or modern, poetry or prose, Petrarch or Proust), places the learning of Latin under God's purview (I.14.23). To study the alphabet becomes a religious act, in that it draws the child closer to the truest truth. God is grammar

(I.13.22). Ethics is meter (III.7.14). Words, of course—again following Augustine—have helped propagate false images, corrupt
(and all-too-human) gods, as we find in Virgil and Terence. But
the fault lies not with the words, which are cups; the fault lies
with the wine we pour into them; with the meanings inculcated by
misguided teachers:

> Non accuso verba quasi vasa electa atque pretiosa, sed
> vinum erroris, quod in eis nobis propinabatur ab ebriis
> doctoribus, et nisi biberemus, caedebamur nec appellare
> ad aliquem iudicem sobrium licebat. (I.16.26)

> I don't fault words for being choice and precious cups,
> but the wine of error that fills them, forced upon us by
> drunken teachers—and if we didn't drink it, we were
> beaten, and had no sober judge to turn to.

The two elements most clearly transformed here are syntax
and, as implied above, lexicon. The former has become simpli-
fied, dispensing with hypotaxis and logical order and favoring an
oral tone, that of a sermon or a confession; the latter imports new
words from the Greek (which will enter modern vernaculars, for
instance *scandalum*, "offense," and the verb form *scandalizo*, "I
offend"; *angelus*, "angel"; *diabolus*, "devil"; *baptizo*, "I baptize";
ecclesia, "church"; *apostolus*, "apostle"), revives lesser-used vocabulary (including archaisms), or alters the meaning of words
that have long been established in the written tradition. Below is
a particularly illuminating example from Saint Jerome (347–419
or 420 C.E.):

> Avaritiae quoque tibi vitandum est malum, non quo ali-
> ena non adpetas—hoc enim et publicae leges puniunt—,
> sed quo tua, quae sunt aliena, non serves.

> You must also avoid the vice of avarice, not in the sense
> that you shouldn't want what others have—for this is
> punished by civic laws—but in the sense of not clinging
> too tightly to your own belongings, which [in reality]
> belong to others [or in truth, to God].

We're reading here from a much-celebrated letter (XII.31, to
Eustochium): the "virginity" letter (from 384). The term *avaritia*
is already used in classical Latin, to mean both "covetousness"
(to want what belongs to others) and "avariciousness" (to cling to
your own belongings). Though the first is more common, here the
author asserts the second; or, to follow Augustine's image, he fills
the cup with a "better" drink, one that corresponds to the new
ethics of Christianity and, as the closing words suggest, goes well
beyond mere earthly laws.

The metaphorical nature of the language shifts as well. Not
only does Christian Latin borrow from specialized vocabularies,
such as military terminology—*miles* (soldiers), for example, comes
to mean a Christian fighting in the name of Christ, and *sacra-
mentum* (a soldier's pledge) becomes a religious commitment—
but new imagery is born, making novel and brilliant connections,
and blending the most blatantly incompatible semantic registers.
The symbology grows more complex, the figurative language more
diffuse. Hyperbole abounds, as does paradox—due also to the
influence of biblical writings, which are often impenetrable, as
Augustine notes and approves: since that which is understood only
with difficulty brings greater satisfaction (*De doctrina Christiana*,
I.6.8).

Let's look, while on the subject of paradox, at an emblematic
passage by Tertullian (c. 160–220 C.E.), the author of an early
treatise in defense of Christianity, the *Apologeticum*. Aimed entirely at overturning the pagan viewpoint, the work indeed brims
with paradox and oxymoron:

Invisibilis est, etsi videatur; incomprehensibilis, etsi per gratiam repraesentetur; inaestimabilis, etsi humanis sensibus aestimetur; ideo verus et tantus est. Ceterum quod videri communiter, quod comprehendi, quod aestimari potest, minus est et oculis, quibus occupatur, et manibus, quibus contaminatur, et sensibus, quibus invenitur, quod vero inmensum est, soli sibi notum est. (XVII.2)

[Our God] is invisible, though we see Him; incomprehensible, though He reveals Himself through grace; inconceivable, though He is conceived by the human senses; therefore is He the true and mighty God. But in general that which can be seen, comprehended, conceived, is worth less even than the eyes that view it, than the hands that contaminate it, than the senses that discover it. That which is immeasurable is known only to itself.

We find the root of a similar argument in the speeches of Christ himself. As in this example, one of many found in the Gospels:

Tollite iugum meum super vos [. . .] et invenietis requiem animabus vestris; iugum enim meum suave, et onus meum leve est. (Matthew II.29–30)

Take my yoke upon you [. . .] and you will find peace for your souls; for my yoke is easy and my burden light.

In those places where the gap between Christian Latin and the classical tradition opens widest, the congruence between analogical components that we find in Virgil and Cicero gives way to an associative language—avant-garde, digressive, even visionary. If Augustine, as we saw with the wine image, is still capable of forming coherent metaphors, developing an initial analogy into a chain of figurative expressions (cups/wine/drunkenness/sobriety), he's also given to inserting wholly unfamiliar comparisons into his language, which establish strong connections between the incorporeal and the concrete or perceptible, the moral and the physical dimensions. Here are just a few examples, taken from the early books of the *Confessions*: "palmitem cordis mei" ("the grass-shoot of my heart," I.17.27); "in adfectu tenebroso" ("in a dark feeling," I.18.28), a phrase in which we find a characteristic poetical adjective (as in Virgil and Ovid); "voragine turpitudinis" ("chasm of ignominy," I.19.30); "vepres libidinum" ("brambles of lechery," II.3.6); "mortis profunditas" ("precipice of death," II.6.14), where *profunditas* is a relatively new term; "sartago flagitiosorum amorum" ("the frying pan of shameful loves," III.1.1); "anima [. . .] ulcerosa" ("soul covered in lesions," ibid.).

Just as original are his stacks of metaphors, as in this one:

Exarsi enim aliquando satiari inferis in adulscentia et silvescere ausus sum variis et umbrosis amoribus, et contabuit species mea et computrui oculis tuis . . . (II.1.1)

In my youth, I burned with the desire to glut myself with baseness, to branch off into multiple, shadowy loves, and my beauty faded and I rotted before your eyes . . .

So many different contexts in such a short space! Fire (*exardeo*, which is also a new verb), food (*satior*), vegetation (*silvesco*, used previously by Cicero, though not in a moral sense), physical decay (*contabesco* and *computresco*, these too postclassical verbs).

Or else there's this example, later in the work:

Sic aegrotabam et excruciabar accusans memet ipsum solito acerbius nimis ac volvens et versans me in vinculo meo . . . (*Confessions*, VIII.11.25)

Thus was I ill and tormented, accusing myself more
severely than usual, twisting and writhing in my chains . . .

In a single sequence he manages to fit in illness, torment (*ex-
crutior* is a verb from ancient comedy, which we find in Catullus's
famous epigram 85, on the conflict between love and hate), and
prison—each indicating the state of the sinner.

Such sentences are evidence enough of just how far language
has progressed in its science of the inner self. It is more deeply
introspective, more open to moments of self-examination. Which
gives rise to an entirely new critical approach to emotions and
states of the soul; a psychoanalytical language with the power
of a high court: to dictate the laws and conditions of the inar-
ticulate heart; a *topography* of the spirit, no less, which evolves
through daring intellectual excursions. Thus the rise of words like
"abyssi" (II.4.9, a word of Greek origin, which will find a firm
place in many modern languages) or "celsitudinem" (II.6.13, "supreme height"), or expressions such as "gurgite flagitorum" (II.2.2,
"the gorge of vices") and "Tartaro libidinis" (III.1.1, "the hell
of lechery"), which revives a word from paganism. Then there's
the profusion of metaphors that refer to memory, to which Augustine dedicated many brilliant pages. Here too spatial descriptions
predominate: "campos et lata praetoria" ("the fields and the vast
palace," X.8.12), "aula ingenti" ("the large palace," X.8.14), "ingenti sinu" ("the large womb," X.8.14), "thesauro" ("ark," X.8.14),
"penetrale amplum et infinitum" ("the spacious and infinite secret
room," X.8.15), "fundum" ("foundation," X.8.15), "interior loco,
non loco" ("the innermost place, no place," X.9.16), "campis et
antris et cavernis innumerabilibus" ("fields and grottoes and innumerable caverns," X.17.26).

Memory, for Augustine, is formed primarily of images taken
from sensory experiences (it's worth noting that memory is a popular subject of rhetoric, beginning with the pseudo-Ciceronian

Rhetorica ad Herennium, since memory plays a fundamental role in the teaching of oratory, and since it's from there—from rhetoric—that Augustine picks up, despite all of his apparent originality). No one knows how such images came about; but there they are, in the recesses of the mind, drawn forth as need demands, even if the meanings they produced are no longer current. In this way (and now for a series of paradoxes and oxymora that pulse with their own insightful energy), I can see colors even in the dark, or sing without opening my mouth, or tell a lily's scent from a violet's without smelling a thing (X.8.13). Though memory is also composed of abstract notions, which are not images of sensory experiences but things in and of themselves: for example, numbers, lines, one's persuasive ability, grammatical knowledge ("litteratura," X.9.16—a word that will spread to the major European languages under a different meaning, and which we'll find used in this particular sense to mean "grammar," as early as Quintilian, *Institutio oratoria*, II.1.4, and Seneca, *Letters to Lucilius*, 38.20). In describing these notions, Augustine again resorts to spatial metaphors: "miris tamquam cellis reponuntur," "they are stored as if in wondrous closets," and, when needed, "proferuntur," "they are retrieved" (X.9.16). But abstract expressions did not come to us through the doors of flesh ("ianuas [. . .] carnis," X.10.17): which is to say we find them *already* in our memory, sparse and tucked away in the deepest corners; to possess them, then, is an act of both extraction and collection. Hence Augustine's view that the verb for "to think" should be expressed with *cogito*, the frequentative of the verb *cogo*, "I collect/I gather" (X.11.18).

Memory is also made up of recollections of past highs and lows—though the thought of a happy moment doesn't necessarily bring pleasure nor a sad one pain. Memory, in fact, is spirit; therefore it is detached from the body (X.14.21). And yet it's a bodily metaphor that Augustine turns to—one of his most daring metaphors—when clarifying a similar distinction:

> memoria quasi venter est animi, laetitia vero atque tristitia
> quasi cibus dulcis et amarus . . . (ibid.)

> memory is like the stomach of the soul; happiness, rather,
> and sadness like sweet and bitter foods . . .

Such innovation does not come without a price for the innovator. The gain feels like a loss. And the greatest loss of all is the *elegantia*, the high altar of classicism: the musical blend of sound, meaning, and syntax. A perfect example here is Saint Jerome, a staunch defender of new Latin, though he too, like Augustine, was raised on the great pagans. How tortured he is in declaring—again in his letter on virginity—that he's renouncing the apprenticeship of his youth! The comic poets of paganism brought him far more pleasure than the prophets, whose coarse language appalled him ("sermo horrebat incultus"). Augustine too claims that Cicero's elegance made reading the holy texts a trial in his early days (*Confessions*, III.5). And yet, clearly trying to negotiate as best he can, Augustine strips Cicero of his uncontested title as master of style, and claims to have discovered in his work—particularly in his invitation to philosophy, the *Hortensius* (sadly lost to us)—the decisive argument that sparked his conversion to Christianity.[1] This is his attempt to reconcile the two cultures through reason. And indeed, as hinted at in Tertullian (the *Apologeticum* attributes prophet-like characteristics to Solon), this effort of his will expand and eventually triumph, centuries later, with the humanism of Dante, whose entire aim is to find early signs of the Christian message in the great pagans such as Virgil, Ovid, Statius, and Lucan. His influence extends even to Petrarch, the true father of Renaissance humanism, who recalls Augustine's case in his *Familiares* (II.9). Reflecting on the debt that Augustine owes to Cicero, he concludes: "nemo dux spernendus est qui viam salutis ostendit," "spurn no guide who shows the way to salvation."

In a dream—one of the most celebrated dreams of late antiquity, narrated in the above-mentioned letter to Eustochium (XII.30)—Jerome finds himself at the feet of God, awaiting judgment. Things don't bode well for him. God accuses Jerome of not being a Christian, but rather a Ciceronian (one could spend pages exploring this extraordinary intuition, which anticipates the revolutionary theories of the modern age—that the psyche itself is language). After a few good whacks, which, as he discovers upon waking, leave real marks on his skin, he realizes he has a second chance: return to your life, but stay far away from that sinful rubbish. Which is exactly what he does.

In the same period that Jerome is writing his letter on virginity, he is preparing himself for the major undertaking of his literary career, a colossal tribute to that *other* tradition: a Latin translation of the Bible, the so-called *Vulgata*, which earned him his title as the patron saint of translators. Jerome's translation is certainly not the first, but he's determined that it be the most authoritative, the definitive version. And so it will be. The previous Latin translations, as Augustine points out in Book II of his *De Doctrina Christiana*, are rife with errors of every sort. In letter LVII, addressed to Pammachius and dated 395–96 (he begins his translation sometime around 390 and finishes around 405), Jerome gives a polemical account of the principles that guide his translation method—the necessity, that is, of capturing the meaning rather than translating word for word, which is foolish given the lexical and syntactical differences between languages. But then, to whom does he turn for authority? Again to Cicero, who was himself the translator of Greek orators. He also mentions the beloved comedians, who translated and adapted Greek originals. Translation method aside, this letter sheds light on a new and important aesthetic principle of literary Christian Latin: *simplicitas* (a term associated with Seneca, not with Cicero); or rather, *sancta simplicitas*, the language of the apostles—and to speak like them is to live like them—for all men can understand and become followers of Christ.

Here's an example from the Gospel of Luke:

Et postquam venerunt in locum, qui vocatur Calvariae, ibi crucifixerunt eum et latrones, unum a dextris et alterum a sinistris. Iesus autem dicebat: "Pater, dimitte illis, non enim sciunt quid faciunt." Dividentes vero vestimenta eius, miserunt sortes. Et stabat populus exspectans. Et deridebant illum et principes dicentes: "Alios salvos fecit; se salvum faciat, si hic est Christus Dei electus!" Illudebant autem ei et milites accedentes, et acetum offerentes illi et dicentes: "Si tu es rex Iudaeorum, salvum te fac!" Erat autem et superscriptio super illum: "Hic est rex Iudaeorum." Unus autem de his, qui pendebant, latronibus, blasphemabat eum, dicens: "Nonne tu es Christus? Salvum fac temetipsum et nos!" Respondens autem alter increpabat illum dicens: "Neque tu times Deum, quod in eadem damnatione es? Et nos quidem iuste, nam digna factis recipimus! Hic vero nihil mali gessit." Et dicebat: "Iesu, memento mei, cum veneris in regnum tuum." Et dixit illi Jesus: "Amen dico tibi: Hodie mecum eris in paradiso." Et erat iam fere hora sexta, et tenebrae factae sunt in universa terra usque in horam nonam, et obscuratus est sol, et velum templi scissum est medium. Et clamans voce magna Iesus ait: "Pater, in manus tuas commendo spiritum meum"; et haec dicens exspiravit. Videns autem centurio, quod factum fuerat, glorificavit Deum dicens: "Vere hic homo iustus erat!" (23.33–47)

The passage tells the story of Jesus's death. A sublime passage, tragic par excellence, the height of storytelling and apex of the religious mystery; and yet . . . And yet the language never veers from the syntactical linearity and verbal sobriety with which the Gospels recount every moment of the tale (the parables, Jesus's life and miracles). Each phase of the event follows the next paratactically, interrupted here and there by an *et*—the most elementary and passe-partout conjunction of the Latin language. The verbs here don't follow traditional syntax (no conjunction in the interrogative introduced by "quid," and the passive pluperfect uses *fuerat* rather than *erat* as its auxiliary verb). Present participles in the nominative case, rare in classical prose (though common in Greek), recur in formulaic phrases that seem pulled from popular speech. The vocabulary is banal, the word order already much like what we find in the vernacular languages. Here's my translation:

> When they came to the place called Calvary, they there crucified him and the thieves, one to his right, one to his left. And Jesus said: "Father, forgive them, they know not what they do." And they tore his garments and cast lots. And the people looked on. And even the rulers derided him, saying: "He saved others, let him save himself, if he's truly God's chosen Christ." And the soldiers too mocked him, coming up to him and holding out vinegar and saying: "If you're the king of the Jews, then save yourself." And above him was an inscription: This is the king of the Jews. One of the hanging thieves insulted him, saying: "Aren't you Christ? Save yourself and us!" But the other thief rebuked him, saying: "Don't you too fear God, since you're condemned to the same punishment! We, rightly so, since we're getting what we deserve for our actions. But he, he committed no evil." And he said: "Jesus, remember me when you enter your kingdom." And Jesus replied: "I say to you truly: Today you will be with me in paradise." And already it was nearing

the sixth hour [noon], and at the ninth hour [three in the afternoon] darkness covered the earth, and the sun hid itself, and the veil of the temple was torn in half. And lifting up his voice, Jesus said: "Father, I leave my spirit in your hands"; and with these words he died. And when the centurion saw what had happened, he glorified God, saying: "This man was truly righteous."

In *De Doctrina Christiana*, a text of fundamental importance to Christian linguistics, Augustine argues that uncouth, even ungrammatical, speech is preferable to eloquence that hinders comprehension. In fact, Christian Latin develops and defines itself in large part as a didactic tool. It serves to explain the complex truths of sacred texts, to distinguish between good and evil, and to convince. It's not a language given to closing arguments with a trill of musical syllables, as is typical in Cicero—a habit that, besides, Augustine has no patience for—but it is one fit for demonstrating a point with clarity (*evidentia*) and switching the argument and tone (*varietas*) as soon as it's grasped by the reader.

We must keep in mind that Augustine based his linguistic reform yet again on Cicero's example; that he professed himself an anti-Ciceronian while playing the part of a Ciceronian. *Evidentia* and *varietas* are in fact fundamental components of pagan oratory as well, and will find their place in the aesthetic and linguistic discourses of the Renaissance.[2] Which reminds us yet again just how great an influence Cicero had on *all* of Western linguistic culture. The same three stylistic registers espoused by Augustine—low, middle, and elevated—derive, as he admits, from Cicero (*Orator*, 21.69ff.). The first is used to explain, the second to judge, and the third to persuade. However—and here's another important point of departure from Cicero, which will help to shape the vernacular languages—each register has something of the other two, and develops in their shadows, defining and strengthening itself through opposition.[3] Whatever the case, in all of these registers—even the highest of the three—clarity predominates; and none, not even the lowest, concerns itself with anything but matters of great importance, the final aim of any discourse being divine truth. The ranking of one register above another lies not in its abundance of metaphorical images or the difficulty of its lexicon, but in the fervor of the argument: above all else, it is a personal attachment, a spiritual heat ("pectoris ardorem," *De Doctrina Christiana*, IV.20.42), which burns even hotter when one's purpose is to convert.

19

The Duty of Self-Improvement: Juvenal and Satire

"The Latin vogue today is waning, / And yet I'll say on his [Onegin's] behalf / He had sufficient Latin training / To gloss a common epigraph, / Cite Juvenal in conversation . . ."

—Alexander Pushkin[1]

One of the Latin language's most characteristic inventions is "social criticism." Or so I term that utterly (and proudly) Roman genre, which in literary history has been known since antiquity as "satire" (*satura*). This genre requires a colorful vocabulary, a clipped and rapid syntax, and an engrossing rhetoric, for the aim is to observe, to flog, to denounce, ridicule, insult, accentuate. Of course, there's satire and then there's satire. Horace's (65–8 B.C.E.) is hardly aggressive; it's more cheerful than gossipy, feels more like life than an expressionist caricature. Nevertheless, even Horace's satire is born from a strong distaste for the present day and a proud disdain for his contemporaries. In truth, all of Latin literature, as permeated as it is by nostalgia for a better past, has something of satire to it, no matter the genre. Cicero is a satirist when he portrays the defects of Catiline or Verres; Catullus, when in his epigrams he attacks certain people's vices and fixations; and Petronius too, when he turns a spotlight on the debauchery and crass greed of southern society. Even history, to a certain measure, is satire, since it praises the past and pans the present: just look at Sallust or, better yet, Tacitus. Even our starry-eyed genre, the bucolic, shows a tendency toward the "satirical," stuck as it is between a lament for our immaculate origins and a dream of a golden rebirth.

But here I'd like to focus for a minute on the purely linguistic aspects of satire, for which purpose we have the remarkable paradigm of Juvenal (c. 50/65–140 C.E.), a writer of obscure origins, to say the least. Even the biographical information we have is unclear. We know only that he lived through the succession of a few emperors, from Nero to Hadrian, and that, as his poetry attests, he bore witness to widespread, manifold, and irrepressible corruption. In the sixteen satirical pieces of his to survive, not a single aspect of the social world is spared his indignant condemnation. Even natural decay, such as aging, becomes the object of scorn and lends itself to brutal caricature (*Satires*, X.190–209). All goes wrong, all for the very worst: "difficile est saturam non scribere" (I.30). And it doesn't get much worse than this:

> Nil erit ulterius quod nostris moribus addat
> posteritas, eadem facient cupientque minores,
> omne in praecipiti vitium stetit. Utere velis,
> totos pande sinus. Dices hic forsitan "unde
> ingenium par materiae? Unde illa priorum
> scribendi quodcumque animo flagrante liberet
> simplicitas? [. . .]" (I.147–53)

> Posterity will have nothing new to add
> to our habits. Our children will do and want the same.

Every vice has taken root. Raise up your sails,
unfurl them all. Perhaps you'd say: How
will the mind fit its subject? Where's that frankness
the ancients showed in everything they wrote,
their burning spirit? [. . .]

Here it's important to note his use of direct questions, one of satire's most common syntactical devices. Also worth noting is the noun *simplicitas*, placed at the beginning of the line and smartly set up, two lines above, by the demonstrative *illa*: we've already come across this term as a principle of Latin according to Christians (and according to Seneca). And, as it turns out, its meaning in Juvenal is much the same. He too, like Christ's apostles, is after a truth-seeking language, which he can use to instruct his neighbor.

Another common trait of Juvenal's Latin is his use of imaginative hyperbole, which he achieves through an aggregation of precise imagery:

Egregium sanctumque virum si cerno, bimembri
hoc monstrum puero et mirandis sub aratro
piscibus inventis et fetae comparo mulae,
sollicitus, tamquam lapides effuderit imber
examemque apium longa consederit uva
culmine delubri, tamquam in mare fluxerit amnis
gurgitibus miris et lactis vertice torrens. (XIII.64–70)

If I see an honest and respectable man, I compare
this miracle to a two-limbed baby or to somehow finding
a fish beneath the plow or to a pregnant mule,
filled with dismay, as if it were raining stones,
or if a swarm of bees had formed a giant cluster
above a temple, as if a roiling river
whirling with eddying milk flowed into the sea.

He populates his lines with a throng of negative examples, accumulating centuries of history piece by piece. Hundreds of characters, from every time and place, are reduced to mere names, and their names to symbols of vice and perversion. But the discussion never turns abstract, never solidifies into a gallery of "types"—rather, Juvenal forms an inlay of concrete details, of ordinary situations, which effectively portray the daily life of his times. And we watch as these "extras" navigate their life of tools and utensils, food and wine, architecture and rituals, committing shameful acts of every shape and size: they get hammered, piss themselves, vomit, screw until they pass out (even with close relatives and parents), strut, flail, talk trash, consume and conspire, slather on makeup, exercise in the gym—meanwhile, to their own detriment and the detriment of others, committing perjury and falsifying public documents, even practicing cannibalism. The basic unit of expression (the sentence or line) functions as a kaleidoscope, constantly turning and blending the world, coloring his multitude of clashing observations in every shade of light. There's something carnivalesque, something infernal about the way he steeps his poetry in such a whirl of concrete imagery, allusions of a sometimes dubious nature, "objective" contingencies large and small (Dante, as you might have guessed, was familiar with Juvenal and cites him in several places), until the reader must step back and take a breath. When Juvenal writes, he crams his lines with *things*; and these things stand in for spiritual and mental states:

> quidquid agunt homines, votum, timor, ira, voluptas,
> gaudia, discursus, nostri farrago libelli est. (I.85–86)

> all that men experience—desire, fear, anger, pleasure,
> joys and wanderings—is fodder for my book.

These two lines are typical of the tendency to amass details that characterizes satirical Latin. I've translated the word *farrago* as "fodder," its original meaning. Here, however, *farrago* expresses also the idea of an eclectic jumble, which is the meaning that will prevail, though with a completely negative connotation, in the Italian word *farragine* ("jumble," or indeed "farrago," in English). Even more suggestive and forceful, much more so than a list of abstractions, is the word *discursus*: it bears the root *curro* (*corro* in Italian, or "I run") and means an aimless running about (from the prefix *dis-*, as found in the English "disruption"). Which seems, in a sense, something of an apt description for Juvenal's writing.

Juvenal, however, is just as capable of changing the pace. Though he prefers to run, now and then he'll slow things down, examining a certain scene or figure and, as he zooms in, enlarging and distorting his subject. I'm thinking of the grotesque close-ups in Satire VI, all aimed at women: one who, in the name of following her lover to Egypt, forgets her own seasickness and faces agonizing boat trips; one who forces her guests to fast in order to prolong an orgy in the temple, and who then guzzles down wine before the horrified eyes of her husband; one who mauls the Greek language; and another who claims she's an expert in poetry.

On other occasions he uses this "slo-mo" technique to vividly depict and define inner states, for example a criminal's feeling of guilt (XIII.211–44)—a brief psychoanalytical essay in which already we can sense Dostoyevsky and even Freud—or the solidarity and commiseration with the grief of others (XV.131–58). The genius of Latin is here on full display: turning introspective, it depicts real-life circumstances, physical reactions, empirical facts. The criminal, filled with *anxietas*, tosses and turns in his bed, loses his appetite (even for good wine), is plagued with nightmares, mistakes normal shifts in the weather as signs of his doom, falls for traps that even his tortured mind knows not to fall for, and at last learns to distinguish between good and evil. And anyone who partakes in the suffering of another is bound to weep, for nature has endowed us with tears.

But if man is capable of commiseration—if, with his soul, he indeed stands above the beasts, can form societies and band together in solidarity (XV.147–58)—how is it that every age ends in ruin?

Money takes the brunt of the blame. It dominates every relationship. Joy and misery nip at its heels. In its name, the spirit sheds its worth, love for the sacred fades, and all human dignity is lost. Better to be in need, as when Hannibal of Carthage was at the gates of Rome:

> Nunc patimur longae pacis mala, saevior armis
> luxuria incubuit victumque ulciscitur orbem.
> Nullum crimen abest facinusque libidinis ex quo
> paupertas Romana perit. (VI.292–95)

> Now we suffer the ills, far worse than war, of a long peace.
> Luxury's taken hold, wreaking vengeance on the
>   conquered world.
> No crime or unbridled misdeed is lacking—not since
> the death of Roman frugality.

Here we have what must be an impromptu analysis, though it comes off as a carefully considered interpretation. Juvenal, indeed, is no banal and repetitive moralist, as one might gather from a cursory reading of his satires, but an author who takes deep consideration of society's development and has a keen philosophical sense of civic life. *Paupertas*—source of the English words "pauper" and "poverty"—refers to a scarcity of means (*pau* we find in the adjective *paucus*, "little," *poco* in Italian), a lack of money; not indigence. This too, like *simplicitas*, is an essential term. It's no wonder that Juvenal turns to Diogenes as a model—the poor philosopher par excellence, who lived in a barrel, earning the admiration of even the ruler of the world, Alexander the Great (XIV.308–14). Nor does he leave out Epicurus, happy in his little garden, or Socrates, content in his humble home (XIV.319–21). He also celebrates the plain and primitive diet of the ancients, which came at little cost, since all could be found in the garden and the surrounding fields: goats, asparagus, eggs and chickens, grapes, apples, beans, a slice of lard, some heartier meat now and then, taken from a sacrificial victim (XI.64–85).

But then—how many possessions are too many, and who sets the measure? True wealth, in fact, comes from within; above all nobility of soul, against which family title carries no weight. "Stemmata quid faciunt?" (VIII.1), "What good is lineage?" (*Stemma*, a Greek word, means "garland"—*stemma*, therefore, is the garland used to decorate an ancestor's statue, and therefore metaphorically suggests lineage.) Go ahead and line your atrium with all the wax busts you want: "nobilitas sola est atque unica virtus" (VIII.20), "the one and only nobility is virtue." Valued above all are the riches of the soul, "animi bona" (VIII.24): a beautiful metaphor, which we wouldn't be surprised to find in Christian writing. And these overlaps with Christianity, by the way, should not be overlooked. Juvenal, though pagan, presents himself as a true moral reformer, going so far as to defend martyrdom:

Esto bonus miles, tutor bonus, arbiter idem
integer; ambiguae si quando citabere testis
incertaeque rei, Phalaris licet imperet ut sis
falsus et admoto dictet periuria tauro,
summum crede nefas animam praeferre pudori
et propter vitam vivendi perdere causas. (VIII.79–84)

Be a good soldier, a good guardian, and a judge
of sound mind; if ever you're called to testify
in an unclear case, though Phalaris command you to lie
and admit your perjuries, with his bull at hand,
it is a greater evil to hold survival over honor,
and in the name of life, forgo your reason to live.

It pays to know here that Phalaris was the tyrant of Akragas
in Sicily, who killed his enemies by entrapping them in a bronze
bull and lighting a fire beneath it (their howls could be mistaken
for mooing). In other words: die happily for the sake of truth, bear
the chains of torture with a willing heart.

Such confidence, meanwhile, rests on firmly religious grounds,
which Juvenal's mocking caricatures tend to obscure. When the
ideal cuts through, however, the language of satire takes on a
different pace and character entirely—that of sage advice. The
commotion settles, the stage clears, and at last you can hear the
underlying whisper of a peaceful conscience. Just read the end of
Satire X, a miniature masterpiece, or, as it might fairly be called,
a synthesis of centuries' worth of moral wisdom, in which linguistic clarity, a faith in the divine, and rationalism come harmoni-
ously together:

Nil [. . .] optabunt homines? si consilium vis,
permittes ipsis expendere numinibus quid
conveniat nobis rebusque sit utile nostris;
nam pro iucundis aptissima quaeque dabunt di.
Carior est illis homo quam sibi. Nos animorum
inpulsu et caeca magnaque cupidine ducti
coniugium petimus partumque uxoris, at illis
notum qui pueri qualisque futura sit uxor.
Ut tamen et poscas aliquid voveasque sacellis
exta et candiduli divina tomacula porci,

orandum est ut sit mens sana in corpore sano.
Fortem posce animum mortis terrore carentem,
qui spatium vitae extremum inter munera ponat
naturae, qui ferre queat quoscumque labores,
nesciat irasci, cupiat nihil et potiores
Herculis aerumnas credat saevosque labores
et venere et cenis et pluma Sardanapalli.
Monstro quod ipse tibi possis dare; semita certe
tranquillae per virtutem patet unica vitae.
Nullum numen habes, si sit prudentia: nos te,
nos facimus, Fortuna, deam caeloque locamus. (X.346–66)

So men should desire nothing? Hear me out,
let the gods be the judges of what we need,
what best aids our condition; in fact, the gods
will gladly provide what's fitting.
Man is dearer to them than to himself. We, led by our
    heart's
impulse and by a blind and powerful urge,
chase marriage and childbirth; but to them it's known
what children and wife we'll have.
And yet you pray in temples and offer up
the innards and sacred sausages of the whitest piglet,
you should pray for a sound mind in a sound body.
Ask for a resolute soul, one free from the fear of death,
one that holds long life among the least of nature's
gifts, that can bear any burden,
that knows no ire, wants nothing, and upholds
the labors and pains of Hercules above
lovemaking and feasts and all the downy pillows of
    Sardanapalus.
What I propose can be had on your own; the path is one
that leads by virtue to a peaceful life.

There are no other gods, when you have wisdom. It's we,
    dear Fortune,
we who make you a goddess, and prop you up in the sky.

In these splendid lines, we encounter a stew of philosophical schools, from Platonism to Stoicism to Epicureanism. Among so much philosophy one could hardly miss the striking detail of the sausages, *tomacula*, referred to here with a word derived from Greek (*tomé* means "I cut"). Nor the feigned preciousness of the diminutive adjective for pork, *candiduli*—like calling it pork "of the purest white" (we've already seen such disregard for ritual in Lucretius, whose spirit we also find hovering in the lines on the fear of death). There's irony, but there's also a blend of the practical and the theoretical, as when he encourages temperance in every act, large or small, even in buying fish (XI.35–36). Sardanapalus is an ancient Assyrian king, meant to symbolize effeteness and self-decay. Hercules, on the other hand, as always represents self-sacrifice and spiritual elevation (which is why, in Christianity, he'll be revived as a symbol of Christ). Also present here—in its original context, at last, where it carries a far different meaning than when quoted out of context—is one of the most renowned maxims of the Latin language: *mens sana in corpore sano*.

The final lines, in particular, contain the core of an ethical principle that not only had a long tradition at the time that Juvenal was writing, but that would permeate Western culture, finding its highest expression in the Renaissance: the ability to prevail over the whims of chance, *fortuna*, by using wisdom, *prudentia*, which, etymologically (from *pro-videntia*), is a pre-vision.

20

The Loneliness of Love: Propertius

Much of Latin's beauty rests in the fact that Latin is a language of eros, which is of course a primary component of human life and of every culture on earth: a system of metaphors, images, and terms that define and classify the experience of love in all its forms, physical, psychological, and especially cultural, as separate from other languages and spheres of expression, such as politics and war. An entire genre is dedicated to love, the elegy, which again has its origins in Greece, as do all the most important genres of Latin literature, and which paves the way for the great erotic poetry of the vernacular tradition. Its most distinguished representatives, among those whose work has survived, are Tibullus, Propertius, and Ovid, all of whom lived under Augustus. Though we must also give a nod, at the very least, to Cornelius Gallus, a friend of Virgil's, of whose work, however, almost nothing remains. Virgil recalls him in his last eclogue (which inspired John Milton to compose his *Lycidas*), and in truth there's a strong link between bucolic poetry and the love elegy. We see this in Tibullus's first elegy, among the most precious works in Latin poetry, an ingenious blend of the two genres. The elegy, beyond its role as an expression and study of emotion, dares to offer itself as a lover's manual, turning this into a discipline all its own. As is the case with Ovid.

Love, however, also has its place in the comedies, in Virgil's epic, in his *Eclogues*, as I've just mentioned, and even in his *Georgics*, which end with one of the most memorable love stories of the ancient world (the tale of Orpheus and Eurydice); we find it in Catullus's and Horace's poetry; it's in Ovid's *Metamorphoses*, in Apuleius's novel, and so on. Even in his philosophical poem, Lucretius employs the vocabulary of love, right from the poem's opening line, which depicts a postcoital Mars and Venus. Love, in short, is everywhere. It is sensual bliss, it is a yearning, a waiting, a stripping away of all reason. Love, at least in Latin, leads almost inevitably to suffering. Catullus adopts it as his highest ideal, a form of correspondence that is consecrated by the act of marriage (hence his works in honor of the betrothed), though he also shows its destructive aspects, its vexing and disappointing side—infidelity, above all. Even Lucretius's Mars, though we find him resting in Venus's lap after the struggles of war, ends up hurting himself, because love is indeed *vulnus*, "wound." In Book IV of *De rerum natura*, Lucretius provides us with another crudely anti-idealistic depiction of love: what else are lovers but two who can never become one, who seek wholeness in vain through sexual encounter, each straining to enter the other by violence. Frustration prevails, without fail:

> [. . .] etenim potiundi tempore in ipso
> fluctuat incertis erroribus ardor amantum
> nec constat quid primum oculis manibusque fruantur.
> Quod petiere, premunt arte faciuntque dolorem
> corporis et dentes inlidunt saepe labellis
> osculaque adfigunt, quia non est pura voluptas

et stimuli subsunt, qui instigant laedere id ipsum,
quod cumque est, rabies unde illaec germine surgunt.
(IV.1076–83)

[. . .] it's in that very moment of possession
that lovers' love spins out in all directions
and hands and eyes no longer know what pleasure to
    seek first.
And what they find, they press hard and cause pain
to the flesh, their teeth sunk into lips,
planting kisses—for pleasure's not pure,
an eagerness to injure lurks beneath, to harm
that thing from which our madness spawns.

This love-disease is a search for pleasure (*voluptas*), nothing
more. First a drop of sweetness in the heart, then the cold grip of
anguish. And yet Lucretius reminds us that love, especially for
men, cannot be avoided, since it is a physiological condition, an
impulse to ejaculate, which, if ignored, exacerbates pain, causing
an ulcer.

And then there are the thousands of fantasies, the endless
mental projections (*simulacra*) that swarm like ghosts, that bring
no peace or security, but only reignite one's lust with a constant
stream of illusions. The desired person cannot be taken in like
food, but only as an abstract image—the very opposite of what
would satisfy one's desire. Centuries and centuries before Petrarch
or Proust, Latin, through Lucretius, gave expression to the lover's
anguished imagination:

ex hominis vero facie pulchroque colore
nil datur in corpus praeter simulacra fruendum
tenuia; quae vento spes raptast saepe misella.

Ut bibere in somnis sitiens quom quaerit et umor
non datur, ardorem qui membris stinguere possit,
sed laticum simulacra petit frustraque laborat
in medioque sitit torrenti flumine potans,
sic in amore Venus simulacris ludit amantis,
nec satiare queunt spectando corpora coram
nec manibus quicquam teneris abradere membris
possunt errantes incerti corpore toto. (IV.1094–1104)

but of the human face and beautiful complexion
one can enjoy in a body nothing but
vagrant ghosts; scant hope that the wind often dashes.
As in a dream when the thirsty man asks for water but
    no water
is given that could quench the burning thirst in his limbs,
and yet he pines after a mirage of drops and toils in vain
and thirsts as he drinks while down in a surging river.
So in love Venus taunts lovers with ghosts,
and they cannot sate their bodies by looking—though
    they are near—
nor can they draw anything from the supple limbs
as they grope aimlessly across the other's entire body.

What lines! With what bitterness, what sad irony he traces the limits of man's perception! To look but not see, to touch but not grasp. Even his assault on hope—which he describes with a rare diminutive (*misella*)—is a lyrical routing! We can hear the wind that steals it. And again we run into the concept of *error*, which we encountered in the previous excerpt: that aimless groping of another's body, which, worse than an idle search, is a journey down a deceptive path. Because for Lucretius, of course, true pleasure is in thought, in reasoning, not in such illusions like the longing for physical possession.

Let's turn for a minute to Propertius (c. 50–16 B.C.E.), the greatest of the elegiac poets under Augustus: the most profound, who gave most elegant and passionate expression to the language of love. As Catullus had his Lesbia, so Propertius had Cynthia (Ovid, on the contrary, has Corinna and many others).[1] Propertius turns his focus to the sweeter side of love, though not even he could avoid depicting its physical and spiritual tax. Love is *furor*, "madness"; *morbus*, "illness"; *servitium*, "slavery"; *militia*, "war"; *toxicum*, "poison." It steals your words, drains your complexion, your physical strength. And there's no finding the source of such torment. No doctor has the cure:

> omnis humanos sanat medicina dolores:
> solus amor morbi non amat artificem. (*Elegies*, II.1.57–58)

> Medicine cures all human ails:
> love alone rebuffs the master of its suffering.

The tortured lover's walk is a funeral march. The cause, of course, is a woman: beautiful, fickle, unfaithful. One day she wants you, the next she's running off with who knows who, your world turned upside down. Propertius, even without Lucretius's philosophical vision, sees love's fluctuations as part of the broader historical flux:

> omnia vertuntur: certe vertuntur amores:
> vinceris aut vincis, haec in amore rota est. (II.8.7–8)

> Everything changes: certainly loves change:
> you're conqueror or conquered, so turns the wheel of love.

Love, meanwhile, and discussions of love, clearly become a new lens through which to view the decline of Republican freedom. The love elegy portrays the end of an era. It is born, in fact, from the ashes of antiquity's great discourses. It is a fleeing but also a polemical renunciation of higher allegiances, of literary projects that set themselves in dialogue with politics—*military* politics—and the goals of the empire:

> Pacis Amor deus est, pacem veneramur amantes:
> stant mihi cum domina proelia dura mea. (III.5.1–2)

> Love is a god of peace; it's peace we lovers worship:
> my battle is the long battle with my woman.

Virgil, who would seem to us the very embodiment of an imperial mouthpiece, came to the epic form despite himself: several times in his *Eclogues* he contrasts minor and major poetry, declaring his preference for the former. Ovid tried his hand at writing the supreme poem with his *Metamorphoses*, but ends by erecting a monument not to stability and Augustan order but to perennial crisis. In his elegies—despite the surrounding pressures—Propertius expresses his disregard for any such grandiose poetry quite consciously, and even with an expressly antipolitical intent, countering the Virgilian ideology of the dynastic epic with a more personal ideology:

> nec mea convenient duro praecordia versu
> Caesaris in Phrygios condere nomen avos.
> Navita de ventis, de tauris narrat arator,
> enumerate miles vulnera, pastor ovis;
> nos contra angusto versamus proelia lecto;
> qua pote quisque, in ea conterat arte diem. (II.1.41–46)

> to write hard lines in praise of Caesar's name,
> straight back to his Phrygian roots, is not for me.

The sailor speaks of winds, the plowman oxen,
the soldier counts his wounds, the shepherd sheep;
me, I tell of struggles in a narrow bed:
let men spend their day at the art at which they excel.

His opposition to Virgil—an immense literary superego from
the very start, destined only to grow in notoriety over the coming
millennia—erupts in the final elegy of Book II:

me iuvet hesternis positum languere corollis,
quem tetigit iactu certus ad ossa deus;
Actia Vergilium custodis litora Phoebi,
Caesaris et fortis dicere posse ratis,
qui nunc Aeneae Troiani suscitat arma
iactaque Lavinis moenia litoribus.
Cedite Romani scriptores, cedite Grai!
nescio quid maius nascitur Iliade. (II.34.59–66)

Me, whom the god struck clear to the marrow, I'm one
for lying and languishing among yesterday's garlands.
Let Virgil sing the shores of Actium, with their guardian
    Phoebus,
and Caesar's sturdy ships; Virgil, who
now evokes the arms of Aeneas of Troy,
and the walls that line Lavinium's shores.
Give way, O Roman writers! Give way, you Greeks!
Something greater than the *Iliad* is born.

Just beneath this passage, Propertius lays out the exact
literary canon—a sort of antitradition—in which he envisions
his own poetry: Varro, Catullus, Calvus, Gallus. All poets who
wrote on a range of topics but who are here singled out for their
love poetry. And of course he can't go without mentioning his re-

nowned Greek predecessor, the Alexandrian poet Callimachus, whose work influenced Roman poets as early as Ennius. Propertius invokes him in the first elegy of Book III, along with Philitas, Callimachus's teacher (only a few fragments of this poet and Homeric philologist remain), reaffirming his faith in concise, polished poetry: "non datur ad Musas currere lata via," "the road to the Muses is not broad" (III.1–14). The topic of exigency comes up again in the ninth elegy of Book III, where the poet, while out at sea, declares his preference for rivers, once again mentioning Callimachus and Philitas (III.9.35–44). I cannot help quoting at this point the incipit of Ezra Pound's celebrated "Homage to Sextus Propertius"—a splendid example of modernism's classical heritage:

> Shades of Callimachus, Coan ghosts of Philetas
> It is in your grove I would walk,
> I who come first from the clear font
> Bringing the Grecian orgies into Italy,
> and the dance into Italy.

Callimachus and Philitas (or Philetas, according to Pound's spelling), who was from Cos, are here not just part of the modern poet's rendition of Propertius's ancient poem, but a testament to Pound's own willingness to insert his work within the legacy of Greece and Rome.

Addressing Ponticus (an epic poet by now consigned to oblivion), Propertius proudly defends his minor poetic vein, which will bring him no shortage of glory, serving as an example to other hapless lovers (I.7). He also revives the myth of the "initiation rite" dream—by then firmly associated, as we saw, with Ennius, the acclaimed father of Latin epic poetry (III.3.6). Stretched out in the shade of Mount Helicon, home to the Muses, the poet is dreaming of the ancient kings of Alba Longa when suddenly Apollo appears (it's worth noting here that the first line of the poem uses two words found in Virgil's pastoral poetry, *recubans* and *umbra*). The god encourages him to shift his focus, to find themes more suited to his intellect, to forge a new path. At this point they're joined by Calliope, one of the nine Muses, who more or less repeats Apollo's advice (quit writing about war, in other words). She then wets his lips with holy water, to signify the completion of the initiation process.

Propertius, we must remember, also wrote elegies about Rome's past—splendid elegies on antiquity and archaeology (collected in Book IV). His poetry, nonetheless, is for the large part concerned with love; love that asserts itself against history and genealogy; love that is, as it might be termed, anti-Roman. This constitutes a radical departure from a predecessor like Catullus, who sees in love—despite all the difficulties a relationship with a woman brings—the perfect integration between the individual and society, between province (his own upbringing) and city. Catullus may condemn love's deterioration, the breaking of bonds and promises, but he believes deeply in love. Which brings him great suffering. Propertius spares himself such belief. There is no love, in his view, that doesn't cause anguish: "omnis [. . .] timetur amor" (I.11.18), "all love is fear." Infidelity is the rule, not the exception: "nemo est in amore fedelis" (II.34.3), "no lover is faithful." His suffering is born not simply from displeasure or from disappointing circumstances, though these may seem the subject of his poetry, but from a profound sense of bewilderment, a distrust from the very outset. Lesbia, in the end, will stand for Catullus as a missed opportunity to achieve his high ideal—the ideal, though, will remain. Cynthia is never an ideal: she's merely a beautiful woman who causes suffering and from whose bondage he must free himself. Though there's pain in both cases, the historical significance of the pain has changed. It has passed from a protest against the corruption of the present day to an acceptance of our destined solitude.

Nor is such acceptance without its dose of nostalgia (which, as we've seen, is a fundamental aspect of Roman culture and one of its most enduring legacies). The archaeological elegies from Book IV that we spoke of earlier, which lament a Rome that is no longer, can be read with respect to the first three books as a grand dirge for the death of the ideal. An ode to the happiness of origins— a happiness born of love—appears in elegy 13 of Book III as well. After denouncing lust, the frivolity of women, and the infidelity of wives, Propertius embarks on an ode to the serenity of early farm life, when girls were content to receive flowers and fruit from their suitors; when we made our beds in the grass, beneath the shade of trees. Now nature gives home only to the sad lament of the poet torn from his lover. Here are the marvelous opening lines, which Petrarch may well have had in mind when writing his "Solo et pensoso . . .":

Haec certe deserta loca et taciturna querenti,
et vacuum Zephyri possidet aura nemus. (I.18.1–2)

Places like these, deserted and deaf to laments,
where the breath of Zephyr fills the empty wood.

At the close of this same elegy, he returns to exalt the connection between the heart's desolation and the desolation of the countryside:

pro quo, divini fontes, et frigida rupes
et datur inculto tramite dura quies;
et quodcumque meae possunt narrare querelae,
cogor ad argutas dicere solus aves. (I.18.27–30)

in exchange, I get sacred fountains and cold rocks,
and a wink of sleep by some deserted trail;

and whatever story my laments may tell,
I must tell it alone, in the presence of the trilling birds.

Solus: in this single adjective rests the entire poetics of marginalization, estrangement, exclusion, the unheard lament. In Propertius's elegies, *solus* appears with symbolic frequency, resounding like a declaration, *principium individuationis*, proclaiming a true form of identity. To conclude, I quote this spectacular line:

solus ero, quoniam non licet esse tuum. (II.9.46)

I'll be alone, if I cannot be yours.

21

More on Happiness:
The Lesson of Horace

And so we come to Horace (65–8 B.C.E.), the greatest poet, along with Virgil, of the Augustan age; synonymous with language's beauty and an enduring symbol, to this day, of what it means to be a poet.

Rather than the epic, he favored short poems (following in the footsteps of Greek lyricists) and compact verse portrayals of social customs, or satire, as just discussed. Here we'll focus on his lyric poetry.

Ancient and profoundly classical, Horace feels contemporary in every age. His voice emanates from afar, and yet it reaches us with impressive clarity, inviting dialogue. Every century has sent him its share of fan mail. At the dawn of humanism, Petrarch wrote him a letter brimming with admiration (*Familiares*, XXIV.10), perhaps the most beautiful of those he sent to the ancient authors, focusing on his lyrical output (for Dante, Horace was solely a satirical author, *Inferno*, IV.89). Still more letters were dispatched from the twentieth century. Primo Levi, reflecting on modernity's presumed achievements, felt the need to evoke Horace's name; and the Russian poet Joseph Brodsky, though he

seemed to prefer Ovid, used him to take the pulse of modern poetry.[1] In the conclusion to *Twilight of the Idols*, which we recalled
earlier for its tribute to Sallust, Nietzsche gives us this splendid
homage to Horace:

> I had the same experience on first coming into contact
> with Horace. From that day to this no poet has given
> me the same artistic delight as I derived from the very
> first from an Horatian ode. In certain languages what is
> achieved here is not even desirable. This mosaic of words
> in which every word, as sound, as locus, as concept,
> pours forth its power to left and right and over the whole,
> this minimum in the range and number of signs which
> achieves a maximum of energy of these signs—all this is
> Roman and, if one will believe me, noble *par excellence*.
> All other poetry becomes by comparison somewhat too
> popular—a mere emotional garrulousness.[2]

The long influence of Horatian poetry, particularly in English,
extends to the present day. At the turn of the third millennium, an
American poet, J. D. McClatchy, led an interesting experiment: he
compiled a complete volume of Horace's odes by asking the most
important poets writing in English to each translate one.[3] We can
hear echoes of Horace even in Italy's beloved poet Eugenio Montale:
his famed opening line "Non chiederci . . . ,"[4] a poetics in and of
itself, is drawn from an opening line in Horace, "Tu ne quaesieris."
In fact, there's a bit of Horace throughout Montale's work, even in the
title of his later collection, *Satura* (satire), and in the opening of his
acclaimed sonnet "Ut pictura poesis"—a quote taken from Horace's
letter to the Pisos, which we'll come back to soon.[5]

As a matter of fact, Horace saw it all coming—even made it
so. In one of his most passionate odes, which concludes the third

book, he declares that thanks to his poetic fame he would outlive the pyramids.

Horace seems to hold an appeal even for those with less lyrical tastes. In 2013, the British author Harry Eyres published a book entitled *Horace and Me*—which does all it can to give Horace his place in the modern landscape.[6]

If I were writing a book called *Horace and Me*, perhaps I'd begin by saying that Horace stands for us first and foremost as a symbol against vulgarity, in all its forms: bragging, indiscretion, gossip, materialism, overindulgence, idiocy, following the herd. Nor does his disdain for the herd derive from noble roots (his father, in fact, was a freedman), but rather from a genuine awareness of contemporary society and the world's evils. One of his most emblematic lines, "Odi profanum vulgus et arceo" (*Odes*, III.1.1), "I hate the profane rabble, and keep it at a distance," is not simply the contempt of a man who thinks himself superior, but his idea of what makes a human being: a man who cultivates his mind and spirit, and there finds himself in a sacred space. Indeed, the adjective *profanus* is the opposite of *sacer*, "sacred": it's composed of the prefix *pro-*, "in front of," and *fanum*, "temple"; a man who is profane is excluded from ritual, is uninitiated. Horace attributes his social distinction to the excellent education that his freedman father had the foresight and generosity to provide for him (*Satires*, I.6.76–80). A learned man, Horace befriended learned men, eventually finding his way into the circle of Maecenas, confidant and literary advisor to Augustus. Horace dedicates a few of his poems to Maecenas, including Satire 6 from Book I—where, in addition to an homage to his enlightened father, we also find the memory of their timid first encounter, spurred by the recommendations of Virgil and Varus:

ut veni coram, singultim pauca locutus
infans namque pudor prohibebat plura profari,
non ego me claro natum patre, non ego circum
me Satureiano vectari rura caballo,
sed quod eram narro. Respondes, ut tuus est mos,
pauca; abeo, et revocas nono post mense iubesque
esse in amicorum numero. Magnum hoc ego duco,
quod placui tibi, qui turpi secernis honestum
non patre praeclaro, sed vita et pectore puro.
    (*Satires*, I.6.56–64)

when I met you there in person, I croaked a few words,
an infant, indeed shame prevented me from saying more.
I did not say that I was born of a famous father, that I
gallop around the fields on a Tarentian steed
but I said who I was. Your reply, as always,
was brief. I left, and you called me nine months later,
to count me among your friends. That you found me
    worthy
I think a great privilege—you, who judge a man
not by his father, but by pureness of life and heart.

This well-arranged portrait stages a drama of class mobility, casting it as a peaceful memory, but also an archetypal scene, one that will recur with such frequency, and so problematically, throughout the cultural history of the West (and not only the West). Here, Horace enacts no less than the encounter between poetry and power. It doesn't seem that Horace quite bowled Maecenas over on their first meeting. Nor that Maecenas raced to welcome him into his private circle of friends. Nevertheless, after considerable delay, the moment of consecration occurs. Though in truth he'd already been self-consecrated. The arbiter, in the end, can only recognize what's already there in the poet—what comes from within, from an undistinguished father, from the transformation he made through education. In other words, Horace is already Horace: his public birth (the nine-month waiting period seems to reflect a real pregnancy) supersedes his private one. This insistence on the private realm is typical of Horace. Typical as well, in the excerpt above, is his insistence on language. Note the many expressions that refer to speech: *locutus*, *infans* (*in* + *fans*, "non-speaker"), *profari*, *narro*, *respondes*. The thematic fulcrum, more precisely, is "saying and not saying at once," with the word *pauca* used in reference to both characters. Each has his own reasons for saying so little: the poet feels inferior (or at least he'll admit as much to posterity) and Maecenas has a reputation of being laconic. How could they ever have understood each other with so much left unsaid? Perhaps they didn't at all, but simply enjoyed each other's company; each character played his part dutifully. Poets, after all, can convey themselves to the powerful without really speaking.

Since antiquity, Cicero and Virgil ranked as the foremost models of literary language, standing as embodiments of Latin style, one for prose and the other for poetry (and they would remain so through the Italian Renaissance). Horace, no less a master with words (thinking again of Nietzsche's assessment) and never afraid to declare himself as such, symbolizes something more: Horatianism, a category that stretches beyond language, a *spiritual* category, a status that neither Virgil nor Cicero, for all their influence, ever achieved. Horace presented himself as a psychological mold, a "character": a man who, not without irony, tried to let life run its natural course; who guarded himself from the gossip mill; who took no moment for granted and knew what belonged to youth and what to old age.

However intellectual, the Horatian "type" is not a philosopher by profession, like Seneca or Lucretius. He is a man for whom self-education comes first, and who learns by the most strenuous and essential means possible: by living authentically, without hopes or regrets, here and now, with that same immediacy with which words take shape in the mouth, and that same care with which one arranges them in a sentence—or better yet, in a line of poetry. My use of a linguistic metaphor here is no accident: in word order and precise meaning, Horace sees the gears and cogs of life itself. In his epistle to Florus, he even goes so far as to claim that the true art of composition is not a verbal art but the art of living:

> ac non verba sequi fidibus modulanda Latinis,
> sed verae numerosque modosque ediscere vitae.
>   (*Epistles*, II.2.143–44)

> and [knowledge is] not bowing to words that bend on the
>   Latin lyre,
> but learning the bars and rhythms of life itself.

Again we have the theme of self-education, *ediscere*, composed of *discere* (source of the English word "disciple"). Learning to live, in fact, is a form of apprenticeship: *the poet is he who lives well*.

In no other author of antiquity do writing and life correspond so ideally; indeed, so perfectly. Discipline and naturalness, therefore; decorum and spontaneity: this is Horace's Latin. For him, as it will be for Petrarch, every stylistic trait is a measure of time, because it takes time, because *it is moment*. It's no wonder that such an "autobiographical" poet, who speaks so often of his experiences, also excels in composition theory, with a deep historical, as well as technical, understanding of the art. He knows exactly what role Latin poetry has played in the course of history, as we find evidence of in several odes, and is well aware of just how much responsibility and vigilant scrupulousness it takes to be a poet. Let's look here at another important passage from his epistle to Florus:

vemens et liquidus puroque simillimus amni
fundet opes Latiumque beabit divite lingua;
luxuriantia compescet, nimis aspera sano
levabit cultu, virtute carentia tollet,
ludentis speciem dabit et torquebitur, ut qui
nunc Satyrum, nunc agrestem Cyclopa movetur.
    (II.120–25)

strong and clear and much like the purest river,
he'll spread abundance, enriching Latium with a rich
    language;
he'll check all excess, polish any coarseness
with a careful hand, discarding all that's deprived of
    force,
and giving the impression of play—when in truth he
    writhes, as if dancing
now like a Satyr, now like a bumpkin Cyclops.

Horace even left us a treatise on the art of writing—another
letter, the so-called epistle to the Pisos (his dedicatees), known
also as his *Ars poetica*, a work much treasured in the Renaissance.
It's a manifesto on linguistic rationalism, and it still has much to
teach. He invites the poet to practice order, unity, coherence, self-
awareness, study; to avoid peculiarities and eccentricities; to not
content oneself, to not let one's instinct run overboard, to revise
and to heed the advice of harsh critics. And never to rush into
publishing—because a word once printed sticks, while, as long as
the text remains unpublished, one can always choose to scrap it.

Poetry, yes, is a natural gift, but it is also and above all a
project; and the poet, no matter how inspired, must always have a
clear sense of intention. *Ars poetica* is filled with ingenious phrasings, which have in time become dogmas: "lucidus ordo" (41, a
luminous arrangement of parts), "callida [. . .] iunctura" (47–48,

unusual word combinations, to give well-worn terms a new flavor), "limae labor" (291, the labor of correction), "ut pictura, poesis" (361, as is painting so is poetry). Here are the lines where "ut pictura, poesis" appears:

Ut pictura, poesis: erit quae, si propius stes,
te capiat magis, et quaedam, si longius abstes.
Haec amat obscurum, volet haec sub luce videri,
iudicis argutum quae non formidat acumen;
haec placuit semel, haec deciens repetita placebit.
    (vv. 361–65)

Poetry is like painting: some things catch you
more if you stand in front of them, other things from a
    distance.
One favors shadow, one wants to be seen in light,
untroubled by the sharp wit of the critics;
some please once, some will please even after ten times.

These are the lines that perhaps best exemplify Horace's critical and aesthetic genius. But the entire *Ars poetica* is a masterpiece of intelligence and expressive force. And what a sense of history he demonstrates when speaking of language! Words come and go, like leaves, like all things human (60–62); we drop them, we pick them back up, we invent new ones. The poet, even when drawing on tradition, is at root an observer, one who captures life and who never dismisses the age's current practices, or *usus* (71). Hence the poet's ability to distinguish before and after, his keen sense of the age of those around him. Time is his clay. Everything in its right moment. Nothing out of place, nothing out of order. All punctual, all right where it must be, in perfect accord with everything else.

    Horace's Latin stands as a paradigm of economy. He doesn't

digress, he doesn't add, he doesn't exaggerate. He tends to avoid archaisms, which in Virgil—as in Ennius—are abundant (even if a few sneak their way into his epistle to Florus and the *Ars poetica*). There's nothing "easy" about Horace's Latin, not even when it seems to be dictated by occasion, as in the *Odes*, where his art reaches truly new heights—comparable in its concentration and precision of detail to what Tacitus accomplishes in his prose—leaving Western tradition some of the most beautiful works composed by any author, ancient or modern. Though carefully crafted, his Latin nonetheless offers something immediate, something quotable, which catches our eye even among the most intricate verbal lacework, communicating one truth or another:

> vitae summa brevis spem nos vetat incohare longam
>   (I.4.15)

> short life leaves no allowance for long hope

> quid sit futurum cras fuge quaerere . . . (I.9.13)

> never ask what tomorrow brings . . .

> compesce mentem . . . (I.16.22)

> restrain your soul . . . [that is, keep your emotions in check]

> [. . .] valet ima summis / mutare et insignem attenuat deus, / obscura promens . . . (I.34.12–14)

> [. . .] god can exchange the lowest for the highest, unseat the remarkable man, and uplift the obscure . . .

Aequam memento rebus in arduis / servare mentem . . .
(II.3.1–2)

Remember to keep a calm soul in difficult times . . .

rebus angustis animosus atque / fortis appare . . .
(II.10.21–22)

in tight situations, show your strength and courage . . .

dona praesentis cape laetus hora . . . (III.8.27)

accept happily the gifts of the present moment . . .

[. . .] nil cupientium / nudus castra peto et transfuga
divitum / partis linquere gestio . . . (III.16.22–24)

[. . .] naked I seek the camp of those who want nothing, a
deserter I long to abandon the ranks of the rich . . .

[. . .] multa petentibus / desunt multa . . . (III.16.42–43)

[. . .] for those who want much, much is lacking . . .

[. . .] ille potens sui / laetusque deget, cui licet in diem /
dixisse: "Vixi" . . . (III.29.41–43)

[. . .] he who, day after day, can say, "I lived," lives happily
and as master of himself . . .

pulvis et umbra sumus. (IV.7.16)

we are dust and shadow.

And so many more. Running like a current through all of
these truths is a sigh for the passage of time. One day follows another, new moons die off; youth fades; the years go by . . . Without
this sense of temporal anguish, Horace would be merely a good
moralist.

Even gleaning lines, as I've just done—however randomly—
the reader of Horace's *Odes* arms himself with a handbook on
happiness. To live life fully: that is his secret. And, in doing so, to
avoid excess, which is not fullness, but a miscalculation, a lack no
different from insufficiency.

22

Conclusion as Exhortation: Study Latin!

We have come to the end of our account. Throughout these pages, I have tried to communicate the beauty of Latin, and the reasons— historical, linguistic, literary, political, philosophical—why this ancient language is still essential to our lives today. It's natural, then, to say that I also think we could all greatly benefit from studying it. I don't believe there is one right way to do so: follow your inclinations and choose whatever aspect of Latin you most feel drawn to. Go to a library, take an evening course, start from the work of an author you find particularly appealing: Catullus's poems? Apuleius's novel? Ovid's stories of transformation? Turn to editions where the English translation comes with the Latin text en face. Make comparisons between the two languages, circle Latin words you find interesting, look them up in a dictionary . . . It won't take long before you realize how much Latin you use when you speak English—that is, how much of who you are linguisti- cally you owe to this Useless Language! Above all, enjoy the study of Latin as such, as language. Because Latin is not just enriching, or thought-provoking, or mind stretching (as useful as those qualities may be). I must say here what I've thus far left implicit: studying

Latin is an extraordinarily rewarding experience in itself. To put it quite simply: Latin is fun.

What do I mean by fun? Not, of course, the same uncomplicated joy as an easy pastime, or a simple joke. Something altogether deeper: working toward meaning, and understanding meaning as a process, not as a given. It might still be seen as a game, but one whose rules you have to work out, whose prize reveals itself only—and joyfully—after long and thoughtful effort.

Learning Latin means immersing oneself in the pleasure of this meaning-making process. It takes focus, attention, and alertness to the ambiguities of syntax and the semantic richness of individual words. It's a highly exciting process of selection and decision making. Logic is involved, but logical skills alone are not enough. Learners of Latin must use intuition and imagination, be ready to take chances and to be daring. Meaning is never ready-made, not even outside the boundaries of literature. It always emerges from some kind of negotiation between individuals, it belongs to a (social, cultural, psychological) context. That's why we can easily make mistakes both in reading and in listening to others: we either assume too much or do not pay enough attention to all that is relevant; we forget how complicated and ambiguous linguistic communication can be. Latin is here to remind us that meaning is not to be taken for granted; that words are complex entities, almost like living creatures, and therefore have memories and intentions of their own. A sentence is a public space where past experiences and present needs converge, striving to form new messages. As readers and learners, we participate in this public space. This comes with a strong sense of responsibility: in the end, it is truth itself that is at stake! Translating or reading Latin means understanding and detecting the truth, and then letting it speak once again in our own language after so many centuries. Interpretive effort, then, turns into the pleasure of discovery, of recovery, of illumination, one of the most gratifying experiences the human heart can have.

One must also consider that Latin—a highly literary language—does not construct its messages as most modern languages do. Latin resists linearity, straightforwardness, immediacy. On the contrary, it pursues allusiveness and multiplicity. The syntax can be elaborate or omissive, and in idiosyncratic ways; its morphology is highly varied; its vocabulary is packed with semantic nuances that become clear only in the context of the sentence. Once again, context is crucial! By which I mean that when we read Latin we need to consider things comparatively, one in relation to another, creating a coherent whole, while considering differences and even conflicts between the parts. And isn't this what we do every day to make society function? Which is why Latin has such a priceless lesson to teach us: to weigh every element, even the minutest or commonest monosyllable, even the slightest difference in spelling; to become aware of the intricate relationships through which words dialogue with one another; to take a sentence not as a face-value utterance but as an artistic and, as such, a multifaceted performance, combining sense, rhythm, and aesthetic prowess. Learning Latin affords us the special gratification of experiencing this complexity, which is ultimately part of one of the highest ambitions of being human: achieving linguistic beauty.

Latin may come across as difficult. But not to worry. All art is difficult, and Latin is art, verbal art, just as Picasso's painting, Mozart's music, or Einstein's models of the universe are artistic constructions in their own ways. Painting, music, science too could all be said to be difficult, as could any great form of representation and thought. In truth, nothing is easy when creativity and intuition are involved. If a great piece of literature comes across as easy, we should ask ourselves: What's escaping me here? What am I not getting that I *should* be getting? What's under the misleading surface? Where's the trick? Difficulty is part of the game: it makes the reward all the more satisfying.

Easiness, then, is just an illusion, or perhaps it is a feature of something else: passion. When we are passionate about, say, classical music or physics, we apply ourselves with unrestrained commitment. And it's this passion that makes the commitment a pleasure, or at least more pleasurable than doing something we're forced to do. We may be passionate about classical music, and not about physics (or the other way around). In this case, studying one will be more pleasurable than the other, and feel like less of a chore. In other words: it will seem easier. In school, little distinction is made between the subjects we are passionate about and the ones we must study—it's something we have to discover on our own.

So the question really is: How do I become passionate about something? And that's much harder to answer. At the beginning of this book, I admitted that I couldn't really say why I've loved Latin ever since I was a child, even before I started learning it. Passion, probably, begins as a search for happiness. We look for happiness and something tells us that we will find it in this or that particular activity. And so we give it a try. Passion can also emerge as simple curiosity. Humans are curious creatures. Thanks to curiosity we stay young, because we take nothing for granted, not even what we already know through experience. Curiosity means we keep asking questions until we realize we have changed our minds, fallen in love, or fallen quite out of it. We could even call it wonder: that feeling of admiration that enlarges our faith in the possibilities of reality. One thing is for sure: we can't know if we're passionate about something, or not, unless we know of its existence, are exposed to it, can try it for ourselves, or listen to arguments in its favor. I cannot make you love Latin, nor can any teacher. But I can try to impart some of my own passion, show you why I love it, and try to spark a similar interest in you. Schools can teach it, universities offer it as an elective. The rest is up to your curiosity, your own quest for happiness.

Learning Latin demands attention and memory. And there's a pleasure in developing one's attention and memory—the pleasure of playing with words, of discovering how differently humans can think and how many new thoughts and sentences can come to our minds, once we learn how to shift to new grammatical models and semantic processes. Translation will not just illuminate the content and form of the original. It will also give us the skill of perceiving the very structure of our own language, indicating paths to hidden meanings, etymologies, burgeoning metaphors of which most of us are now no longer aware, and will prompt us to cultivate verbal accuracy, intellectual exactitude, conceptual depth. Latin will open our eyes to so many secrets, bringing to the fore a fundamental notion: that the history of languages is made not of one straight line, which permits no alternatives, but is a growing mnemonic adventure, where new outcomes do not completely override past solutions, and meaning over time meanders through endless compromises, negotiations, and also unresolved tensions between competing representations. One brief example: Who, without any Latin, would think that "minister"—as in prime minister—is not such a distinguished title, after all? In Latin, the word means "servant." Social inferiority is clearly expressed by the first part of the word, *minus* (that much we can still understand in English). Through the study of Latin, we will also become all the more aware of the countless similarities, and differences, among modern languages—especially in the field of vocabulary. Besides showing us the original meaning of numerous words in modern languages, Latin teaches us that the same Latin word may end up taking on different meanings in different languages. *Parentes*, for example, produces "parents" in English and in French, and *parenti* in Italian. The English and French derivatives retain the original meaning (mother and father). The Italian word, instead, acquires a different, although "related," meaning: that of "relatives" (*parents*, I admit, may also mean "relatives" in French, though *proches*, from *proximi*, "the very near," is more common). These differences notwithstanding, it's clear that all of us—English-speaking and non-English-speaking people alike—may share more than we perceive at first sight. Anyone with a little Latin knows that our similarities outnumber our differences.

One last consideration. Latin offers an inexhaustible wealth of images and representations that speak of mankind—of us, therefore. That wealth is the ultimate purpose of one's training in the Latin language. Indeed, the belief that an ancient author still has something to say to us today is without doubt valid, even necessary. Yet the impulse to update and domesticate should be avoided: studying Latin and reading the ancients teach us, and must teach us, the fundamental importance of historical distance, without which we lose our temporal and cultural sense of place. We read and translate the ancients best when we go in search of a historical experience, when we attempt to measure the distance, which is filled with mirages and shifting perspectives, like a landscape viewed from afar and from ever-changing points of view. We can draw interpretations and responses from an ancient author, but we must always keep in mind that those interpretations and responses correspond to radically different times and cultural contexts, and therefore cannot be applied literally to our present needs. The ancients speak for the ancients. And what we learn, in essence, by discovering who they are, is to speak of ourselves. We too, in a sense, become a little ancient; it isn't they who become modern. Through studying, reading, writing, and loving Latin, we step into the river of history, and there we find a deeper understanding of where we began and where we want to go.

Notes

Ode to a Useless Language
1. See my book *Rinascimento* (Turin: Einaudi, 2010).

1. A Home
1. Jorge Luis Borges, "Funes the Memorious," in *Labyrinths: Selected Stories & Other Writings*, ed. Donald A. Yates and James E. Irby (New York: New Directions, 1964), 61.
2. Some years ago I wrote a brief grammar book of my own: *Latino* (Milan: Alphatest, 1999).

3. Which Latin?
1. The international bibliography of Latin history—both popular and scholarly, high and low quality—is ample. Here I'll note only the German author Jürgen Leonhardt's excellent book, *Latein: Geschichte einer Weltsprache* (Munich: Verlag C. H. Beck, 2008), which itself contains a useful bibliography (English trans. by Kenneth Kronenberg, *Latin: Story of a World Language*, Cambridge, MA, and London: Belknap Press of Harvard University Press, 2013).
2. See Luciano Canfora, *Ideologie del classicismo* (Turin: Einaudi, 1980).

4. A Divine Alphabet
1. Two good sources on the historical development of Latin: Leonard R. Palmer, *The Latin Language* (London: Faber and Faber, 1954), and James Clackson and Geoffrey Harrocks, *The Blackwell History of the Latin Language* (Chichester: Wiley-Blackwell, 2011).
2. "The I Tatti Renaissance Library," in *On Famous Women*, ed. and

trans. Virginia Brown (Cambridge, MA, and London: Harvard University Press, 2001), 54–55.

3.   For a good introduction to Indo-European, I recommend James Clackson, *Indo-European Linguistics: An Introduction* (Cambridge: Cambridge University Press, 2007). For a classic work in Italian on the subject, see Vittore Pisani, *Glottologia indoeuropea* (Turin: Rosenberg & Sellier, 1984 [first edition, 1949]).

5. Understanding Latin with Catullus

1.   Catullus, *Carmina: il libro delle poesie* (Milan: Feltrinelli, 2014 [with my introduction]).

6. Cicero's Star-Studded Sky

1.   *Intervalla* can mean "interval/pause" or "distance"; *distinctio,* either "punctuation" or "difference"; and *conversio* "revolving" or the repetition of the same word at the end of a clause.
2.   In society, the accord between civil sectors is itself an extension of the cosmic harmony (*De re publica*, end of Book II).
3.   For more on the importance of the unsaid or the incompletely stated in ancient rhetoric, see my *Lacuna* (Turin: Einaudi, 2014).

7. Ennius's Ghost

1.   Horace in his *Epistles* I.19.7, and—as we'll see—Propertius in his *Elegies*, III.3.6.
2.   I here quote from *Poeti latini arcaici. Livio Andronico, Nevio, Ennio,* ed. Antonio Tragila (Turin: UTET, 1986), 436.
3.   Ibid., 394.
4.   Note here his use of the archaic *sam* instead of *eam* (an archaism that will have readers raising an eyebrow for generations to come, though without quite knocking Ennius from his pedestal) and of the Graecism *sopiam*. The infinitive verb *reserare* lacks an object, though one can imagine that what he's opening up are the founts or doors of the Muses (in *Aeneid*, VII.613, Virgil uses the verb specifically to mean the opening up of a protected area); or else, I'd suggest, the secret knowledge that Homer grants to the poet. In the *Metamorphoses* (XV.145), in fact, Ovid uses the verb *reserare* to mean "reveal" in a very similar context.
5.   *Poeti latini arcaici*, 446.

8. Caesar, or the Measures of Reality

1. Bertolt Brecht, *The Business Affairs of Mr. Julius Caesar*, trans. Charles Osborne, ed. Tony Phelan and Tom Kuhn (London: Bloomsbury Methuen Drama, 2016), 23.

9. The Power of Clarity: Lucretius

1. Primo Levi, *The Search for Roots: A Personal Anthology*, trans. Peter Forbes (Chicago: Ivan R. Dee, 2002), 136.
2. For more, see my book *Lacuna* (Turin: Einaudi, 2014).

11. Syntactic Goose Bumps, or Virgil's Shivering Sentences

1. Gian Biagio Conte, *Anatomia di una stile: L'enallage e il nuovo sublime*, in Gian Biagio Conte, *Virgilio: L'epica del sentimento* (Turin: Einaudi, 2002), 59 (complete essay, 5–63).
2. Giorgio Pasquali, one of the twentieth century's great scholars of classical literature, spoke of this "allusive art." See Giorgio Pasquali, *Arte allusiva*, in *Pagine stravaganti di un filologo*, vol. II, ed. Carlo Ferdinando Russo (Florence: Le Lettere, 1994), 275–82.
3. *Imitatio* will again find favor in the course of the Renaissance: see my *Umane parole* (Milan: Bruno Mondadori, 1997), and my *Rinascimento* (Turin: Einaudi, 2010), 224–53.
4. Seamus Heaney, *Aeneid Book VI* (London: Faber & Faber, 2016), 16.
5. See E. L. Harrison, "Cleverness in Virgilian Imitation," in *Classical Philology* 65, no. 4 (October 1970), 241–43. And for a very different perspective, see Gian Biagio Conte, *Memoria dei poeti e sistema letterario* (Palermo: Sellerio, 2012 [first edition, Turin: Einaudi, 1971]), 106–10.
6. I here refer the reader to my introduction to Catullus, *Carmina: il libro delle poesie* (Milan: Feltrinelli, 2014).

12. The Master of Diffraction, Tacitus, and Sallust's Brevity

1. I've also written on Tacitus's style in *Lacuna* (Turin: Einaudi, 2014), 83–85 and passim.
2. See *Lacuna*, 87.
3. Friedrich Nietzsche, *Twilight of the Idols; and, the Anti-Christ*, trans. R. J. Hollingdale (London: Penguin, 1990), 116.

13. Ovid, or the End of Identity

1. Giacomo Leopardi, *Zibaldone*, ed. Michael Caesar and Franco
    D'Intino (New York: Farrar, Straus and Giroux, 2013), 1422–23.
2. Robert Lowell, *Ovid's* Metamorphoses, in *Collected Prose*, ed. Robert
    Giroux (New York: The Noonday Press, 1987), 157.
3. Italo Calvino, *Ovidio e la contiguità universale*, in *Saggi 1945–*
    1985, ed. Mario Barenghi (Milan: Meridiani Mondadori, 1995),
    vol. I, 12 (full essay, 904–16).
4. I comment on Ovid's late style in my monograph *Con Ovidio. La*
    felicità di leggere un classico (Milan: Garzanti, 2017), 98–100.
5. More on the theme of physical transformation in my *Con Ovidio*,
    149–82.

14. Breathing and Creaking: Reflections on Livy

1. See Giuseppe Billanovich, "Petrarch and the Textual Tradition
    of Livy," in *Journal of the Warburg and Courtauld Institutes* 14,
    no. 3/4 (1951), 137–208.

15. The Word *Umbra*: Virgil's *Eclogues*

1. Giacomo Leopardi, *Canti*, trans. Jonathan Galassi (New York:
    Farrar, Straus and Giroux, 2010), 107.
2. See the first chapter of my *Rinascimento* (Turin: Einaudi, 2010).

16. Seneca, or the Serenity of Saying It All

1. James Ker, *The Deaths of Seneca* (New York and Oxford: Oxford
    University Press, 2009).
2. Rebirth serves as the theme of one of the letters as well. *Letters to*
    Lucilius, 36.10–11.

17. Deviances and Dental Care: Apuleius and Petronius

1. John F. D'Amico, "The Progress of Renaissance Latin Prose: The
    Case of Apuleianism," in *Renaissance Quarterly* 37, no. 3 (Fall
    1984). See also Julia Haig Gaisser, *The Fortunes of Apuleius & the*
    Golden Ass: A Study in Transmission and Reception (Princeton and
    Oxford: Princeton University Press, 2008).
2. Letter to Louise Colet, June 27–28, 1852.
3. Walter Pater, *Marius the Epicurean*, ed. Michael Levey (London:
    Penguin Books, 1986), 40.

4. This is precisely what Petronius's characters do, according to Huysmans: "And all this is told in an extraordinarily vigorous style, precise in coloration, a style that draws from every dialect, that borrows expressions from every language Rome has known, that pushes back all the boundaries, that ignores all the trammels of the so-called Golden Age, letting each man speak his own tongue." J. K. Huysmans, *Against Nature (À rebours)*, trans. Margaret Mauldon, ed. Nicholas White (Oxford: Oxford University Press, 1998), 25.

5. Allusion to Catullus 39.

18. Brambles, Chasms, and Memories: Augustine's Linguistic Reformation

1. See Marco Tullio Cicerone, *Ortensio*, critical text, introduction, translation, and commentary by Alberto Grilli (Bologna: Patron, 2010).

2. For *varietas*, see Cicero, *De oratore*, III.25.98–100. I speak of *varietas* in the last chapter of my *Rinascimento*. For *evidentia*, which is to place an object before one's eyes using words, see Cicero, *De partitione oratoria*, VI.20; *Academica*, II.17; *De oratore*, III.53.202; *Orator*, XL.139.

3. On the humble style of Christian Latin, see Erich Auerbach's classic essay *Sermo humilis*, in Erich Auerbach, *Literary Language and Its Public in the Late Latin Antiquity and in the Middle Ages*, trans. Ralph Manheim (Princeton: Princeton University Press, 1993), 25–66.

19. The Duty of Self-Improvement: Juvenal and Satire

1. Alexander Pushkin, *Eugene Onegin: A Novel in Verse*, trans. James E. Falen (Oxford: Oxford University Press, 2009), 7.

20. The Loneliness of Love: Propertius

1. On Ovid's revolutionary departure from the once-beloved paradigm, see my *Con Ovidio. La felicità di leggere un classico* (Milan: Garzanti, 2017), 73–89.

21. More on Happiness: The Lesson of Horace

1. Primo Levi, *The Complete Works of Primo Levi*, ed. Ann Goldstein (New York: Liveright, 2015), page 2355; Joseph Brodsky, "Letter to

Horace," in *On Grief and Reason: Essays* (New York: Farrar, Straus and Giroux, 1998), 428–58.

2. Friedrich Nietzsche, *Twilight of the Idols; and, the Anti-Christ*, trans. R. J. Hollingdale (London: Penguin, 1990), 116.

3. Horace, *The Odes: New Translations by Contemporary Poets*, ed. J. D. McClatchy (Oxford and Princeton: Princeton University Press, 2002).

4. *Non chiederci la parola che squadri da ogni lato / l'animo nostro informe*—"Don't ask us for the word to frame / Our shapeless spirit on all sides" (translation from Eugenio Montale, *Collected Poems 1920–1954: Ossi di seppia / Cuttlefish bones, Le occasioni / The occasions, La bufera e altro / The storm, etc.*, trans. Jonathan Galassi (New York: Farrar, Straus and Giroux, 1998).

5. See Corrado Confalonieri, *Satura—titoli di un titolo. Montale dal recto al verso nel segno dei classici* (Parma: Uninova, 2012).

6. Harry Eyres, *Horace and Me: Life Lessons from an Ancient Poet* (New York: Farrar, Straus and Giroux, 2013).

Acknowledgments

This book would not exist without the faithful exhortations of my agent, Marco Vigevani, and Michele Fusilli and Paolo Zaninoni, the nonfiction editor and editorial director, respectively, at Garzanti. I want to express to them here my sincere gratitude.

I'd also like to thank my friend and fellow Latinist Beppe Pezzini (now Lecturer in Latin at the University of St. Andrews), a critical source of inspiration to me when in the autumn of 2014, at Oxford, I began thinking about the structure of this book. I think fondly of our post-lunch conversations at the café in Magdalen College, with an open and collaborative spirit, and not without the guileless contribution of nature, clouds, ponds, ducks, even a ferret.

Special thanks to Nicolas Moureaux, my eternal companion in conversation and happiness.

Index of Names

BOOKS BY

Randall Jarrell

THE WOMAN
AT THE
WASHINGTON
ZOO

THE WOMAN

AT THE

WASHINGTON

ZOO

POEMS & TRANSLATIONS

RANDALL

JARRELL

NEW YORK ATHENEUM PUBLISHERS
1960

Most of these poems have already been published in ACCENT, THE AMERICAN SCHOLAR, ART NEWS, ENCOUNTER, THE KENYON REVIEW, THE LADIES HOME JOURNAL, THE NATION, PARTISAN REVIEW, POETRY, THE PRAIRIE SCHOONER, THE TIMES LITERARY SUPPLEMENT, *and* THE VIRGINIA QUARTERLY REVIEW. *The translations from Rilke were made with the permission of* INSEL-VERLAG, *Wiesbaden.*

To Mary

CONTENTS

THE WOMAN
AT THE
WASHINGTON
ZOO

THE WOMAN AT THE WASHINGTON ZOO

The saris go by me from the embassies.

Cloth from the moon. Cloth from another planet.
They look back at the leopard like the leopard.

And I. . . .
                 this print of mine, that has kept its color
Alive through so many cleanings; this dull null
Navy I wear to work, and wear from work, and so
To my bed, so to my grave, with no
Complaints, no comment: neither from my chief,
The Deputy Chief Assistant, nor his chief—
Only I complain. . . . this serviceable
Body that no sunlight dyes, no hand suffuses
But, dome-shadowed, withering among columns,
Wavy beneath fountains—small, far-off, shining
In the eyes of animals, these beings trapped
As I am trapped but not, themselves, the trap,
Aging, but without knowledge of their age,
Kept safe here, knowing not of death, for death—
Oh, bars of my own body, open, open!

The world goes by my cage and never sees me.
· And there come not to me, as come to these,
The wild beasts, sparrows pecking the llamas' grain,
Pigeons settling on the bears' bread, buzzards
Tearing the meat the flies have clouded. . . .
                                Vulture,
When you come for the white rat that the foxes left,

Take off the red helmet of your head, the black
Wings that have shadowed me, and step to me as man:
The wild brother at whose feet the white wolves fawn,
To whose hand of power the great lioness
Stalks, purring. . . .
                        You know what I was,
You see what I am: change me, change me!

CINDERELLA

Her imaginary playmate was a grown-up
In sea-coal satin. The flame-blue glances,
The wings gauzy as the membrane that the ashes
Draw over an old ember—as the mother
In a jug of cider—were a comfort to her.
They sat by the fire and told each other stories.

"What men want. . . ." said the godmother softly—
How she went on it is hard for a man to say.
Their eyes, on their Father, were monumental marble.
Then they smiled like two old women, bussed each other,
Said, "Gossip, gossip"; and, lapped in each other's looks,
Mirror for mirror, drank a cup of tea.

Of cambric tea. But there is a reality
Under the good silk of the good sisters'
Good ball gowns. *She* knew. . . . Hard-breasted, naked-
  eyed,
She pushed her silk feet into glass, and rose within
A gown of imaginary gauze. The shy prince drank
A toast to her in champagne from her slipper

And breathed, "Bewitching!" Breathed, "I am bewitched!"
—She said to her godmother, "Men!"
And, later, looking down to see her flesh
Look back up from under lace, the ashy gauze
And pulsing marble of a bridal veil,
She wished it all a widow's coal-black weeds.

A sullen wife and a reluctant mother,
She sat all day in silence by the fire.

4

Better, later, to stare past her sons' sons,
Her daughters' daughters, and tell stories to the fire.
But best, dead, damned, to rock forever
Beside Hell's fireside—to see within the flames

The Heaven to whose gold-gauzed door there comes
A little dark old woman, the God's Mother,
And cries, "Come in, come in! My son's out now,
Out now, will be back soon, may be back never,
Who knows, eh? *We* know what they are—men, men!
But come, come in till then! Come in till then!"

THE END OF THE RAINBOW

Far from the clams and fogs and bogs
—The cranberry bogs—of Ipswich,
A sampler cast upon a savage shore,
There dwells in a turquoise, unfrequented store
A painter; a painter of land- and seascapes.

At nine o'clock, past Su-Su
—Asleep on the threshold, a spirited
Dwarf Pekinese, exceptionally loving—
The sun of Southern California streams
Unlovingly, but as though lovingly,
Upon the spare, paint-spotted and age-spotted hand's
Accustomed gesture.
                            Beyond the mahlstick a last wave
Breaks in Cobalt, Vert Emeraude, and Prussian Blue
Upon a Permanent White shore.

Her long hair, finer and redder once
Than the finest of red sable brushes, has been brushed
Till it is silver. The hairdresser, drunk with sunlight,
Has rinsed it a false blue. And blue
Are all the lights the seascapes cast upon it, blue
The lights the false sea casts upon it. Su-Su
—Su-Su is naturally black.

Five sheets of plate-glass, tinted green
And founded on the sand, now house the owner
Of the marsh-o'erlooking, silver-grey, unpainted salt-box
To which, sometimes, she writes a letter
—Home is where the dead are—

And goes with it, past CALIFORNIA,
And drops it in a mail-slot marked THE STATES.
The Frog-Prince, Marsh-King
Goggles at her from the bottom of the mail-slot.

There is brandy on his breath.
The cattails quivering above his brute
Imploring eyes, the tadpoles feathering
The rushes of his beard—black beard brought down
In silver to the grave—rustle again
In flaws or eddies of the wet wind: "Say.
Say. Say now. Say again."

                              She turns away
Into the irrigated land
With its blond hills like breasts of hay,
Its tall tan herds of eucalyptus grazing
Above its lawns of ice-plant, of geranium,
Its meadows of eternal asphodel.

The dark ghosts throng by
Shaking their locks at her—their fair, false locks—
Stretching out past her their bare hands, burnt hands.
And she—her face is masked, her hands are gloved
With a mask and gloves of bright brown leather:
The hands of a lady left out in the weather
Of resorts; the face of a fine girl left out in the years.

Voices float up: seals are barking
On the seal-rocks as, once, frogs were croaking
On rushy islands in the marsh of night.

Voices—the voices of others and her voice
Tuned flat like a country fiddle, like a Death

Rubbing his bow with resin at a square-dance—
Voices begin: . . . *A spider a frying-pan, and tonic pop,*
And—fancy!—put tomatoes in their chowder.
Go slow. Go slow. You owe it to yourself.
Watch out for the engine. You owe it to yourself.
Neither a borrower nor a lender be.
Better to be safe than sorry.
Better to be safe than sorry. Say to yourself,
Is it my money they're asking or me?
It must have been the money.
                                        The harsh
Voice goes on, blurred with darkness: *Cheat*
Or be cheaten. Let
And live let.

                    Great me. Great me. Great me.
Proverbs of the night
With the night's inconsequence, or consequence,
Sufficient unto the night. . . . *Every maid her own*
Merman—and she has left lonely forever,
Lonely forever, the kings of the marsh.
She says to Su-Su, "Come to your Content."
—*A name in the family for more*
Than seven generations. And Su-Su
—Su-Su is Su-Su IV.

Twelve o'clock: she locks
The door that she has painted, walks away
Straightforwardly, her Su-Su frisking
Before, on the leash that she has braided; eats
At a little table in a sunny courtyard
A date milkshake and an avocadoburger.

Thus evil communications
Corrupt good manners. . . .

              Little Women, Little Men,
Upon what shores, pink-sanded, beside what cerulean
Seas have you trudged out, nodded over, napped away
Your medium-sized lives!

              Poor Water Babies
Who, summer evenings, sent to bed by sunlight,
Sat in your nightdress on a rag-rug island
Seeming some Pole, or Northwest Passage, or Hesperides
Of your bedchamber's humped, dark-shining Ocean:
The last sunbeam shone
Upon the marble set there at the center
Of that grey-glassed, black-eaved, white-dormered chamber
Until, not touched by any human hand,
Slowly,
Fast, faster, the red agate rolled
Into the humpbacked floor's scrubbed corner.
From your bed that night, you looked for it
And it was gone—gone, gone forever
Out into darkness, far from the warm flickering
Hemisphere the candle breathed
For you and your *Swiss Family Robinson*, marooned
With one down pillow on an uninhabited
Hair mattress. . . .

Su-Su is looking: it's the last of lunch.
She takes a piece of candy from her purse
—Dog-candy—and says, "Beg, sir!" --
              Su-Su begs.

They walk home in all amity, in firm
And literal association. She repeats: *With dogs*
You know where you are; and Su-Su's oil-brown,
                                        oil-blue stare
—The true Su-Su's true-blue stare—
Repeats: *With people you know where you are.*

Her thin feet, pointed neither out nor in
But straight before her, like an Indian's,
And set upon the path, a detour of the path
Of righteousness; her unaccommodating eyes'
Flat blue, matt blue
Or grey, depending on the point of view—
On whether one looks from here or from New England—
All these go unobserved, are unobservable:
She is old enough to be invisible.

Opening the belled door,
She turns once more to her new-framed, new-glassed
Landscape of a tree beside the sea.
It is light-struck.

If you look at a picture the wrong way
You see yourself instead.
                        —The wrong way?
A quarter of an hour and we tire
Of any landscape, said Goethe; eighty years
And he had not tired of Goethe. The landscape had,
And disposed of Goethe in the usual way.

She has looked into the mirror of the marsh
Flawed with the flight of dragonflies, the life of rushes,
And seen—what she had looked for—her own face

Staring up into her; but underneath,
In the depths of the dark water, witnessing
Unmoved, with a seal's angelic
More-than-human less-than-human eyes, a strange
Animal, some wizard ruling other realms,
The King of the Marsh.
                        She says: "He was a—*strange* man."

And the voice of a departed friend, a female
Friend, replies as crystal
Replies to a teaspoon, to a fingernail:
"A *strange* man. . . . But all men are, aren't they?
A man is like a merman." "A merman?"
"Mermen were seals, you know. They called them silkies."
"You mean the Forsaken Merman was a *seal?*"
"What did you think it was, a merman?
And mermaids were manatees." "The things you know!"
"The things you don't know!"

                    The Great Silkie,
His muzzle wide in love, holds out to her
His maimed flippers, and an uncontrollable
Shudder runs through her flesh, and she says, smiling:
"A goose was walking on my grave.
—And the Frog-Prince?" "Oh, I don't know.
If you ask me the Frog-Prince was a frog."

These days few men, few women, and no frogs
Enter "my little studio-shop," "my little paint-store,"
To buy paint; paintings; small black dogs;
Pieces of Pilgrim Rock; pomander-apples
In rosemary; agates; a marsh-violet pressed
In *Compensation*—red goatskin, India paper,

Inscribed in black ink, "For my loving daughter";
A miniature of Great-Great-Great-
Grandfather Wotkyns, pressed to death in Salem
For a wizard; a replica, life-sized, of a female friend
In crystal—wound, the works say, "Men!";
A framed poem signed *Beddoes:* she has dreams to sell.

She has spent her principal on dreams.
Some portion, though, is left—left to her in
                        the Commonwealth
Of Massachusetts, in trust to the end of time.
But life, though, is not left in trust?
Life is not lived, in trust?
True, true—but how few live!
The gift for life, the gift of life
Are rarer, surely, than the gift of making
In a life-class, a study from the life
Of some girl naked for an hour, by the hour;
Of making, from an egg, a jug,
An eggplant, at cross-purposes on drapery,
A still-life; of rendering, with a stump,
Art-gum, and four hardnesses of charcoal, life
Whispering to the naked girl, the naked egg, the naked
Painter: "What am I offered for this frog?"

A kiss? The Frog-Prince, kissed,
Is a prince indeed; a king, a husband, and a father;
According to his State, a citizen; according to
                        his God, a soul;
According to his—*fiancée*, a risk
Uncalculated, incalculable; a load
Whose like she will not look upon again; a responsibility
She is no longer saddled with, praise Heaven!

[Applause.] And, smiling as she used to smile,
She murmurs as she used to murmur: "Men!"

She looks into the mirror and says: "Mirror,
Who is the fairest of us all?"

According to the mirror, it's the mirror.

Great me. Great me. Great me. The voices tune themselves
And keep on tuning: there is no piece, just tuning.
. . . But there are compensations; there is *Compensation.*
She reads it (it, or else the Scriptures
With a *Key* by Mrs. Eddy) when she wakes
In the night as she so often does: the earth
Lies light upon the old, and they are wakeful.

She reads patiently: the bed-lamp lights
Above her sunlit, moonlit, starlit bed
The little slogan under which she sleeps
Or is wakeful: HE WHO HAS HIMSELF FOR FRIEND
IS BEST BEFRIENDED—this in gothic.
One sees, through the bars of the first *H*, a landscape
Manned with men, womaned with women,
                                        dogged with a dog,
And influenced—Content says—by the influence
Of *The Very Rich Hours of the Duke of Burgundy.*
The hours of the earth
—The very rich hours, the very poor hours,
                                 the very long hours—
Go by, and she is wakeful.

She wakes, sometimes, when she has met a friend
In the water; he is just standing in the water, bathing.
He has shaved now, and smells of peppermint.

He holds out to her
With hands like hip-boots, like her father's waders,
A corsage of watercress: the white bridal-veil-lace flowers
Are shining with water-drops. In their clear depths
She sees, like so many cupids, water babies:
Little women, little men.
He pulls his feet with a slow sucking sound
From the floor where he is stuck, like a horse in concrete,
And, reaching to her, whispers patiently
—Whispers, or the wind whispers, water whispers: "Say.
Say. Say now. Say again."

                    A slow
Delicious shudder runs along her spine:
She takes off her straw sailor.
Red again, and long enough to sit on,
Her hair floats out to him—and, slowly,
                              she holds out to him
In their white, new-washed gloves, her dry
Brown leather hands, and whispers: "Father,
If you come any closer I'll call Father."

He melts, in dark drops, to a little dark
Pool drying on the floor, to Su-Su. It is Su-Su!
She holds out to the little dark
Grave drying in the grass, her little dry
Bouquet of ice-plant, of geranium,
And reads: *In Loving Memory of Su-Su
I, II, III, IV*.
She says: "That four is a mistake.
One two three is right, but leave out four."

The Prince is dead. . . . The willows waver
Above the cresses of his tomb.

—His tomb?
The Frog-Prince is married to a frog, has little frogs,
Says sometimes, after dinner, in his den:
"There was a mortal once. . . ." And his Content
Goes through the suburbs with a begging-bowl
Of teak, a Wedgewood cowbell, ringing, ringing,
Calling: *Untouched! Untouched!*
                                        The doors shut themselves
Not helped by any human hand, mail-boxes
Pull down their flags, the finest feelers
Of the television sets withdraw.
                                        Beside her, Death
Or else Life—spare, white, permanent—
Works out their *pas de deux:* here's Death
Arranging a still-life for his own Content;
Death walking Su-Su; Death presenting
To the trustees of the estate, a varied
Portfolio; Death digging
For gold at the end of the rainbow—strikes water,
Which is thinner than blood; strikes oil,
That water will not mix with—no, nor blood;
Pauses, mops his skull, says: *The wrong end.*

At home in Massachusetts gold, red gold
Gushes above the Frog-Prince, Princess, all the Princelets
Digging with sand-pails, tiny shovels, spoons, a porringer
Planned, ages since, by Paul Revere. They call:
                                        "Come play! Come play!"
Death breaks the ice
On her Hopi jar and washes out the brushes;
Says, as he hands her them: *Life's work. It's work.*
Out here at the wrong end of the rainbow
Say to yourself: What's a rainbow anyway?

She looks into the mirror, through the rainbow
—The little home-made rainbow, there in tears—
And hears the voices the years shatter into
As the sunlight shatters into colors: *Me. Me. Me,*
The voices tune themselves.
She says: "Look at my life. Should I go on with it?
It seems to you I have . . . a real gift?
I shouldn't like to keep on if I only. . . .
It seems to you my life is a success?"

Death answers, *Yes. Well, yes.*

She looks around her:
Many waves are breaking on many shores,
The wind turns over, absently,
The leaves of a hundred thousand trees.
How many colors, squeezed from how many tubes
In patient iteration, have made up the world
She draws closer, like a patchwork quilt,
To warm her, all the warm, long, summer day!
The local colors fade:
She hangs here on the verge of seeing
In black and white,
And turns with an accustomed gesture
To the easel, saying:
"Without my paintings I would be—
                                    why, whatever *would* I be?"

Safe from all the nightmares
One comes upon awake in the world, she sleeps.
She sleeps in sunlight, surrounded by many dreams
Or dreams of dreams, all good—how can a dream be bad
If it keeps one asleep?

The unpeopled landscapes
Run down to the seal-less, the merman-less seas,
And she rolls softly, like an agate, down to Su-Su
Asleep upon the doorsill of the seas.
The first Su-Su, the second Su-Su, the third Su-Su
Are dead?
            Long live Su-Su IV!

The little black dog sleeping in the doorway
Of the little turquoise store, can dream
His own old dream: that he is sleeping
In the doorway of the little turquoise store.

IN THOSE DAYS

In those days—they were long ago—
The snow was cold, the night was black.
I licked from my cracked lips
A snowflake, as I looked back

Through branches, the last uneasy snow.
Your shadow, there in the light, was still.
In a little the light went out.
I went on, stumbling—till at last the hill

Hid the house. And, yawning,
In bed in my room, alone,
I would look out: over the quilted
Rooftops, the clear stars shone.

How poor and miserable we were,
How seldom together!
And yet after so long one thinks:
In those days everything was better.

THE ELEMENTARY SCENE

Looking back in my mind I can see
The white sun like a tin plate
Over the wooden turning of the weeds;
The street jerking—a wet swing—
To end by the wall the children sang.

The thin grass by the girls' door,
Trodden on, straggling, yellow and rotten,
And the gaunt field with its one tied cow—
The dead land waking sadly to my life—
Stir, and curl deeper in the eyes of time.

The rotting pumpkin under the stairs
Bundled with switches and the cold ashes
Still holds for me, in its unwavering eyes,
The stinking shapes of cranes and witches,
Their path slanting down the pumpkin's sky.

Its stars beckon through the frost like cottages
(Homes of the Bear, the Hunter—of that absent star,
The dark where the flushed child struggles into sleep)
Till, leaning a lifetime to the comforter,
I float above the small limbs like their dream:

I, I, the future that mends everything.

WINDOWS

Quarried from snow, the dark walks lead to doors
That are dark and closed. The white- and high-roofed
  houses
Float in the moonlight of the shining sky
As if they slept, the bedclothes pulled around them.
But in some the lights still burn. The lights of others' houses.

Those who live there move seldom, and are silent.
Their movements are the movements of a woman darning,
A man nodding into the pages of the paper,
And are portions of a rite—have kept a meaning—
That I, that they know nothing of. What I have never heard
He will read me; what I have never seen
She will show me.
                    As dead actors, on a rainy afternoon,
Move in a darkened living-room, for children
Watching the world that was before they were,
The windowed ones within their windowy world
Move past me without doubt and for no reason.

These actors, surely, have known nothing of today,
That time of troubles and of me. Of troubles.
Morose and speechless, voluble with elation,
Changing, unsleeping, an unchanging speech,
These have not lived; look up, indifferent,
At me at my window, from the snowy walk
They move along in peace. . . . If only I were they!
Could act out, in longing, the impossibility
That haunts me like happiness!

Of so many windows, one is always open.

Some morning they will come downstairs and find me.
They will start to speak, and then smile speechlessly,
Shifting the plates, and set another place
At a table shining by a silent fire.
When I have eaten they will say, "You have not slept."

And from the sofa, mounded in my quilt,
My face on *their* pillow, that is always cool,
I will look up speechlessly into a—

It blurs, and there is drawn across my face
As my eyes close, a hand's slow fire-warmed flesh.

It moves so slowly that it does not move.

AGING

I wake, but before I know it it is done,
The day, I sleep. And of days like these the years,
A life is made. I nod, consenting to my life.
. . . But who can live in these quick-passing hours?
I need to find again, to make a life,
A child's Sunday afternoon, the Pleasure Drive
Where everything went by but time; the Study Hour
Spent at a desk, with folded hands, in waiting.

In those I could make. Did I not make in them
Myself? The Grown One whose time shortens,
Breath quickens, heart beats faster, till at last
It catches, skips. . . . Yet those hours that seemed, were
   endless
Were still not long enough to have remade
My childish heart: the heart that must have, always,
To make anything of anything, not time,
Not time but—
          but, alas! eternity.

NESTUS GURLEY

Sometimes waking, sometimes sleeping,
Late in the afternoon, or early
In the morning, I hear on the lawn,
On the walk, on the lawn, the soft quick step,
The sound half song, half breath: a note or two
That with a note or two would be a tune.
It is Nestus Gurley.

It is an old
Catch or snatch or tune
In the Dorian mode: the mode of the horses
That stand all night in the fields asleep
Or awake, the mode of the cold
Hunter, Orion, wheeling upside-down,
All space and stars, in cater-cornered Heaven.
When, somewhere under the east,
The great march begins, with birds and silence;
When, in the day's first triumph, dawn
Rides over the houses, Nestus Gurley
Delivers to me my lot.

As the sun sets, I hear my daughter say:
"He has four routes and makes a hundred dollars."
Sometimes he comes with dogs, sometimes with children,
Sometimes with dogs and children.
He collects, today.
I hear my daughter say:
"Today Nestus has got on his derby."
And he says, after a little: "It's two-eighty."
"How could it be two-eighty?"

"Because this month there're five Sundays: it's two-
    eighty."

He collects, delivers. Before the first, least star
Is lost in the paling east; at evening
While the soft, side-lit, gold-leafed day
Lingers to see the stars, the boy Nestus
Delivers to me the Morning Star, the Evening Star
—Ah no, only the Morning *News*, the Evening *Record*
Of what I have done and what I have not done
Set down and held against me in the Book
Of Death, on paper yellowing
Already, with one morning's sun, one evening's sun.

Sometimes I only dream him. He brings then
News of a different morning, a judgment not of men.
The bombers have turned back over the Pole,
Having met a star. . . . I look at that new year
And, waking, think of our Moravian Star
Not lit yet, and the pure beeswax candle
With its red flame-proofed paper pompom
Not lit yet, and the sweetened
Bun we brought home from the love-feast, still not eaten,
And the song the children sang: *O Morning Star*—

And at this hour, to the dew-hushed drums
Of the morning, Nestus Gurley
Marches to me over the lawn; and the cat Elfie,
Furred like a musk-ox, coon-tailed, gold-leaf-eyed,
Looks at the paper boy without alarm
But yawns, and stretches, and walks placidly
Across the lawn to his ladder, climbs it, and begins to
    purr.

I let him in,
Go out and pick up from the grass the paper hat
Nestus has folded: this tricorne fit for a Napoleon
Of our days and institutions, weaving
Baskets, being bathed, receiving
Electric shocks, Rauwolfia. . . . I put it on
—Ah no, only unfold it.
There is dawn inside; and I say to no one
About—
        it is a note or two
That with a note or two would—
                say to no one
About nothing: "He delivers dawn."

When I lie coldly
—Lie, that is, neither with coldness nor with warmth—
In the darkness that is not lit by anything,
In the grave that is not lit by anything
Except our hope: the hope
That is not proofed against anything, but pure
And shining as the first, least star
That is lost in the east on the morning of Judgment—
May I say, recognizing the step
Or tune or breath. . . .
              recognizing the breath,
May I say, "It is Nestus Gurley."

THE GREAT NIGHT

(*Rainer Maria Rilke*)

Often I looked at you—stood at the window I had started
The day before, stood and looked at you. The new city
    still
Seemed something forbidden; the landscape, not yet won
    over,
Darkened as though I was not. The closest things
Didn't bother to make me understand. The street
Crowded itself up to the lamp post; I saw that it was
    strange.
Out there a room was clear in lamplight—
Already I was part; they sensed it, closed the shutters.
I stood there. And then a child cried. And I knew
The mothers in the houses, what they were—knew, sud-
    denly,
The spring of all our tears, the spring that is never dry.
Or a voice sang, and went a little beyond
Whatever I had expected; or an old man coughed,
Full of reproach, as though his flesh were in the right
Against the gentler world. Then a clock struck the hour—
But I counted too late, and it got by me.
As a boy, a stranger, when at last they let him,
Can't catch the ball, and doesn't know any of the games
The others are playing together so easily,
So that he stands and looks off—where?—I stand, and
    suddenly
See that *you* have made friends with me, played with me,
    grown-up
Night, and I look at you. While the towers
Were angered, while with averted fates

A city encompassed me, and the unguessable hills
Were encamped against me, and in closing circles
Strangeness hungered round the chance-set flares
Of my senses: then was it, O highest,
That you felt it no shame to know me, that your breath
Went over me, that there passed into me
Your grave and from far apportioning smile.

THE GROWN-UP

(*Rainer Maria Rilke*)

All this stood on her and was the world,
And stood on her with all things, Pain and Grace,
As trees stand, growing and erect, all image
And imageless as the ark of the Lord God,
And solemn, as if set upon a State.

And she bore it; bore, somehow, the weight
Of the flying, fleeting, far-away,
The monstrous and the still-unmastered,
Unmoved, serene, as the water-bearer
Stands under a full jar. Till in the midst of play,
Transfiguring, preparing for the Other,
The first white veil fell smoothly, softly,

Over her opened face, almost opaque,
Never to raise itself again, and giving somehow
To all her questions one vague answer:
In thee, thou once a child, in thee.

WASHING THE CORPSE

(*Rainer Maria Rilke*)

They had got used to him. But when they brought
The kitchen lamp in, and it was burning
Uneasily in the dark air, the stranger
Was altogether strange. They washed his neck,

And since they had no knowledge of his fate
They lied till they had put together one,
Always washing. One of them had to cough,
And while she was coughing she left the heavy

Sponge of vinegar on his face. The other
Stopped a minute too, and the drops knocked
From the hard brush, while his dreadful
Cramped hand wanted to demonstrate
To the whole household that he no longer thirsted.

And he did demonstrate it. Coughing shortly,
As if embarrassed, they went back to work
More hurriedly now, so that across the dumb
Pattern of the wallpaper their contorted shadows

Writhed and wallowed as though in a net
Until the washing reached its end.
The night, in the uncurtained window-frame,
Was relentless. And one without a name
Lay clean and naked there, and gave commandments.

EVENING

(Rainer Maria Rilke)

The evening folds about itself the dark
Garments the old trees hold out to it.
You watch: and the lands are borne from you,
One soaring heavenward, one falling;

And leave you here, not wholly either's,
Not quite so darkened as the silent houses,
Not quite so surely summoning the eternal
As that which each night becomes star, and rises;

And leave you (inscrutably to unravel)
Your life: the fearful and ripening and enormous
Being that—bounded by everything, or boundless—
For a moment becomes stone, for a moment stars.

CHILDHOOD

(adapted from Rainer Maria Rilke)

The time of school drags by with waiting
And dread, with nothing but dreary things.
O loneliness, O leaden waiting-out of time. . . .
And then out. The streets are gleaming and ringing,
All the fountains flash up from the squares.
In the parks the world is enormous.
And to walk through it all in one's little suit
Not at all as the others go, have ever gone:
O miraculous time, O waiting-out of time,
O loneliness.

And to gaze far out into it all:
Men and women, men, men—black and tall
And going slowly, as if in their sleep,
Beside the sudden white and blue and red
Children; a house here, now and then a dog,
And one's fear changing silently to trust:
O senseless grief, O dream, O dread,
O bottomless abyss.

And then to play with top or hoop or ball
Beneath the paling branches of the park
Or sometimes, blind and wild in the reeling
Rush of tag, to brush against the grown-ups,
But to go home with them when it is dark
With little stiff steps, quiet, held fast to:
O knowledge ever harder to hold fast to,
O dread, O burden.

And to kneel beside the great gray pond
Hour on hour with one's little sail-boat,
Forgetting it because so many more,
Lovely and lovelier, glide through darkening rings,
And to have to think about the little pale
Face that shone up from the water, sinking:
O childhood, O images gliding from us
Somewhere. But where? But where?

LAMENT

(*Rainer Maria Rilke*)

All is far
And long gone by.
I believe the star
That shines up there
Has been dead for a thousand years.
I believe, in the car
I heard go by,
Something terrible was said.
In the house a clock
Is striking. . . .
In what house?
I would like to walk
Out of my heart, under the great sky.
I would like to pray.
And surely, of all the stars,
One still must be.
I believe I know
Which one endures;
Which one, at the end of its beam in the sky,
Stands like a white city.

THE CHILD

(Rainer Maria Rilke)

Without meaning to, they watch him play
A long time; once or twice his profile
Turns and becomes a live, full face—
Clear and entire as a completed

Hour that is raised to strike its end.
But the others do not count the strokes.
Exhausted with misery, enduring their lives,
They do not even see that he endures:

Endures everything, now and always,
As—near them, as though in a waiting-room,
Wearily, dressed in his little dress—
He sits and waits till his time comes.

DEATH

(*Rainer Maria Rilke*)

There stands death, a bluish liquid
In a cup without a saucer.
An odd place for a cup:
Stands on the back of a hand. And one can see
Quite plainly, there on the glassy slope,
The place where the handle broke off. Dusty. And HOPE
On the side in used-up letters.

The drinker that drank the drink
Read it out, long, long ago, at breakfast.

This being of theirs!
To get rid of them you have to poison them?

Except for that, they'd stay? They munch away
At their own frustration so insatiably?
One has to pull the present from their mouths,
The hard present, like a dental plate.

Then they mumble. Mumble, mumble. . . .

. . . .
Star
Seen from a bridge once: O falling star,
Not to forget you. Stand!

REQUIEM
FOR THE DEATH OF A BOY

(Rainer Maria Rilke)

Why did I print upon myself the names
Of Elephant and Dog and Cow
So far off now, already so long ago,
And Zebra, too. . . . what for, what for?
What holds me now
Climbs like a water line
Up past all that. What help was it to know
I was, if I could never press
Through what's soft, what's hard, and come at last
Behind them, to the face that understands?

And these beginning hands—

Sometimes you'd say: "He promises. . . ."
Yes, I promised. But what I promised you,
That was never what I felt afraid of.
Sometimes I'd sit against the house for hours
And look up at a bird.
If only I could have turned into the looking!
It lifted me, it flew me, how my eyes
Were open up there then! But I didn't love anybody.
Loving was misery—
Don't you see, I wasn't we,
And I was so much bigger
Than a man, I was my own danger,
And, inside it, I was the seed.

A little seed. The street can have it.
The wind can have it. I give it away.

Because that we all sat there so together—
I never did believe that. No, honestly.
You talked, you laughed, but none of you were ever
Inside the talking or the laughing. No.
The sugar bowl, a glass of milk
Would never waver the way you would waver.
The apple lay there. Sometimes it felt so good
To hold tight to it, a hard ripe apple.
The big table, the coffee-cups that never moved—
They were good, how peaceful they made the year!
And my toy did me good too, sometimes.
It was as reliable, almost, as the others,
Only not so peaceful. It stood halfway
Between me and my hat, in watchfulness forever.
There was a wooden horse, there was a rooster,
There was the doll with only one leg.
I did so much for them.
I made the sky small when they saw it
Because almost from the start I understood
How alone a wooden horse is. You can make one,
A wooden horse, one any size.
It gets painted, and later on you pull it,
And it's the real street it pounds down, then.
When you call it a horse, why isn't it a lie?
Because you feel that you're a horse, a little,
And grow all maney, shiny, grow four legs—
So as to grow, some day, into a man?
But wasn't I wood a little, too,
For its sake, and grew hard and quiet
And looked out at it from an emptier face?

I almost think we traded places.
Whenever I would see the brook I'd race it,

And the brook raced, too, and I would run away.
Whenever I saw something that could ring, I rang,
And whenever something sang I played for it.

I made myself at home with everything.
Only everything was satisfied without me
And got sadder, hung about with me.

Now, all at once, we're separated.
Do the lessons and the questions start again?
Or, now, ought I to say
What it was like with you?—That worries me.
The house? I never got it right, exactly.
The rooms? Oh, there were so many things, so many.
. . . Mother, *who* was the dog really?
That in the forest we would come on berries—
Even that seems, now, extraordinary.

Surely there're some other children
Who've died, to come play with me. They're always
    dying;
Lie there in bed, like me, and never do get well.

Well. . . . How funny that sounds, here.
Does it mean something, still?
Here where I am
No one is ill, I think.
Since my sore throat, so long ago already—

Here everyone is like a just-poured drink.

But the ones who drink us I still haven't seen.

THE WINTER'S TALE

(*Henrikas Radauskas*)

Guess what smells so. . . . You didn't guess.
Lilies? Lindens? No. Winds? No.
But princes and barbers smell so,
The evening smells so, in a dream.

Look: a line goes through the glass
Bending quietly; and the hushed
Light, in the tender mist,
Is gurgling like a brook of milk.

Look: it's snowing, it's snowing, it's snowing.
Look: the white orchard is falling asleep.
The earth has sunk into the past.
Guess who's coming. . . . You didn't guess.
Princes and barbers are coming,
White kings and bakers,
And the trees murmur, covered with snow.

THE ARCHANGELS' SONG

(from Goethe's FAUST*)*

RAPHAEL:

> The sun sings out, as of old,
> Against the spheres' unchanging sound;
> Yet once more, with thunderous footsteps,
> He works out his predestined round.
> Though no angel fathoms him, his face
> Gives strength to them upon their way;
> The inconceivably exalted works
> Are glorious as on the first day.

GABRIEL:

> Swift, past all understanding swift
> Is the splendor of earth's whirling flight:
> The brilliance of Paradise is changed
> For the awful darkness of the night.
> The ocean foams up, overwhelming,
> The great rocks tremble with the force,
> And rocks and ocean are swept onward
> In the spheres' swift, eternal course.

MICHAEL:

> In rivalry the tempests roar
> From sea to land, from land to sea,
> And, raging, forge out for the earth
> Fetters of wildest energy.
> Before the path of the thunderbolt
> The lightnings of desolation blaze.
> And yet thine angels, Lord, adore
> The tranquil footsteps of thy days.

ALL THREE:
    Since none can fathom thee, thy face
    Gives strength to us upon our way,
    And thine exalted works, O God,
    Are glorious as on the first day.

FOREST MURMURS

(*Eduard Mörike*)

Stretched out under the oak, in the wood's new leaves,
I lay with my book. To me it is still the sweetest;

All the fairy tales are in it, the Goose Girl and the Juniper
Tree
And the Fisherman's Wife—truly, one never gets tired of
them.

The curly light flung down to me its green May-shine,
Flung on the shadowy book its mischievous illustrations.

I heard, far away, the strokes of the axe; heard the cuckoo
And the rippling of the brook, a step or two beyond.

I myself felt like a fairy tale; with new-washed senses
I saw, O so clear! the forest, the cuckoo called, O so
strange!

All at once the leaves rustle—isn't it Snow-White coming
Or some enchanted stag? Oh no, it's nothing miraculous:

See, my neighbor's child from the village, my good little
sweetheart!
She'd nothing to do, and ran to the forest to her father.

Demurely she seats herself at my side, confidentially
We gossip of this and that; and I tell her the story

(Leaving out nothing) of the sorrows of that incom-
parable
Maiden her mother three times threatened with death.

Because she was so beautiful, the Queen, the vain one,
   hated her
Fiercely, so that she fled, made her home with dwarfs.

But soon the Queen found her; knocked at the door as a
   peddler,
Craftily offering the girl her wonderful things to buy;

And forgetting the words of the dwarfs, the innocent
   child
Let her in—and the dear thing bought, alas! the poisoned
   comb.

What a wailing there is that night, when the little ones
   come home!
What work it takes, what skill, before the sleeper awakes!

But now a second time, a third time, in disguise,
The destroyer comes. How easily she persuades the
   maiden;

Laces in the tender body, strangling it, till she has choked
The breath in the breast; brings, last, the deadly fruit.

Now nothing is any help; how the dwarfs weep!
The poor darling is locked in a crystal coffin, they set it

There on the mountain side in sight of all the stars—
And inside it, unfading forever, the sweet shape sleeps.

So far had I come: all at once, from the thicket behind
   me,
The song of the nightingale arose in radiant splendor,

Rained through the boughs like honey, sprinkling its fiery
Barbed sounds down over me; I shuddered in terror, in
    delight—

So one of the goddesses, flying above him unseen,
Betrays herself to a poet with her ambrosial fragrance.

But soon, alas! the singer was silent. I listened a long time
But in vain; and so I brought my story to its end.—

Just then the child pointed and cried: "She's here already,
It's Margaret! See, she's brought Father the milk, in her
    basket."

Through the branches I could make out her older sister;
Leaving the meadow, she had turned up into the wood.

Bronzed and stalwart, the maid; noon blazed on her
    cheeks.
We'd have frightened her if we could, but she greeted us
    first:

"Come along, if you like! Today you don't need any meat
Or soup, it's so warm. My meal is rich and cool."

And I didn't struggle. We followed the sound of the
    wood-axe.
How willingly I should have led, instead of the child, her
    sister!

Friend, you honor the Muse who, ages ago, to thousands
Told her stories, but now for a long time has been silent.

Who by the winter fireside, the loom and the work-bench,
Proffered to the folk's creating wit her delectable food.

Her kingdom is the impossible: impudent, frivolous, she
  ladles together
All that's unlikeliest, gleefully gives her prizes to half-wits.

Allowed three wishes, her hero will pick the silliest.
To honor her, now, let me make to you this confession—

How at the side of the girl, the sweet-spoken, the never-
  silent,
Catching me unawares, the passionate wish overwhelmed
  me:

If I were a hunter, a shepherd, if I were born a peasant,
If I handled an axe, a shovel—you, Margaret, would be
  my wife!

Never then would I complain of the heat of the day;
The plainest food, if you served it, would seem a feast.

Each morning, in its magnificence, the sun would meet
  me—
Each evening, in magnificence, blaze over the ripening
  fields.

Fresh from the woman's kiss, my blood would grow sweet
  as balsam;
Boisterous with children, my house would blossom on
  high.

But on winter nights, when the drifts pile high—by the
  fireside,
O Muse, maker of the stories of men! I would invoke
  thee.

JAMESTOWN

Let me look at what I was, before I die.
Strange, that one's photograph in kindergarten
Is a captain in a ruff and a Venusian
—Is nothing here American?
John Smith is squashed
Beneath the breasts of Pocahontas: some true Christian,
Engraving all, has made the captain Man,
The maiden the most voluptuous of newts.
Met in a wood and lain with, this red demon,
The mother of us all, lies lovingly
Upon the breastplate of our father: the First Family
Of Jamestown trembles beneath the stone
Axe—then Powhatan, smiling, gives the pair his blessing
And nymphs and satyrs foot it at their wedding.
The continents, like country children, peep in awe
As Power, golden as a Veronese,
Showers her riches on the lovers: Nature,
Nature at last is married to a man.

The two lived happily
Forever after. . . . And I only am escaped alone
To tell the story. But how shall I tell the story?
The settlers died? All settlers die. The colony
Was a Lost Colony? All colonies are lost.
John Smith and Pocahontas, carving on a tree
We Have Gone Back For More People, crossed the sea
And were put to death, for treason, in the Tower
Of London? Ah, but they needed no one!
Powhatan,
Smiling at that red witch, red wraith, his daughter,

Said to the father of us all, John Smith:
"American,
To thyself be enough! . . ." He was enough—
Enough, or too much. The True Historie
Of the Colony of Jamestown is a wish.

Long ago, hundreds of years ago, a man
Met a woman in a wood, a witch.
The witch said, "Wish!"
The man said, "Make me what I am."
The witch said, "Wish again!"
The man said, "Make me what I am."
The witch said, "For the last time, wish!"
The man said, "Make me what I am."
The witch said: "Mortal, because you have believed
In your mortality, there is no wood, no wish,
No world, there is only you. But what are you?
The world has become you. But what are you?
Ask;
Ask, while the time to ask remains to you."

The witch said, smiling: "This is Jamestown.
From Jamestown, Virginia, to Washington, D.C.,
Is, as the rocket flies, eleven minutes."

THE LONELY MAN

A cat sits on the pavement by the house.
It lets itself be touched, then slides away.
A girl goes by in a hood; the winter noon's
Long shadows lengthen. The cat is gray,
It sits there. It sits there all day, every day.

A collie bounds into my arms: he is a dog
And, therefore, finds nothing human alien.
He lives at the preacher's with a pair of cats.
The soft half-Persian sidles to me;
Indoors, the old white one watches blindly.

How cold it is! Some snow slides from a roof
When a squirrel jumps off it to a squirrel-proof
Feeding-station; and, a lot and two yards down,
A fat spaniel snuffles out to me
And sobers me with his untrusting frown.

He worries about his yard: past it, it's my affair
If I halt Earth in her track—his duty's done.
And the cat and the collie worry about the old one:
They come, when she's out too, so uncertainly. . . .
It's my block; I know them, just as they know me.

As for the others, those who wake up every day
And feed these, keep the houses, ride away
To work—I don't know them, they don't know me.
Are we friends or enemies? Why, who can say?
We nod to each other sometimes, in humanity,

Or search one another's faces with a yearning
Remnant of faith that's almost animal. . . .
The gray cat that just sits there: surely it is learning
To be a man; will find, soon, *some especial*
Opening in a good firm for a former cat.

THE TRAVELER

As she rides to the station
There is always something she has left behind.
Here is her hatbox; where is her hat?
Or she is blind—but the others are blind,
Not one thinks: Where are her eyes?
This plush smells—how does she smell it?
Her head hangs on a hanger in the closet
And calls as an engine calls, the engine
Cries as a head cries: *Shall I spare this city?*
The rails answer: *Raze it, raze it.*
She thinks as a child thinks:
When the sun sets, it is to count my loss.

Here in the station, in the other station,
On the track, appearing each instant,
That is made to her destination,
Her purse is heavier than she can know,
Her streaked breasts shake with a double heart.
When she steps at last to the stone of the station
Her arm drags, her step is slow.
She carries her head in her hand like a hatbox
Of money, of paper money:
A headful of money not even she will take.

When the moon rises, it is to count her money.
She sits on the bed of a bedroom counting her money:
Her look glazes, her breath is slow.
The wind moves to her
Softly, through parting curtains,

And a bill on the floor, a bill on the comfort,
As though they were living, stir.
When the wind says, *Shall I spare this city?*
She gives no answer.

A GHOST, A REAL GHOST

I think of that old woman in the song
Who could not know herself without the skirt
They cut off while she slept beside a stile.
Her dog jumped at the unaccustomed legs
And barked till she turned slowly from her gate
And went—I never asked them where she went.

The child is hopeful and unhappy in a world
Whose future is his recourse: she kept walking
Until the skirt grew, cleared her head and dog—
Surely I thought so when I laughed. If skirts don't grow,
If things can happen so, and you not know
What you could do, why, what is there you could do?

I know now she went nowhere; went to wait
In the bare night of the fields, to whisper:
"I'll sit and wish that it was never so."
I see her sitting on the ground and wishing,
The wind jumps like a dog against her legs,
And she keeps thinking: "This is all a dream.

"Who would cut off a poor old woman's skirt?
So good too. No, it's not so:
No one could feel so, really." And yet one might.
A ghost must; and she was, perhaps, a ghost.
The first night I looked into the mirror
And saw the room empty, I could not believe

That it was possible to keep existing
In such pain: I have existed.

52

Was the old woman dead? What does it matter?
—Am I dead? A ghost, a real ghost
Has no need to die: what is he except
A being without access to the universe
That he has not yet managed to forget?

THE METEORITE

Star, that looked so long among the stones
And picked from them, half iron and half dirt,
One; and bent and put it to her lips
And breathed upon it till at last it burned
Uncertainly, among the stars its sisters—
Breathe on me still, star, sister.

CHARLES DODGSON'S SONG

The band played *Idomeneo:*
  A child's felicity
Held Stendhal, sitting with the Empress
  Eugenie on his fat knee.

Clerk Maxwell's demon was possessed;
  He lay for half his days
And never moved a single molecule.
  Mill, haunted by the silent face

Of Bentham—it was made of wax—
  Read Wordsworth, and at last could weep.
I sought for love, and found it in girls' gloves:
  There's none outside, you know. "That bird's dead,
    Father,"

Said Darwin's son. Dejectedly
  The Father broke his spear, looked deep
Into the Cause of things: but it was only
  A hippopotamus asleep.

DEUTSCH DURCH FREUD

I believe my favorite country's German.

I wander in a calm folk-colored daze; the infant
Looks down upon me from his mother's arms
And says—oh, God knows what he says!
It's baby-talk? he's sick? or is it German?
That *Nachtigallenchor:* does it sing German?
Yoh, yoh: here mice, rats, tables, chairs,
Grossmütter, Kinder, der Herrgott im Himmel,
All, all but I—
        all, all but I—
                speak German.

Have you too sometimes, by the fire, at evening,
Wished that you were—whatever you once were?
It is ignorance alone that is enchanting.
Dearer to me than all the treasures of the earth
Is something living, said old Rumpelstiltskin
And hopped home. Charcoal-burners heard him singing
And spoiled it all. . . . And all because—
If only he hadn't known his name!

In German I don't know my name.
                       I am the log
The fairies left one morning in my place.
—In German I believe in them, in everything:
The world is everything that is the case.
How clever people are! I look on open-mouthed
As Kant reels down the road *im Morgenrot*
Humming *Mir ist so bang, so bang, mein Schatz—*
All the nixies set their watches by him

Two hours too fast. . . .
                              I think, *My calendar's*
Two centuries too fast, and give a sigh
Of trust. I reach out for the world and ask
The price; it answers, *One touch of your finger.*

In all *my* Germany there's no *Gesellschaft*
But one between *eine Katze* and *ein Maus.*
What's business? what's a teaspoon? what's a sidewalk?
Schweig stille, meine Seele! Such things are not for thee.
It is by Trust, and Love, and reading Rilke
Without *ein Wörterbuch*, that man learns German.
The Word rains in upon his blessed head
As glistening as from the hand of God
And means—what does it mean? Ah well, it's German.
Glaube, mein Herz! A Feeling in the Dark
Brings worlds, brings words that hard-eyed Industry
And all the schools' dark Learning never knew.

And yet it's hard sometimes, I won't deny it.
Take for example my own favorite daemon,
Dear good great Goethe: *ach*, what German!
Very idiomatic, very noble; very like a sibyl.
My favorite style is Leupold von Lerchenau's.
I've memorized his *da und da und da und da*
And whisper it when Life is dark and Death is dark.
There was someone who knew how to speak
To us poor *Kinder* here *im Fremde.*
And Heine! At the ninety-sixth *mir träumte*
I sigh as a poet, but dimple as *ein Schuler.*
And yet—if it's easy is it German?
And yet, that *wunderschöne Lindenbaum*
Im Mondenscheine! What if it is in Schilda?

It's moonlight, isn't it? *Mund, Mond, Herz,* and *Schmerz*
Sing round my head, in *Zeit* and *Ewigkeit,*
And my heart lightens at each *Sorge,* each *Angst:*
I know them well. And *Schicksal! Ach,* you Norns,
As I read I hear your—what's the word for scissors?
And *Katzen* have *Tatzen*—why can't I call someone
    Kind?
What a speech for Poetry (especially Folk-)!

And yet when, in my dreams, *eine schwartzbraune Hexe*
(Who mows on the Neckar, reaps upon the Rhine)
Riffles my yellow ringlets through her fingers,
She only asks me questions: *What is soap?*
I don't know. *A suitcase?* I don't know. *A visit?*
I laugh with joy, and try to say like Lehmann:
"Quin-quin, es ist ein Besuch!"
                          Ah, German!
Till the day I die I'll be in love with German
—If only I don't learn German. . . . I can hear my
    broken
Voice murmuring to *der Arzt: "Ich—sterber?"*
He answers sympathetically: *"Nein—sterbe."*

If God gave me the choice—but I stole this from
    Lessing—
Of German and learning German, I'd say: Keep your
    German!

The thought of *knowing* German terrifies me.
—But surely, this way, no one could learn German?
And yet. . . .
               It's difficult; is it impossible?
I'm hopeful that it is, but I can't say
For certain: I don't know enough German.

THE GIRL DREAMS THAT
SHE IS GISELLE

Beards of the grain, gray-green: the lances
Shiver. I stare up into the dew.
From her white court—enchantress—
The black queen, shimmering with dew,

Floats to me. In the enchainment
Of a travelling and a working wing
She comes shying, sidelong, settling
On the bare grave by the grain.

And I sleep, curled in my cold cave. . . .
Her wands quiver as a nostril quivers:
The gray veilings of the grave
Crumple, my limbs lock, reverse,

And work me, jointed, to the glance
That licks out to me in white fire
And, piercing, whirs *Remember*
Till my limbs catch. Life, life! I dance.

THE SPHINX'S RIDDLE
TO OEDIPUS

Not to have guessed is better: what is, ends,
But among fellows, with reluctance,
Clasped by the Woman-Breasted, Lion-Pawed.

To have clasped in one's own arms a mother,
To have killed with one's own hands a father
—Is not this, Lame One, to have been alone?

The seer is doomed for seeing; and to understand
Is to pluck out one's own eyes with one's own hands.
But speak: what has a woman's breasts, a lion's paws?

You stand at midday in the marketplace
Before your life: to see is to have spoken.
—Yet to see, Blind One, is to be alone.

JEROME

Each day brings its toad, each night its dragon.
Der heilige Hieronymus—his lion is at the zoo—
Listens, listens. All the long, soft, summer day
Dreams affright his couch, the deep boils like a pot.
As the sun sets, the last patient rises,
Says to him, *Father;* trembles, turns away.

Often, to the lion, the saint said, *Son.*
To the man the saint says—but the man is gone.
Under a plaque of Gradiva, at gloaming,
The old man boils an egg. When he has eaten
He listens a while. The patients have not stopped.
At midnight, he lies down where his patients lay.

All night the old man whispers to the night.
It listens evenly. The great armored paws
Of its forelegs put together in reflection,
It thinks: *Where Ego was, there Id shall be.*
The world wrestles with it and is changed into it
And after a long time changes it. The dragon

Listens as the old man says, at dawn: *I see*
—*There is an old man, naked, in a desert, by a cliff.*
He has set out his books, his hat, his ink, his shears
Among scorpions, toads, the wild beasts of the desert.
I lie beside him—I am a lion.
He kneels listening. He holds in his left hand

The stone with which he beats his breast, and holds
In his right hand, the pen with which he puts
Into his book, the words of the angel:
The angel up into whose face he looks.
But the angel does not speak. He looks into the face
Of the night, and the night says—but the night is gone.

He has slept. . . . At morning, when man's flesh is young
And man's soul thankful for it knows not what,
The air is washed, and smells of boiling coffee,
And the sun lights it. The old man walks placidly
To the grocer's; walks on, under leaves, in light,
To a lynx, a leopard—he has come:

The man holds out a lump of liver to the lion,
And the lion licks the man's hand with his tongue.

THE BRONZE DAVID
OF DONATELLO

A sword in his right hand, a stone in his left hand,
He is naked. Shod and naked. Hatted and naked.
The ribbons of his leaf-wreathed, bronze-brimmed bonnet
Are tasseled; crisped into the folds of frills,
Trills, graces, they lie in separation
Among the curls that lie in separation
Upon the shoulders.
                Lightly, as if accustomed,
Loosely, as if indifferent,
The boy holds in grace
The stone moulded, somehow, by the fingers,
The sword alien, somehow, to the hand.
                     The boy David
Said of it: "There is none like *that*."
                   The boy David's
Body shines in freshness, still unhandled,
And thrusts its belly out a little in exact
Shamelessness. Small, close, complacent,
A labyrinth the gaze retraces,
The rib-case, navel, nipples are the features
Of a face that holds us like the whore Medusa's—
Of a face that, like the genitals, is sexless.
What sex has victory?
The mouth's cut Cupid's-bow, the chin's unwinning dim-
    ple
Are tightened, a little oily, take, use, notice:
Centering itself upon itself, the sleek
Body with its too-large head, this green
Fruit now forever green, this offending

63

And efficient elegance draws subtly, supply,
Between the world and itself, a shining
Line of delimitation, demarcation.
The body mirrors itself.
                    Where the armpit becomes breast,
Becomes back, a great crow's-foot is slashed.
Yet who would gash
The sleek flesh so? the cast, filed, shining flesh?
The cuts are folds: these are the folds of flesh
That closes on itself as a knife closes.

The right foot is planted on a wing. Bent back in ease
Upon a supple knee—the toes curl a little, grasping
The crag upon which they are set in triumph—
The left leg glides toward, the left foot lies upon
A head. The head's other wing (the head is bearded
And winged and helmeted and bodiless)
Grows like a swan's wing up inside the leg;
Clothes, as the suit of a swan-maiden clothes,
The leg. The wing reaches, almost, to the rounded
Small childish buttocks. The dead wing warms the leg,
The dead wing, crushed beneath the foot, is swan's-
    down.
Pillowed upon the rock, Goliath's head
Lies under the foot of David.

Strong in defeat, in death rewarded,
The head dreams what has destroyed it
And is untouched by its destruction.
The stone sunk in the forehead, say the Scriptures;
There is no stone in the forehead. The head is helmed
Or else, unguarded, perfect still.
Borne high, borne long, borne in mastery,

The head is fallen.
                              The new light falls
As if in tenderness, upon the face—
Its masses shift for a moment, like an animal,
And settle, misshapen, into sleep: Goliath
Snores a little in satisfaction.

To so much strength, those overborne by it
Seemed girls, and death came to it like a girl,
Came to it, through the soft air, like a bird—
So that the boy is like a girl, is like a bird
Standing on something it has pecked to death.

The boy stands at ease, his hand upon his hip:
The truth of victory. A Victory
Angelic, almost, in indifference,
An angel sent with no message but this triumph
And alone, now, in his triumph,
He looks down at the head and does not see it.

Upon this head
As upon a spire, the boy David dances,
Dances, and is exalted.
                              Blessed are those brought low,
Blessed is defeat, sleep blessed, blessed death.

Randall Jarrell

was born in Nashville, Tennessee in 1914 and graduated from Vanderbilt University. He now lives with
his wife and two daughters in Greensboro, North Carolina, where he is Professor of English at the Woman's
College of the University of North Carolina. Mr. Jar-
rell has also taught at Sarah Lawrence and Kenyon
Colleges, the Universities of Texas, Illinois, Indiana
and Cincinnati, and at Princeton University. At various
times he has been poetry critic of the Nation, Partisan
Review and The Yale Review, and as poet, novelist
and critic his work has received many awards. For two
years he was Consultant in Poetry at the Library of
Congress. He is a member of the National Institute of
Arts and Letters and a chancellor of The Academy
of American Poets. His books include six volumes of
poems, of which one is his *Selected Poems* (1955), a
work of fiction *Pictures from an Institution*, and a
book of essays, *Poetry and the Age*.